John Freeman's legacy

'The best brigade major in the Eighth Army.'
– Field Marshal Bernard Montgomery

'All the best young men are on the other side.'
– Winston Churchill (former Prime Minister, in tears after Major Freeman's
maiden speech opening the 1945 parliament on behalf of the Labour government)

'He would have made a wonderful Prime Minister.'
– Dr Henry Kissinger

'He is the most dangerous one of all of us, a man of Saturn.'
– Nye Bevan MP (a Labour leader)

'After years of studying his complex personality, I decided he was
afraid of giving himself too fully to anything or anyone. I once
told him his motto ought to be *Je me sauve* [I protect myself].'
– Barbara Castle MP (a former lover)

'John has the capacity to put up the shutters that is excelled
by nobody except a shopkeeper during riots.'
– Professor Norman MacKenzie (writer and academic)

'John is the only man who has ever made himself celebrated
by turning his arse on the public.'
– Kingsley Martin (editor of the *New Statesman*, referring to
Freeman's back-to-camera interviewing on *Face to Face*)

'It's astounding and sad – and not surprising in a fast-changing world – that our heroes are nobodies to our grandchildren. People of our generation revered John Freeman as one of the foundation stones of early television. If I learned one thing from him it was the art of doing an interview without proving what a clever chap you were. It's a piece of advice often ignored by the current generation of interviewers. I worked with him at ITV and without ever getting close to him – did anyone? – constantly admired his ability to inspire a mixture of admiration and awe from the staff. He was a great man and the present generation who know not of him don't know what they are missing.'
— **Michael Parkinson**

'One of the three best ambassadors I ever served with.'
— **Lord Renwick** (former ambassador to the USA)

'He was very formidable – definitely not a man you would tell lies to. He would have made a gobsmacking QC.'
— **Lord Grade** (former executive chairman of ITV)

'A man of many epiphanies to remind us what England was once about.'
— **Paul Johnson** (writing in *The Spectator* on Freeman's eightieth birthday)

'John was well known but hard to know well; and that's exactly how he wanted it.'
— **Catherine Freeman** (Freeman's third wife)

John Freeman by Feliks Topolski for Face to Face.

A VERY PRIVATE CELEBRITY

THE NINE LIVES OF
JOHN FREEMAN

HUGH PURCELL

The Robson Press

First published in Great Britain in 2015 by
The Robson Press (an imprint of Biteback Publishing)
Westminster Tower
3 Albert Embankment
London SE1 7SP
Copyright © Hugh Purcell 2015

ISBN 978–1-84954-861–8

10 9 8 7 6 5 4 3 2 1

A CIP catalogue record for this book is available from the British Library.

Set in Adobe Garamond Pro

Printed and bound in Great Britain by
CPI Group (UK) Ltd, Croydon CR0 4YY

Contents

Introduction

'I WISH EVERYBODY would forget I was alive,' he said. And most people did. But living a very private life in south-west London, until nearing his centenary, was one of the most extraordinary public figures of twentieth-century Britain: an achiever and thrower-away of high office after high office; a celebrity who sought anonymity. 'John Freeman', said an old friend, 'has spent his life moving through a series of rooms, always shutting the door firmly behind him and never looking back.'

He was a chameleon. In the 1940s he was a war hero, then an MP who reduced Churchill to tears. In the 1950s he was tipped as the future Labour leader, but resigned from politics and became a famous TV interviewer. In 1961 he left the BBC to become editor of the *New Statesman* – at that time, the most influential political weekly. Four years later, he resigned and became a diplomat, first as

High Commissioner to India and then as ambassador to Washington. In 1971, he resigned again to become chairman of London Weekend TV and then of ITN. In 1984, he resigned once more and moved to California as a visiting lecturer, until his return to the UK in 1990. In retirement, he became a well-known figure on the bowls circuit of south-west London. No one knew about his past.

In very old age he still did not look back. He said in 2010: 'I don't remember the past because I've always put it behind me. Not just now, I've always been like that. I like to think about the present and even the future, but my past is a closed book, even to me.'

John Freeman was a man who believed in changing his life, and his wife, every ten years. He had four wives and three families, his last child being born when he was seventy-two. His lovers included the politician Barbara Castle, the writer Edna O'Brien, the film star Eva Bartok, the singer Billie Holliday, and the actress Rosalie Crutchley. It's possible he did not remember them either.

> Not only was his past a closed book, but his present was very private too, in so far as he could shield it from outsiders. He was patholog-ically private, a point well made by Dominic Lawson of the *Daily Mail* in the opening lines of his obituary written in December 2014:
>
> On Saturday morning, in a military nursing home, two months before his 100th birthday, John Freeman died. If he had anything to do with it, my article would end at this point; indeed, he would have regarded the last three words of its first sentence to be the ideal obituary notice.

The paradox of Freeman, the private celebrity, was symbolised by the TV series that made him famous in 1959: *Face to Face*. The viewer never saw Freeman's face. He sat with his back to the camera, in the shadow, smoke from a cigarette curling up between the fingers of his right hand. 'John is the only man who has made himself celebrated by turning his arse on the public,' said Kingsley Martin, former editor of the *New Statesman*. Freeman was the grand inquisitor, exposing the real personality behind the public figure – but never his own.

Thirty years later, the BBC repeated *Face to Face* and sent the radio psychiatrist Anthony Clare and myself to California to film an introductory interview with Freeman, in which the roles were reversed. The programme was a failure. Freeman had an intimidating physical presence and a manner that combined an old-fashioned, somewhat insincere charm with a complete put-down: 'I'm sorry, I don't want to sound rude to you, but that's the sort of portentous question I don't think I want to answer.' As always, he gave nothing away.

An old friend of Freeman's had warned me: 'John has the capacity to put up the shutters that is excelled by nobody except a shopkeeper during a time of riots.' After the interview I noticed that the interior of Freeman's house in Davis was like a hotel room – devoid, as far as I could see, of personal memorabilia.

I became fascinated by John Freeman's life, particularly by his chameleon-like quality to change it every decade or so, and I wanted to write his biography. His third wife, Catherine, was discouraging: 'Don't think he has mellowed and will say, "Now is the time to review my life"; he hasn't and he won't.' Nevertheless, I persisted and asked Freeman, with the proviso that if he objected I would go no further. His reply was one I didn't expect: 'I do not feel able to take any part in the project you propose.' But did that Olympian response leave the door open for others to take part? I asked Nigel Lawson, former Chancellor of the Exchequer and a friend of Freeman, to intercede on my behalf, as he had once thought a biography should be written. He tried and failed: 'Unsurprisingly, knowing him, he is not prepared to approve your project, even grudgingly. However, he did make clear that, equally, he does not disapprove and will not sue.' So, despite feeling that chill air of non-approval on the back of my neck, I obtained a commission from a publisher in 2004 and began to research.

It was not easy. John Freeman's *Who's Who* entry had become briefer and briefer over the years and nearly all his early contemporaries were dead. He had written no autobiography, kept no diary and even destroyed private correspondence. Yet his story quickly became tantalising.

Like other celebrities who give nothing away about themselves, anecdotes stuck to him that might be accurate but could be myth. Was it true that as a schoolboy he had heard Mahatma Gandhi speak and decided to become a socialist? Was it true that as a staff officer at Lüneburg Heath in May 1945 he had conducted the German generals to surrender to Field Marshal Montgomery? The answers lay in his school and war records, which I required his permission to access. And why would he withhold that? It seemed little enough to ask. He'd had a distinguished education as a scholar and head of house at Westminster School, followed by a heroic, decorated war with the Desert Rats – Monty called him 'the best brigade major I have'. Or was this also a myth?

I wrote to him again. Once more his reply combined flowery charm with blunt dismissal:

> Before I return a dusty answer to your letter, I want to tell you how much I appreciate the charm and courtesy with which you have written. I made it plain to you from the start that anything you write would be without my cooperation, and that remains the case – absolutely – I have no intention of changing that decision now. When I retired I resolved to put that life completely out of my mind – to forget it all in fact.

I was deflated by his answer, but all the more intrigued. His final sentence both disturbed and excited me. Why was he so pathologically private? Why was he determined to forget what other old men would be proud to remember?

I pressed ahead, hoping, frankly, that Freeman would pass away while I was writing. He was ninety. His death would enable me to access his records and encourage those friends who respected his privacy to talk to me. By 2013, however, Freeman was in his ninety-ninth year and appearing to fulfil his wish that 'everybody would forget I was alive'. By then, I had completed a long essay entitled 'Face to face with an enigma: the extraordinary life of John Freeman'. I could not wait any longer. I offered it to the *New Statesman* (which was about to celebrate its centenary), as Freeman had been editor there when its readership was at its highest in the 1960s. The present editor, Jason Cowley, liked my essay – always an encouragement to a writer – and published it in the first week of March.

The results exceeded my expectations. My worries that no one would be interested in this figure from the past were completely dispelled. The essay was the 'most read' on the online *New Statesman* for months and has been at the top of the Google rankings for 'John Freeman' ever since. When Freeman eventually died in December 2014, the lengthy obituaries and accompanying feature articles proved without doubt that he continues to fascinate the British public. Several acknowledged my *New Statesman* article – fairly, I think, for I am now the only person who knows the details of the public life of this most private of celebrities.

For the past decade, on and off, I have been researching and writing John Freeman's biography. For a long time I searched for a title. 'Private Celebrity' suggested itself, and 'Nine Lives' refers, of course, to his chameleon-like quality of moving from life to life, leaving little baggage behind. All these lives stand for his professional roles, except the last: 'the ordinary man'. I believe he worked at this in the same self-aware way he worked at his previous roles – as one to be mastered to the best of his ability. There is a whimsical reason for my subtitle too: John Freeman loved cats – particularly his Abyssinian pair, Pushkin and Dulcie, whom he named after the Coleridge poem 'Kubla Khan' (from the lines: 'It was an Abyssinian maid / And on the dulcimer she played'). There was something feline about him too; he walked on his own through his many lives, conscious of his own attractions but showing little interest in others'.

My challenge was to answer the question 'Who was John Freeman?' and in this quest I became certain of two things. The first is that there was sufficient written and oral material to attempt an answer. He was true to his word that he had no intention of writing memoirs and had never kept a diary ('not a single paper', in fact). This, of course, was frustrating. But, fortunately, Freeman was a professional communicator and much of his life is on the public record. Each of his nine lives has its own, very different archive. There is his head of house ledger at school; his brigade major's official weekly war diary; his speeches and articles as government minister; his Flavus diary in the *New Statesman* for over a decade and many, many articles for that journal and also for the *News of the World*. Then there are his television programmes (in transcript or recording), particularly *Face to Face*, his diplomatic despatches and his TV chairman memoranda. Even his lectures as university professor are preserved in a California museum. Only Freeman's ninth life lacks a written archive – when he was trying hard and self-consciously to be 'an ordinary man'. But about that, the bowls players of Priory Park in Barnes have much to say.

There is no shortage of writing about Freeman either. My favourite sources are diaries, with their gobbets of gossip and anecdote;

Woodrow Wyatt, Hugh Dalton, Richard Crossman and Tom Driberg
do not disappoint. A close second come the press portraits in which,
for over half a century, journalists in the UK and the USA have
tried to come 'face to face' with Freeman. Most have failed. Some
have partly succeeded, particularly those portraits written by friends
and colleagues such as Norman MacKenzie, Tom Driberg, Anthony
Howard, Francis Hope and Wesley Pruden.

Such was the ubiquity of Freeman that he is indexed in innumer-
able biographies and histories too – I have half a bookcase full. These
include Carl Jung's *Man and His Symbols* (Freeman wrote the introduction), Henry Kissinger's *White House Years* and David Frost's *An
Autobiography*. He is also, famously, the scarcely disguised 'love object'
in Edna O'Brien's short story of that title.

Over the last decade, I have interviewed numerous family members,
friends and colleagues of Freeman. Some of them pre-deceased him:
the politician Michael Foot; his *New Statesman* colleagues Anthony
Howard and Norman MacKenzie; his first lover, Susan Hicklin (née
Cox). They and others, like the statesman Dr Henry Kissinger, the
writer Paul Johnson and the diplomat Lord Renwick, knew him over
many years. Above all, John's third wife Catherine has been hugely supportive and helpful in pointing me towards important contributors to
this story. My thanks are also due to Judith Freeman, his fourth wife
and the mother of his two younger children, for allowing me access
to his army service record.

My second certainty is that in writing this biography I have discovered much that is new. The beginning was not promising. Freeman
wrote to me: 'I cannot see why my life is of any possible interest to
anybody.' His eldest son Matthew said, 'That became his mantra' –
a warning shot across the bows of any biographer. In my view, this
dismissive attitude was less a case of modesty or the reticence of a

pre-war gentleman than one of perversity. Here, after all, was a man admired by Field Marshal Montgomery; a populariser of Carl Jung; the eponymous lover of Edna O'Brien in 'The Love Object'; a close friend of Henry Kissinger; and a respected boss of Rupert Murdoch – to name but a few from his hall of fame.

Freeman makes a challenging subject for a biographer. I discovered that he was not only dismissive of different episodes in his life, but he seemed to mislead on purpose. For instance, he told both his wife Catherine and his friend Tom Driberg that he had wasted his time at Oxford, doing little except drink heavily and court girls. In fact he edited the university paper *Cherwell* under a disguised name and he was also Flavus, the political diarist who interviewed Ellen Wilkinson on the Jarrow March, reported the fight between Oswald Mosley's Blackshirts and students at Carfax Hall in Oxford, and attended meetings in support of the Republic in the Spanish Civil War. In other words, he was already politically engaged as a socialist and a participant in the dramas of the 1930s.

Many years later he told friends that when he was a visiting professor at Davis University in California, he had little to do except give a few guest lectures and enjoy campus life – nothing of interest there apparently. In actual fact, he was a full-time member of the political science faculty, teaching the undergraduate syllabus to young Californians, and setting and marking exams. For an ex-ambassador to the United States, in his seventies by then and well past retirement age, this was yet another remarkable role change.

I believe that I have uncovered a life of massive achievement, as well as a constant attempt to hide it. John Freeman was an extraordinary man. As Dominic Lawson wrote in Freeman's obituary: 'It is safe to utter the cliché, "We will never see his like again."'

Chapter 1

Young man about town

ON 26 JUNE 1959, John Freeman interviewed one of the founding fathers of psychoanalysis on *Face to Face* – Carl Gustav Jung. Freeman began in his usual, brisk, interrogatory style:

> FREEMAN: How many grandchildren have you?
>
> JUNG: Oh, nineteen.
>
> FREEMAN: And great-grandchildren?
>
> JUNG: I think eight and I suppose one is on the way.
>
> FREEMAN: Now, can I take you back to your own childhood? Do you remember the occasion when you first felt consciousness of your own individual self?

Presumably Freeman had done his homework, for Jung was not disconcerted by this unusual question. He gave an extraordinary answer:

> That was in my eleventh year. Suddenly, on my way to school, it was just as if I had been walking in a mist, and I stepped out of it and I knew: *I am*. And then I thought: *But what have I been before?* And then I found that I had been in a mist, not knowing how to differentiate myself from things. I was just one thing among many things.

Would that Freeman had been similarly introspective when he gave his *Face to Face* type interview to the psychiatrist Anthony Clare in 1988, but, as usual, 'the shutters were up'. However, there are sufficient clues in his own childhood that have encouraged psychiatrists, including the late Anthony Clare, to speculate about his personality.

John Horace Freeman was born on 19 February 1915 in one of those grand stucco Regency houses on the south side of Regent's Park near the centre of London. His father Horace was a successful chancery barrister of Lincoln's Inn and his mother Beatrice, née Craddock, was the daughter of a prosperous butcher's family, whose premises were on nearby Marylebone High Street. In fact, John was born in Grandmother Craddock's house.

Soon his family moved out, to the salubrious but dull suburb of Brondesbury, into a large Edwardian house on Walm Lane with eight bedrooms, two or three servants, two cars and a sizeable garden (though with only one bathroom, as was the norm in those days). Presiding over meals at the dining-room table was a portrait in oils of Horace's father James by Edward Handley-Read, which was once exhibited at the Royal Academy. James Freeman was born in the year of the Battle of Waterloo, one of fifteen children, and became a teacher in Newbury, Berkshire. He, in turn, was descended from Lincolnshire or East Anglian farmers, which, bearing in mind John's conspicuous red hair, suggests a Viking inheritance.

The painting of James showed him at breakfast reading *The Times*. On the wall opposite was a copy of the famous *The Derby Day* painting by William Powell Frith (1819–1909). Next door, an extensive library included all the works of Charles Dickens, which John read before he was twelve. He was attracted more to the storylines (according to a relative) than to the implied social criticism. Not that all his reading was serious: he later confessed to a childhood liking for horror comics such as those about the fictional Chinese poisoner Dr Fu Manchu. His father had a taste for classical poetry, particularly the *Aeneid*, which he encouraged his two sons John and James (born in 1917) to study. This adds to the impression of an *haute bourgeoisie* family enjoying the security and comfort of late Edwardian life after the watershed of 1910. John described his parents as 'Asquithian Liberals, that is to say they considered themselves as being in their day progressive, but they would find themselves at present [in the 1960s] on the extreme right wing of the Tory Party.'

He did, however, bear emotional scars. His father Horace had a cold, analytical mind and discouraged closeness, at least until his last years. Apparently, he and his sons had dinner together once a week, otherwise by appointment. He did not leave either of them money in his will. John once said that from the age of six he disliked his father and despised his mother – 'a pretty but silly woman' he called her. He must have had a loveless and lonely childhood, but he was extraordinarily self-sufficient. He first smoked when he was four and soon after devised an electric alarm system in his bedroom that warned if his parents were around. He rode the trains to school on his own, climbing from carriage to carriage. He roamed around London. He used to recount the story of taking himself off to the Royal Court

Theatre in Sloane Square and asking at the box office: 'Is this a suitable play for a boy of seven?' Theatre was to be an abiding interest throughout his life.

His relations with his brother James, two years his junior, were also cool. He seldom chose to see him when they were adults, saying, 'I've never liked James ever since I saw him deliberately destroying my copy of *Alice in Wonderland* in his cot.' There was more to it than that, for John was convinced that his father preferred James to him – another clue for psychologists.

That was probably true because, while John was an unruly child, James was a well-behaved and academically inclined boy who did everything that was expected of him. After the war, during which he fought in Burma and won the Military Cross, James followed his father to the chancery bar and specialised in industrial relations. He was also a practising Anglican. At his funeral, where there were many prayers, a eulogy and *Pie Jesu* from Faure's 'Requiem', sung by his daughter, John was heard muttering: 'I don't want any of this sort of thing when it's my turn.' In the event, he was to get his wish.

Anthony Clare was not the only psychiatrist to refer to the significance of Freeman's childhood. He had submitted to a polite mauling in that *Face to Face* interview, so perhaps he was licking his wounds when he considered that Freeman had the characteristics of a social psychopath. He referred me to the *Psychiatric Dictionary* (published by the OUP), which defines a social psychopath as having 'a poorly developed sense of empathy leading to unfeeling and insensitive behaviour but disguised as a superficial charm and absence of "nervousness", an egocentricity and incapacity for love'. This, continues the *Psychiatric Dictionary*, has as its aetiology 'emotional deprivation early in life'. Social psychopathy is more characteristic of leaders than of the rest of us, according to a study at Surrey University:

Surveys of high achievers like prime ministers, US presidents and leading entrepreneurs have shown that nearly one-third lost a parent before
the age of fourteen (compared with 8 per cent of the general population). Left high and dry at a young age they have resolved to snatch
hold of their destiny; adversity is the key to exceptional achievement.[1]

Be that as it may, when John was thirteen he won an exhibition, later
a scholarship, to Westminster School and began five very happy years
there. When he left in 1933, he wrote: 'I only hope that my successors
have as calm a voyage [as I had] and will look back on their life at
Westminster with as much pleasure as I do.' In old age, he reminisced
with Nigel Lawson about the good times at their alma mater, relating
with relish how he had lost his virginity to an under-matron at the
age of fifteen. In middle age, he described to his drinking companion
Tom Driberg how his favourite Westminster watering holes had been
the Two Chairmen pub in Queen Anne's Gate and, more daringly, the
bar of a celebrated Edwardian haunt in Soho called Romano's. There
is no sense here of Freeman as a lonely and loveless teenager; rather
it is of a worldly boy enjoying a sophisticated and tolerant school at
the heart of the nation's life.

Freeman's years at Westminster were not hedonistic; they were formative. Whereas many public schoolboys left school culture-bound,
as Christian officers and gentlemen ready to serve their country as
future leaders, only for university to encourage them to work out who
they really were and what they wanted from life, for Freeman it was
the reverse. Westminster taught him the civilising values of tolerance
and courtesy, which never left him, but also awakened a social and
political consciousness. When he was seventeen he joined the Labour
Party after a shocking experience that led him to write in his house
magazine 'the outstanding fact of the year' was that the school 'had

heard the voice of England's forgotten people'. He was referring to the hunger march that massed outside the school gates in Palace Yard on 1 November 1932.

The worldliness of Westminster was partly due to its location right next to the Houses of Parliament and Westminster Abbey. It was also due to the headmaster, Dr Harold Costley-White – later a Canon of Westminster Abbey and then Dean of Gloucester Cathedral. He was quietly determined to teach a strong sense of public responsibility and a code of courtesy, as well as the importance of intellectual self-confidence. To this end, he revived the debating society in Freeman's last year. The opening proposition was: 'This house would welcome the establishment of a dictator.' Freeman spoke against, proposing Lloyd George as an evil dictator in a mocking speech that contrasted him with the Roman consul Lucius Quinctius Cincinnatus, who displayed all the civic virtues before resigning his office and returning home to plough his fields.

Westminster School made every use of its proximity to Parliament. In 1931, Mahatma Gandhi – in London for the Round Table Conference on Indian independence (this is when Churchill called him 'a half-naked fakir') – spoke to the school's political and literary society on 'Indian Self-Government'. A sketch of the event by John Bowle hangs in the school library. Freeman was listening, and the desirability of Indian independence became one of his consistent beliefs. Soon after, he met Krishna Menon, who was campaigning aggressively in the United Kingdom for the cause, and Freeman is also on record as saying that the first political speaker to make an impact on him was Stafford Cripps, who was committed to ending British rule in India. Finally, Freeman provided his own postscript. When he was High Commissioner to India in the 1960s, he looked back upon that schoolboy meeting with Gandhi: 'I remember the sense of surprise, awe – and perhaps "melting" is the word – which his visit evoked.'

Other speakers to the political and literary society also showed a distinct left-wing bias. In 1933, the communist journalist Claud Cockburn gave a talk entitled 'A Journalist in Germany' and the headmaster described 'My Visit to Russia'. In 1934, the year after Freeman left, Professor Harold Laski spoke on 'Liberty' and Professor Julian Huxley on 'Science and Society'. Such talks must have been heady stuff for an impressionable teenager.

The climax of Costley-White's liberal intentions was the formation of the United Front of Progressive Forces (UFPF), based at Westminster School. John had left by then, but his brother James was on the executive committee. In common with other leading public schools such as Wellington, where Freeman's contemporary Esmond Romilly had started a widely publicised pacifist journal (*Out of Bounds: Public Schools' Journal Against Fascism, Militarism and Reaction*), Westminster made up for the establishment's seeming indifference to fascism by actively campaigning against it. Esmond Romilly was by now working in a communist bookshop in London and starting a society for 'escaped' public schoolboys. He was shortly to cycle off to Spain and join what became the International Brigades. It would have been typical of Westminster's encouragement of public debate to invite the Romilly brothers, Esmond and Giles, to speak at the school. In any event, the manifesto of the Westminster UFPF was announced in February 1936 amid 'scenes of enthusiasm unparalleled at Westminster'. It committed its members to:

Uncompromising resistance to fascism, conservatism and war...

Vigorous efforts to secure international disarmament...

The nationalisation of armaments and the coal industry...

The abolition of the Means Test, slum clearance…
The drastic reform of the House of Lords…

The audience of fifty to sixty boys and staff then rose to its feet and gave the first rendering of the 'United Front Song':

Lift up your voices now. Singing for freedom,
Peace and fraternity, more for the poor;
Work for the workless and justice for all men,
Progress in unity! No more war!

Over the next five weeks, UFPF (nicknamed not unfairly as 'ufpuff') held three public demonstrations and two more meetings, and thus 'ended a term of remarkable vitality and enthusiasm'.[2]

Compared to this ecstatic report, the school magazine, *The Eliz-abethan*, makes dull reading. It is the predictable digest of sport, chapel and Officers' Training Corps (OTC). The July 1932 edition includes a rowing profile of the seventeen-year-old John Horace Free-man ('Red' to his friends because of his hair, not yet his politics), who was in the first VIII and continued to be the following year: 'A delightful man to have in the crew. A tremendously hard worker and very keen. At present he rows like the village blacksmith. Next year his aim must be "maximum power with maximum at ease".'

To brawn may be added a big head, according to the Busby House ledger of 1931: 'JF has plenty of brains and common sense but is inclined to that opinion himself, which alienates his elders.' His class-room achievements were high though not uniform. Records show that his mathematics results were truly abysmal in his early years, for he obtained nought out of 100 in two exams – a fact he was inclined to boast about later on. Perhaps he made up for this by reading extensively. He said in later years that Edward Gibbon's *Decline and Fall of the Roman Empire* and George Bernard Shaw's plays had helped form his political views – a tribute to Westminster's encouragement of self-education.

It was Dr Costley-White who revived rowing ('water' in the school slang) and this is how the young Freeman got to know him. His obituary in *The Times* centred on his Christian faith: 'Costley-White was a man of deep religious convictions, which permeated all his work. He was a forceful and fluent preacher; he had a keen and active mind and was a lover of music, a subject he did much to encourage at Westminster.' He left the school to become a distinguished Church of England clergyman. Since Freeman later acknowledged his debt to his former headmaster, the question arises as to whether this influence extended to Freeman's faith too.

The answer must be 'no'. The Christian religion (Church of England) was routine at Westminster, and the fifteen-year-old Freeman submitted to Confirmation as a *rite de passage*, administered to him by the Archbishop of Canterbury. He recalled feeling the weight of the 'apostolic hands' on his head and noted that they trembled. Instead of accepting this as a transmission of the Holy Spirit, he remembered thinking: 'The old boy's not long for this world.' Nor was he: the Archbishop died a few months later in 1930.

Although Freeman felt no confirmation of faith as a result of this experience, nor did he feel indifference. Years later, he told his High Anglican friend Tom Driberg that although he lacked 'the gift of faith', he 'had no difficulty in doing anything officially expected in this field'. Perhaps sympathetic agnosticism summed up his attitude, or was it just the relaxed tolerance that stemmed from Westminster? Incidentally, his mother was a regular churchgoer, though his father was 'a total agnostic'. Additionally, Freeman's third wife was a Catholic, so all three of their children were baptised as Catholics, with his approval.

In later years he showed respect towards other people's Christian beliefs. He wrote in the *New Statesman* in 1963:

> I've always been intrigued by (and respectful of) the views of Christian socialists. Their essential belief, after all, receives much countenance from the Gospels – though precious little from the churches – and the notion of the equality of men before God is profoundly attractive and the very foundation of the respect for individuals which should be the purpose of socialist morality.

The Gospels appealed to him much more than the conservatism of the Church of England: *Tranquilla Non Movere* should be its motto, he wrote on another occasion.[3]

It was a feature of public schools at this time, and for at least thirty years afterwards, that the school prefects had more authority and status than the assistant masters. For example, at many schools the prefects could administer corporal punishment, while the teachers could not. This odd inversion went back to Thomas Arnold, the headmaster of Rugby 100 years before, whose 'praeposter' system (literally 'placed before') installed the senior boys as the custodians of discipline, subject only to his control. The tradition was tellingly satirised by Lindsay Anderson's film *If...* (1968), in which it led to a violent school insurrection that must appeal to the fantasies of public school boys whenever they watch it. It was also common practice for the head of house to write a confidential ledger about his term of office, open only to his successors. The Busby House ledger of Westminster School for 1932–33 (now open to researchers) gave me the first insight into the private world of John Freeman.

What is more personal and unique than handwriting? Freeman's changed little over seventy years and it is instantly distinctive. It is firm, fluent, but notably unformed, as though he was not interested in what it looked like, only in what he wrote. It is self-confident and regular, more administrative than creative. Seeking to open up this most private of individuals, I sent samples of his handwriting from different eras to a professional graphologist for her interpretation. She knew nothing about John Freeman, other than his autograph, so her analysis was perceptive. In summary:

> A love of adventure, particularly in the sphere of competitive achievement. His constant need to be active, though, could cause him to feel restless. Kind and friendly with family and close friends, but with acquaintances and business colleagues unlikely to reveal feelings. Sensitive to criticism but unlikely to express emotion.
>
> A compulsive need to achieve but an absence of warmth. Dispassionate, he experiences life as an onlooker. Socially likes to be correct, has charm at his disposal but is not pliable. Thinks for himself and takes a stand on principles. Egotistical, he feels himself to be special – above others. Strong leadership qualities, works well under pressure and appears not to suffer from stress. Works systematically, a good organiser, thrives on difficult assignments and is easily bored. An intelligent person with sharpness and speed of thought, keen perception that enables him to arrive at solutions quickly.

The overall tone of Freeman's ledger entries is one of authority. Freeman could have been the housemaster of Busby's – not that he had any time for Busby's actual housemaster: 'Hilary is the worst housemaster I ever came across or heard of and his wife in my opinion is an unpleasant, snobbish and silly woman.' He dismissed the outgoing matron as 'an inefficient old bitch', thus showing an earthy expression that did not desert him with the years. No one could accuse him of misogyny, however: 'The new woman is a perfect jewel. I hope future generations of Busbyites will value her as highly as we do.' Bearing in mind his affair with the under-matron, I wonder whether the value he placed was more personal.

Freeman's intentions as head of house were to implement the philosophy of the headmaster. His approach was almost paternal:

> I have done as much as I can to stimulate interest in the debating society and the League of Nations union. Intelligent opinion is more important than achievement at games … I am convinced that the Corps (the OTC) is a bad and unnecessary institution. I have decided to abolish personal fagging, which I consider to be an idiocy. Fags should be treated like decent human beings and if this had happened before then the house would have been much happier.

Reading this, I had to remind myself that Freeman was still a boy at school, very much a teenager. Little wonder his girlfriends at Oxford said he was a grown-up among students, self-possessed and quietly arrogant.

In later years, Freeman said that abolishing personal fagging (the allocation of junior boys as virtual servants to their seniors) was his legacy to Westminster. He wrote the next term (Lent, 1933):

> As indicated, I have abolished fagging and no harm has been done. There is no sign of juniors becoming uppish. Whether fagging implants a respect for authority I am doubtful! People in the Under report that life is more peaceful and pleasant and the standard of work and discipline is better than before. Incessant and useless petty punishments are futile for monitors and fags.

Freeman's most prominent entry in the ledger concerns an event that 'although it has no direct connection with the history of the house, may be worth recording'. History has proven him right:

> On the evening of Tuesday 1 November [1932] a great army of hunger marchers attempted to force an entry into the House of Commons. These marchers had come to London from all parts of England and Scotland some days before and there had already been two dem-onstrations – one in Hyde Park, where a great deal of damage and injury had been done, and one of a more peaceful nature in Trafalgar Square. Then they requested that a deputation should be allowed to appear before the bar of the House of Commons. This request was foolishly refused with the result that about 10,000 unemployed assem-bled at Parliament Square. Strict orders were given that nobody from Westminster was to go outside Dean's Yard. I went out alone to see what could be seen. After one or two truncheon charges the square was empty and the marchers were driven into the mouth of Victoria Street. A police barricade was thrown round with a Police HQ in the middle, from which Lord Trenchard directed operations by flashlight signals. As the crowd became confined between the Abbey railings and the Guildhall, it became rather ill tempered. However, under the control of Wal Harrington more serious rioting was avoided. All this time the crowd was being driven steadily along Victoria Street by mounted police. We heard a great deal of rioting in Great Smith Square, where rioters broke through the police cordon. All evening Dean's Yard was used as a Police Reserve HQ with mounted police exercising their horses. It was all quite exciting.

At this point I was expecting to read that the school had 'heard the voice of England's forgotten people'. In fact, Freeman ends unpredictably:

'But for the extreme tact and bravery of the police, the results might have been more serious – perhaps it's a pity they weren't.' A successor head of Busby's annotates in the margin: 'Either a sadistic, snobbish or blatantly stupid point of view.'

Freeman probably wrote his 'forgotten people' epitaph in the Busby House magazine (as opposed to the ledger), which is missing from the library now, but was possibly available just after the war, when the journalist Anthony Howard, who used the quote in his newspaper profile of Freeman in 1961, was also head of Busby House. The image remains of young Freeman wandering around on his own in the midst of a very large-scale riot and watching the confrontation between desperate marchers and mounted police – a confrontation unequalled until the miners' strike of the mid-1980s. It must have been a formative experience.

It was Freeman who revived the Busby magazine, writing in the ledger with unintended precocity: 'I have sacked the old printer, found a new one, organised advertising and asked all old Busbyites to contribute. I am editing it myself as I am the most suitable person.' He ends: 'Looking back over the whole year, I can see that I had a very happy year as head of Busby's. I honestly believe that the other members of the house enjoyed themselves too.' There can be but few occasions in later years when Freeman wrote so unguardedly, but then he cannot have conceived of a biographer accessing his report seventy-five years later.

There follows a long break in the sequence of the ledger. A subsequent head of Busby's accounted for it:

> This is due entirely to J. H. Freeman, who, in spite of continuous demands from subsequent heads of house, to which he either turned a deaf ear or returned a vague promise, persisted in keeping the ledger. After five years of absence it was in danger of becoming a myth. The

ledger was eventually recovered by Hayward who visited Freeman several times at Oxford.

The missing years of the ledger could be taken as a metaphor for Freeman's missing years at Oxford University.

John Horace Freeman, says the university register, was in residence as a Commoner at Brasenose College (1933–37), where he was awarded a third-class degree in Classics. To be specific, he was given a pass in Mods and a third in Greats, which was just better than a fail. The college magazine, *The Brazen Nose*, adds that he rowed for the first VIII during his first year. Apart from that entry, he may as well not have existed until he was awarded an honorary fellowship in 1969.

In later years he did nothing to dispel this reputation for undistinguished anonymity. He told Catherine that he went up to Oxford determined not to read another book, and he wasted his time gambling and drinking in order to spend his father's money accordingly. This confessed dissipation led later friends like Norman MacKenzie (an assistant editor at the *New Statesman* 1944–62) to wonder whether Freeman then and later had a wild streak that needed to be rigorously, not to say icily, controlled. 'Quite possibly,' said Catherine when I put this to her in 2003. 'He's capable of a furnace of feeling, which is why he tamps everything down and is so ultra-controlled.'

On 19 October 1935, the editor of *Cherwell* wrote a leader asking: 'Is Oxford Degenerate?' The author obviously thought so, and with good reason – which applied to Freeman as much as anybody else:

Ours is essentially a tragic generation. Born in the turmoil and bloodshed, the suicidal folly and the bestiality of a great war, passing our lives in the midst of the social and economic upheaval that resulted, we are likely to die prematurely in another and yet more violent conflict.

The security, the peace and the wealth, which might have been ours and which other generations before us have known, have been sacrificed on the altars of honour and national pride.

It is small wonder then if we are a degenerate and an embittered generation; small wonder that we at Oxford, more fully alive than most of our contemporaries to our situation, are branded as unmoral and unprincipled by our immediate predecessors.

A report in the *Gloucester Echo* of 9 April 1934 confirmed this image of the well-off, dissolute Freeman, one of the 'gay young things' of the era:

The Hon Henry Cecil of Stowlangtoft Hall, near Bury St Edmunds, younger brother of Lord Amherst of Hackney, who was injured in a motor car accident near Thetford, Norfolk, on Saturday, has recovered consciousness, and his condition today was comfortable. Mr Cecil was accompanied by a friend, Mr John Freeman, who was slightly injured.

They were lucky to escape. Their car crashed through a wire fence, turned a somersault, and landed upside down on the railway line 17 ft below. There was very little visibility at the time (early on Sunday morning) due to a mist. They had been returning from a dance at Euston Hall, the seat of the Duke of Grafton.

Freeman's injuries were not slight. It was discovered later that he had fractured his skull, as a result of which he spent two months in a nursing home and gave up rowing. According to his army medical report he suffered from giddiness for several years afterwards.

One of Freeman's close acquaintances at Oxford was Woodrow Wyatt, whose career would be linked with his over the next half-century, through university, the army, Labour politics, broadcasting, journalism and female friends. In 1986, they met at a dinner party given by Lady Montagu. Freeman told her, 'I've known Woodrow for nearly fifty years,' and Woodrow replied, 'Yes, I've known all your wives and you have known all mine.'[4]

They each had four. Wyatt's first wife was Susan Cox, whose first lover was John Freeman. In the absence of Freeman's autobiography, I offer Woodrow and Susan's scene-setter of university life at Oxford.

Woodrow Wyatt was accepted by Worcester College in 1936, after he wrote a twenty-minute essay entitled 'My Thoughts on Hyde Park'. He had little intention of studying: 'If your prime object in going to Oxford or Cambridge is to study, you might as well go to a red-brick university where you can get all the textbooks and routine instruction you want.' The first dinner in hall, he sat next to an Old Etonian. 'Look at their bottoms in the showers,' he would say of other Worcester undergraduates. 'You can see how common they are.' Dinner was dull, he continued:

> Unless someone was 'sconced'. I forget what prompted this ritual – perhaps extreme obscenity, the breach of a convention or just fun brought a challenge to drink a sconce. A huge sconce or pot, holding two or three pints of beer, was brought in ceremonially. If the subject of the sconce could drink the whole pot in a single continuous swallow, he won. The challenger had to pay for his beer. Frequently the victors, white in the face, left hall soon afterwards.[5]

Drinking expensive wine was a matter of status: 'A member of New College was Alan Hare [later a famous philosopher]. He asked me for a drink in his rooms. At twelve in the morning we drank Château Latour. I was deeply impressed.'

Another ritual that condoned self-indulgence was 'sporting your oak', that is shutting the thick outer door of one's room to secure absolute privacy. This may have originated to promote quiet study, but was more of signal to indicate a girl within, hopefully without all her clothes on. One day when the provost called on Wyatt, he found the 'oak sported': 'Later he looked at me sadly. He did not approve of girls and would never have admitted them as members of the college. He never came to see me again.' The girl in question was Susan Cox. She was at Somerville College when university membership of female undergraduates was still being disputed. In fact, the Oxford Union debated the issue in 1936 (although women were not allowed to join the union even if they wanted to). Wyatt wrote an article for a magazine he founded called *The Oxford Comment*, headed 'Oxford Women Are Awful'. He began: 'The average woman undergraduate is wearing ill-fitting clothes, has a shiny face, untidy hair and a sloppy ungainly walk.' He did, graciously, identify Susan Cox as an exception, and rightly so, for she was a tall, golden-haired beauty, with blue eyes and freckles.

Thirty years later, she wrote about the status of female students during her time at Somerville for the *Oxford Magazine*. She was now Susan Hicklin, and her daughter was just starting at the same college. As such, she was called a 'freshman', which was the starting point for her mother's article. She called it 'Two Faces of Eve'. Here it is in summary, interspersed with ditties about the two sexes taken from *Cherwell* magazine when Freeman was writing for it:

> What did the girls at Oxford look like? I did notice there *were* girls about. Sometimes I even spoke to them and they spoke to me. But looking back I seem to sense a disappointment that getting to Oxford hadn't also raised us to the status of men. There was a tendency to refer to girls whom we didn't like as 'females' and those whom we did like as 'chaps'.

I like men
Now and then
I enjoys
Boys.
I keep brandy
Handy
I look best
Undressed

I [Susan Hicklin] sought enlightenment from John Betjeman's *An Oxford University Chest* – a one-man survey that appeared in my last year. 'I suppose it is only right to bring in undergraduettes but it would be wrong to suppose they play a large part in the social life of the university. Wherever women come into undergraduate clubs, they drive men out.'

Although the room was rather small
I knew she wouldn't mind at all.
There was a sofa and a floor
Could any woman ask for more?

The trouble with us in the '30s was that we did not know quite what to aim at. Debs and secretaries were smart – at different ends of the scale; embryo schoolmistresses were not. How were we to avoid looking like either?

My mother solved the problem. She handed onto me a vast deep blue cloak with its high velvet collar. Striding down the Turl with it thrown toga-like over each shoulder, it appealed to me as just the right romantic get-up for the 'dreaming spires' routine. Eyes right! And salute to All Souls with a *Dominus Illuminatio Mea.*

Now that I've done what you desired
I'm feeling cold and very tired,
And any decent woman loathes,
Her honour lost, to lose her clothes.[6]

In 2004 Susan Hicklin spoke to me about Freeman. She and her sister Prudence had known him since their schooldays, when they went to Francis Holland School by Regent's Park in London, near where John was born. First, the young Freeman had an affair with Prudence; then with Susan, when they were undergraduates together. They remained friends into old age.

> He was dashingly handsome with wavy red hair, blue eyes and a slim, fit body. He had a strong physical presence and he must have found womanising very easy. I never asked him if I was his only girl. I was just jolly glad that this Olympian figure took me out sometimes. He had this self-sufficiency, you see, which women find a challenge. I remember once he took me to Henley to watch his brother James row.
>
> He loved beautiful things. He gave me an early edition of *The Country Wife* but he did not write anything in it. He never signed anything.
>
> He was upright and full of principle. He could not bear people who did not do what they said they would do and he could be forbidding. That was John.

I asked her how this squared with Freeman's reputation for dissipation.

> That's not the word I would use. He was certainly hedonistic, determined to enjoy life. He had escaped from a stern father and a force-fed

education and, you see, he must have found Oxford all too easy, particularly attracting women. He actually seemed above things, very grown-up. He wasn't a party person. He told me: 'I'm not very good at playing *la betise* [the clown].' He was not an involvement person, not a joiner. In fact he was a Mr Something-Else. He was gracious, charming, but you could never get the measure of him.

Years later she said mischievously to Catherine Freeman, on meeting her for the first time: 'I was determined that at least one of my sons would have red hair.'

Freeman's life at Oxford was more politically involved and more public spirited than he admitted. Why he completely ignored the truth in his later accounts to friends, as he also did in his army record, is a mystery. He could only have written his dismissive letter to me – 'I can't see how my life can be of any possible interest to anybody' – if he had convinced himself over the years that his perverse modesty or extreme privacy were justified. In fact, at Oxford he even changed his name to deflect attention – and that really is perverse. Here is the missing account of John Freeman's Oxford years.

Freeman, Wyatt and Philip Toynbee (who was at Brasenose with Freeman and became the first communist president of the Oxford Union) were members of the Labour Club. Freeman and Wyatt also helped found the Experimental Theatre Group, inspired by Professor Neville Coghill. This was obviously to Freeman's taste because it encouraged entirely home-grown talent working under an agreement of anonymity. It was set up as a deliberate reaction to Oxford University's Dramatic Society (OUDS), which had enough prestige in 1935 to attract both John Gielgud and G. B. Shaw to supervise the casting of its production of *Richard II*. The principle of the Experimental Theatre Group was that the play itself was important, not the cast who worked on it. This made reviewing a little difficult, but its first production of Dryden's *All for Love*, produced in three weeks, was considered by *Cherwell* 'an excellent production and quite up to OUDS standards'. Later, Freeman listed in his *Who's Who* entry for 1946 that his recreation was drama – a suitable choice for such a chameleon.

Freeman's founding membership of the Experimental Theatre Group is a clue to the identity of Flavus. On 23 May 1936, Flavus showed up for the first time as the pseudonym of the writer of a weekly column in *Cherwell* called 'Morals and Politics'. In Roman times, Flavus was the name of a red-haired conspirator who failed to overthrow the dictator Nero, but Flavus was also the pseudonym used by Freeman when he later edited the 'London Diary' in the *New Statesman*. No coincidence, surely? Flavus disappeared when Freeman stopped being editor of *Cherwell* in April 1937.

On 24 October 1936, Flavus strayed for the only time from morals and politics to a theatre interview. The subject is Dame Sybil Thorndyke, who was staying at the Randolph Hotel. It bears the Freeman style, particularly the somewhat effusive complimenting, which was the Freeman way:

> We talked about Coward and Shaw, actors and critics, Wales, Eurypides and D. H. Lawrence and I asked her what she thought of the Experimental Theatre Club. 'It's a great idea,' she said, 'and if you're doing the job properly we shall soon feel the effect of it.' Ann [daughter of Sybil, also an actress performing in Oxford] came in. She is charming and lovely – may I say that she will have to wait a little while before she is as lovely as her mother?

So Flavus is a member of the Experimental Theatre Club? It must be Freeman.

The political views of Flavus are definitely socialist. On 7 November 1936 he writes:

> The Jarrow marchers have arrived in London and no other working-class demonstration has aroused such widespread sympathy. These courageous marchers are a living indictment of the wanton and callous policy of the national government. They are a living argument for socialism. Never again will the people of Jarrow entrust their interests to a government of profiteers and aristocrats.

This must have been the occasion when Freeman first met Ellen Wilkinson, newly elected as Labour MP for the Jarrow constituency and once a founding member of the Communist Party. She was known as 'Red Ellen', a reference, as with Freeman, to her hair colour and her politics. Freeman said years later that Ellen Wilkinson had been a formative influence on his politics.

Flavus leaves no doubt about where he stands on the Spanish Civil War that had just begun: 'The only possible excuse for a pro-Rebel policy [support for Franco's Nationalists] is the strongest possible political prejudice. The Madrid government [the new Republic] has every conceivable moral and legal right on its side.' (31 October 1936)

It was the rally of Oswald Mosley and his Fascists at the Carfax Assembly Rooms in Oxford that really got Flavus worked up. Like the Fascist Olympia rally of 1933, attended by Philip Toynbee, it was a violent confrontation between individual protest and 'storm-trooper' over-reaction:

> Do you want free speech or not? That question has got to be answered. If you do, you will agree with me in feeling nothing but contempt

and loathing for Sir Oswald Mosley and his half-baked young men. Every lover of freedom will continue to ask questions on these occasions and presumably continue to be beaten up. Fascist tactics have got to be stopped. The most vigorous protests offer the only hope of freedom. (30 May 1936)

There is no political apathy here; no dissipation in booze and sex. Assuming Freeman to be Flavus, in a matter of months he witnessed fascism at first hand, saw the nadir of Britain's social divide, and took sides on 'the last great cause' (the Spanish Civil War).

Cherwell in March 1937 carries a startling paragraph: 'Editor Freeman, who has done most of his editing from London, has been overcome by his cares. Our affable editor goes to town for an operation every Monday and Friday. He has now had enough and is resigning.' The full name of the editor of *Cherwell* is given as George Freeman of Brasenose College. No such person exists in the university register, neither in those years nor in any other. The Association of College Archivists could not trace 'George Freeman' to any college. Without much confidence, I asked Catherine Freeman if John was ever called 'George' at Oxford.

'Georgie – yes, that's what some of the girls did call him.'

Could this be a reference to the nursery rhyme?

> *Georgie Porgie, pudding and pie*
> *Kissed the girls and made then cry*
> *When the boys came out to play*
> *Georgie Porgie ran away.*

Why did John disguise himself as George? Hiding from the public gaze? Deflecting criticism? Perhaps an in-joke? And why did he go down

24

to London every weekend? Possibly this was a reference to the after-effects of his car crash, but, according to Tom Driberg, Freeman now had an extracurricular job in London – selling women's underwear:

> When he was trying to read for Honour Moderations, some impulse prompted him to leave Oxford and go to London; here he earned a living by tutoring and also, for some weeks, by selling ladies' under-wear, door to door, in the East End. Then he went back to Oxford, late for the start of term; his father and his college were sensible about it.

When Driberg asked Freeman why he had done this, he gave his usual answer: to 'supplement his income'.[7] I think the truth is more likely to be journalistic curiosity in London low life – an interest he shared with Henry Mayhew, the author of *London Labour and the London Poor* (1851), who was also the founder of *Punch*, one of Free-man's favourite magazines.

All this must have contributed to Freeman's embarrassing exam results. The second Flavus, writing in the *New Statesman* (18 May 1962), gave a more reasoned excuse:

> When I set out on a somewhat inglorious obstacle race through the Oxford school of Greats more than a quarter of a century ago, I was wholly unversed in the disciplines of logic and they had forgotten to tell me what philosophy itself was about. The result was that I was plunged into a maze of abstractions, which filled me alternately with despair as I failed to grasp their relevance and with manic delight as I constructed some metaphysical sandcastle.

This was by way of saying that subsequently he discovered A. J. Ayer's *Language, Truth and Logic*, which he was reviewing for the *New*

Statesman, and that introduced him to Bertrand Russell, whereby 'the whole business became plain and purposeful: philosophy was not a gentleman's game like Latin verse, but an imperative pursuit of truth about oneself and ones' relation to the external world'.

Freeman left Oxford in May 1937 and, for the next two years, he marked time. There can be no other explanation why he joined the advertising consultancy of Ashley Courtenay Ltd based in Pall Mall, off Trafalgar Square. Another world war was coming and it was hardly the time to start on a lifelong vocation. He regarded it as a mild diversion, worthy of some intellectual input because, he said, writing advertising copy was like writing Latin verse. One of the accounts he handled was for Chubb's locks and safes – 'undoubtedly the best', he used to say. Another was for Lanson champagne, for which he formed a permanent liking. In later years he looked back to Ashley Courtenay Ltd with humorous disparagement: 'If you want to know what it was like, Dorothy Sayers's *Murder Must Advertise* gives a good picture.' He was referring to her hero Lord Peter Wimsey, who made his name with a campaign of free gifts for cigarette coupons, and the slogan 'Whiffle your way round Britain'.

He seems to have enjoyed being in London. He lived on a houseboat, went to the theatre and had many girlfriends, including – Susan Hicklin told me – Winston Churchill's daughter Diana. This is just about possible, although Diana was five years older and had married the Conservative politician Duncan Sandys in 1935. Susan also told me that he befriended the *Punch* magazine humourist E. V. Lucas. I find it easy to see why. Lucas's sense of humour would have been at home in *The New Yorker* (Freeman's favourite magazine), as it was based on observing the human condition with all its quirks and curiosities. He is best known today for his aphorisms, which would also have appealed to Freeman; for example: 'A perfect holiday would be to join a travelling circus as a utility man' or 'There can be no defence like elaborate courtesy'. When Freeman met him he was in his last years, living a solitary life in London. He ate out in clubs and restaurants and resented interference in his private life. Thirty years later, in his Flavus column in the *New Statesman*, Freeman compared Lucas with another 'urbane essayist' he had got to know – A. J. Liebling of *The New Yorker*: 'They both wore the air of worldly pessimism in a becoming (basically cheerful) fashion.'

On 18 August 1938, John Freeman married his first wife, Elizabeth Allen Johnston, in St John's Church, Chelsea. She was twenty-five and her father was a chartered accountant from Surrey. He was twenty-three and an 'advertising consultant', living at Walm Lane, London, NW2. He said later that he had only done it to annoy his father. It was a childless marriage that he later disparaged cruelly. 'I went to war to get away from her,' he used to say and, after the divorce in 1948, 'I wouldn't recognise her now if I saw her across the street.' Susan Hicklin said Freeman treated the marriage as 'a joke'.

A month later, on 30 September, Prime Minister Neville Chamberlain flew back from Munich waving his notorious piece of paper and declaring, 'Peace with honour. Peace in our time.' This was the Munich Agreement that sacrificed Czechoslovakia to Hitler for another year or so of peace. What Freeman thought of this at the time there is no knowing, but Flavus would probably have agreed with everything Freeman wrote in the *New Statesman* in June 1952, when reviewing the memoirs of Viscount Simon:

> Munich was only the last plank in the rotten structure of appeasement, whose foundations Viscount Simon had laid as Foreign Secretary a dozen years before. He seems to have had no inkling of the uncompromising moral judgement that the ordinary people of Britain had

passed on the fascist dictators. It was this tide of passionate feeling, based on principle, which in the later 1930s raised the little men above the level of their rulers.[8]

When Freeman got married he must have had a premonition of the war – a war he would fight in for over four years.

Chapter 2

Brigade major

W HEN THE WAR came, Freeman was determined 'to get in on the ground floor'. This was not through any sentimental patriotism, he added, but because 'that way you could get one of the more interesting jobs'. Presumably he thought he failed in this endeavour because he later told Tom Driberg that he had experienced 'a completely undistinguished war'.[1]

This self-deprecation is so far from the truth as to be perverse. Freeman fought through the war from November 1941 until the end of April 1945, first with the 1st Battalion of the Rifle Brigade (the 'Desert Rats') in north Africa and Italy, and then with the 131st Infantry Brigade in France, Holland and Germany. He won two decorations for gallantry, the second one of which even his family does not know about and is not mentioned on his official army service record. One of Freeman's verbal decorations, so to speak, is that Field Marshal Montgomery called him 'the best brigade major in the Eighth Army' and, although I cannot verify the source of that quote, it comes to me from the historian and journalist Paul Johnson, who knew Freeman well and also served in the Rifle Brigade.

Understandably, Freeman did not like talking about the war. He told his stepdaughter Lizi in the 1950s: 'War is a very bloody business and I've seen men with their heads blown off; you're just like a piece of meat.' He never used his title of major after 1945. Nevertheless, having ploughed through report after report of brigade war diaries signed by J. H. Freeman, as either brigade major or deputy assistant quartermaster-general (DAQMG), I can say with confidence that his war was distinguished, to say the least.

Freeman enlisted with the Coldstream Guards on 27 June 1940 as a rank-and-file guardsman, and was promptly put on a charge for giving a 'wilfully false answer' to his date of birth – it was a year out. This, then, was another occasion on which he gave false information about himself – and there would be several more.

Despite Freeman's laconic references to 'getting in on the ground floor', he must have shared the trepidation of his fellow citizens. Only a few days before, France had surrendered in the face of the Nazi *blitzkrieg*. Only a few weeks before that, the British Army had been evacuated from Dunkirk and Churchill had become Prime Minister, announcing that he had 'nothing to offer except blood, toil, tears and sweat'. That summer the British were left to await their fate, certain that Hitler would order an invasion across the Channel.

Freeman did his basic training – of legendary toughness – at the Caterham depot. After the war, he said he had enjoyed being a guardsman for three reasons: he respected extremely high standards in any organised activity; he liked 'the kind of mindless or irresponsible anonymity of life in the ranks, not intruding at all on one's thoughts'; and, significantly for his later profession, he lived for the first time among working-class men. 'The rough but friendly democracy of the barrack-room appealed to him strongly,' wrote Driberg. So much so that Freeman thought being a guardsman was 'a suitable way to see the war out'.

His commanding officer had other ideas. Sitting tight at Caterham depot had to come to an end. Commanding officer Captain Piggot Brown told him 'pretty sharply' (Freeman's words) that he ought to apply for an officer's commission, as his military conduct was 'very good' and he was 'sober, honest and trustworthy'. Apparently, a 'girl friend's father' suggested the Rifle Brigade, and so Freeman was given a Regular Army Emergency Commission on 21 December 1940.

Second Lieutenant Freeman spent the next ten months with the Rifle Brigade, which was regrouping in England after a bad mauling at Dunkirk. Young subalterns would usually be appointed to command an infantry platoon, but it is notable that the Rifle Brigade was forming a new motor training (MT) battalion, which provided specialist vehicle training for motorised battalions like the Rifle Brigade. Freeman was transferred to the 2nd MT Battalion in June 1941, and that presumably gave him some satisfaction. He later told his family that he had joined the Rifle Brigade because it was mechanised and 'I wouldn't have to walk everywhere'.

The 1st Battalion of the Rifle Brigade embarked for an unknown destination on 28 September 1941. They rounded South Africa, headed for the Red Sea – by which time the destination was no secret – and disembarked at Suez, in the rain, at the end of November. Freeman must have seen the sign that his friend Lieutenant Peter Luke, also of the 1st Battalion of the Rifle Brigade, describes evocatively in his autobiography *Sisyphus and Reilly*:

> Just outside Alexandria, branching off from the main road to Cairo, is a tarmac track, narrow, black and uneven, that bears off west-wards between the Salt Lake of Mariut and the white strand of the sea. At this junction is a sign post bearing the legend 'To the Western Desert'.
>
> The idea that the road is the only one that leads to the war holds me with morbid fascination. Here in Egypt is one sort of life and down the track is another. Here is the Levant, the rich and fertile delta of the Nile, and in it a swarm of eastern peoples: Egyptians, Arabs, Sudanese, Syrians, Mohammedans, Copts, Christians and Jews, living – or trying to live – their multifarious lives. Down there, just a few miles away in a stony desert bordered by the sea, are two northern peoples (with some reluctant Italians), intent on only one thing – making war. The only connection is this tenuous twist of macadam road.[2]

Lieutenant Freeman was in B Echelon of the 1st Battalion. 'Red Free-man came up yesterday from B Echelon,' writes Lieutenant Luke in a letter home in August 1942.[3] The commander of B Echelon was usu-ally a captain (Freeman was promoted to temporary captain on 24 April 1942), responsible for the battalion's workshop vehicles, ammu-nition, fuel and water supply; as such, it was a staff appointment in the rear, behind the fighting forces. It led, in Freeman's case, up the ladder to DAQMG and then brigade major, both of which carried wider and greater responsibilities. Someone early on had decided that Freeman's strengths lay in his organisational control, his efficient management of resources and his maintenance of a clear, cool head for decision-making.

No personal diaries or letters home written by Freeman survive, if he even wrote any. He left no photographs and, after the war, he did not join any Rifle Brigade associations. His official army service record, which I obtained after his death, gives his theatre of war, his rank, and his dates of promotion, but no account of what he actually did as a member of headquarters staff. The official war diaries of the 1st Battalion of the Rifle Brigade, written at the time and now held in the National Archive, are confused and chaotic because that was the nature of the fighting. It is not possible, therefore, to provide a full narrative of Freeman's war in the Western Desert, even if anybody would want to read it. What *is* possible is to take an episodic approach, describing briefly (in cases where evidence definitely exists) some of the dramatic events that Freeman experienced.

In April 1942, Acting Captain Freeman was posted to the headquarters of the 22nd Armoured Brigade, which was defending the Gazala Line to the west of Tobruk. The brigade consisted of four or five battalions, including the 1st Battalion of the Rifle Brigade, a Royal Tank regiment, the County of London Yeomanry (infantry) and the 2nd Regiment of Royal Horse Artillery. In other words, it was a mixed fighting force of about 5,000 men, and Freeman was on the staff providing its operational and logistical needs – a B Echelon function. This was the first of the brigade appointments that would see him through the war. The Gazala Line was a series of defensive 'boxes', each defended by a brigade and laid out across the desert behind minefields and wire, watched by regular patrols between boxes. It was intended to prevent General Rommel and his Afrika Korps from breaking through, capturing Tobruk (which was rich in Allied supplies) and storming across the desert into Cairo, 500 miles to the west.

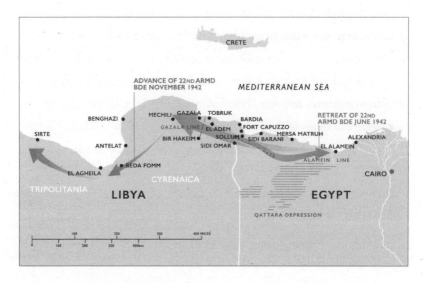

On 25 May, the German offensive began. By brilliant *blitzkrieg* tactics, Rommel outflanked the Gazala Line and pounded towards Tobruk. The Eighth Army retreated even before the panzer divisions arrived, proving the Napoleon dictum that 'in war the moral is to the material as three is to one'. The Allied commander General Ritchie, despite his superior forces, decided to abandon the frontier 'to gain time with distance'. Tobruk fell. Then commenced the headlong flight of the 22nd Armoured Brigade and the rest of the Eighth Army – those who had not been captured or killed – towards Egypt, pursued by the Afrika Korps. The atmosphere was close to panic. In Cairo, staff began to burn records and British civilians crowded on trains to Palestine. Peter Luke was on leave in Cairo and adopted a racing metaphor, displaying the familiar Rifle Brigade cool: 'The Gazala Line ought to have held. They're off in the Msus Stakes [scene of an earlier Rifle Brigade

retreat], Rommel leading the field. All you need is an iodine pencil [for infected wounds] and a pair of running shorts.'[4]

The Eighth Army retreated back over the Egyptian border, as described by the Rifle Brigade official history:

> They [the Afrika Korps] were soon driving hard for Cairo and in front of them, or at any rate driving in the same direction, were three battalions of the Rifle Regiment. It was a time of the utmost confusion. Orders and counter-orders were frequent and complicated. For some distance, the 1st Battalion travelled at night as the centre of three columns, and then discovered that two of them were German. A difficult battle ensued. At one point the 1st Battalion was well behind the leading elements of the enemy. There are stories of companies driving through vast columns of Italians all going the same way. Every day fires appeared on the horizon as dumps of supplies and NAAFI goods were burned. Most of the vehicles were badly in need of repair: fifteen cwts [lorries] would tow each other; carriers would limp and grind along. When the 1st Battalion reached the frontier wire, such was the appearance of the transport that the military police nicknamed them 'the Dodgy Column' ... The regiment was through the wire and, in a collection of vehicles that would have disgraced a circus, was among the last to reach Alamein.[5]

Where was Freeman in this headlong retreat? The official history describes 'the final nightmare': when the supply echelons of the 22nd Armoured, among others, could not replenish petrol because of the enemy surrounding them, so vehicles were abandoned. A rifleman wrote afterwards: 'In addition to the dilapidated state of our transport, we were exposing B Echelon, with our vital supplies, to unacceptable hazards in reaching us.'[6] In London, the chief of the general staff, Alan Brooke, wrote in his diary: 'The Middle East situation is about as unhealthy as it can be, and I do not very well see how it can end.'[7]

By early July, the 22nd Armoured Brigade had arrived at the edge of the Qattara Depression, an area (partly below sea level) of shifting sand dunes interspersed with dangerous salt marshes – a strategic line that could stop any invader. To the north was a bottleneck extending to the coast called the Alamein Line. The Afrika Korps's advance came to a halt of its own volition as they had outrun their supplies, including petrol. With the Royal Air Force controlling the sky and fresh troops re-enforcing the Eighth Army, it was time for both sides to stop.

It was at that point that Lieutenant Luke arrived on the scene: 'We are digging in at Alam el Halfa in the centre of the line. It is to be a last-man-and-last-round operation. *No pasaran* and all that.' Thus began the second episode of Freeman's desert war and his walk-on part in Lieutenant Luke's account. The 1st Battalion of the Rifle Brigade was preparing for the battles ahead and displaying its very own code of desert manners:

> Never stare at individuals through binoculars. It is rude.
>
> Officers may wear what they like within reason, but steel helmets and decorations are not *de rigeur.*
>
> If you are invited out to dinner, take your own wireless truck and your bed-roll. Nobody will want to dig you out of a slit trench in the dark.
>
> When you shit, go a stone's throw away from your nearest neighbour and take a spade. If you are in any doubt as to what is a stone's throw, try crapping near an Australian.[8]

Luke was afflicted with dysentery, so it was Captain Freeman (making his first appearance in *Sisyphus and Reilly*) who came to the rescue:

> On the march my truck had to drive like hell up to the front of the Column so that I could get out, squat, and squitter, while the whole battle group drove past. Sometimes they would barrack and then the lads on my truck would either shout back loyally or hide their faces in shame. Eventually, I got so bad that I was sent back to B Echelon where John Freeman (he was called 'Red' Freeman then – nothing to do with politics, just the colour of his hair) kindly fixed me up with a latrine of my own, made out of petrol tins, and had it placed handy to my bed so that I could stagger from one to the other and, of course, back again.[9]

The Eighth Army then rallied under new command, for General Claude Auchinleck was replaced the next month by General Bernard Montgomery. On his deathbed seventy-two years later, talking to his son Tom, John Freeman recalled hearing the news, which shows what an impact it must have made: 'General Roberts got us together and said, "I know things have been going badly, so HQ are sending out a competent shit to sort out the mess. He's called Montgomery."'

On 13 August, 'Monty', dressed in long shorts to cover his still white knees, addressed his staff for the first time: '*Here* we will stand and fight; there will be no further withdrawal. I have ordered all plans dealing with withdrawal to be burned, at once. If we can't stay here, then let us stay here dead.'[10] To raise morale further, Monty toured the Eighth Army emplacements with Winston Churchill. Lieutenant Luke witnessed it from an embarrassing position:

One bright morning I was sitting on the can, sweating and shivering at the same time, when a staff car drove past about 50 yards away. The occupant was a superior-looking guardee, with a look of impotent fury on his face. Then a very grand staff car with a Union Jack on its bonnet almost ran me down. In it, I had no difficulty in recognising generals Alexander and Montgomery. Between them was a rotund figure in dungarees, topped off by an old fashioned toupee. I was of course in a serious dilemma, glued like that to the can, but, on reflection, since I was not wearing a cap, I think I did the right thing; I sat stiffly to attention and gave a smart eyes-right. Winston Churchill removed the cigar from his mouth and extended it towards me between two fingers in a benign salute.[11]

Soon after the Prime Minister called in on the 22nd Armoured Brigade, Luke noted in his diary (22 August): 'Churchill came to look at our brigade. My platoon only saw his car in the distance surrounded by a fleet of staff cars.' Luke also added a typical reference to Freeman: 'Red Freeman came up yesterday from B Echelon; as usual, full of the latest bits of gossip about who sleeps with who from London to Cairo.'[12]

In his spare moments, Lieutenant Luke would settle down to read:

The sun rises and falls on the pages of *War and Peace*. The glare of the paper hurts my eyes. I lower the book and stare out across the desert where, as far as one can see, and for mile after mile beyond, are identical sand-coloured trucks in wide dispersal. Yet each truck is an island, a home, round which its occupants lead their own domestic lives; a home as recognisable to its owners as any one of a hundred identical houses in a European suburb. But here in the desert, the truck is the individual, and man only one of its working parts. How far in time and space this is from the Russian winter of 1812. Yet is it really so far?[13]

A few nights after, Luke was woken by a boot in the ribs: 'Get up. There's a full-scale attack all along the line.' This was Rommel's offensive at the end of August, intended to break through the Alamein Line to Cairo. As it happened, that first night, the full force of Rommel's depleted panzer divisions was borne by the 22nd Armoured Brigade defending the Alam Halfa Ridge. The next morning, Luke was in the general's mess when 'French Bob' came in, 'gold teeth flashing in the sunlight': '"We've been cut to pieces," he said happily, and it was no great exaggeration. I offered him a consoling gin. "Shin-shin, ol' boy," he said, raising his glass in a toast.'[14]

In fact, although the 22nd Armoured bore the brunt of the enemy's attack, it 'reacted magnificently': 'The panzer columns came under a storm of fire from the tanks and supporting artillery of this all-arms brigade group', forcing them to withdraw.[15] The next day, Montgomery's revitalised Eighth Army counter-attacked, aided substantially by Ultra intelligence intercepts and the Royal Air Force. That was the beginning of the end for Rommel's last offensive in the Western Desert. His next battle, the far bigger El Alamein, would be what he called a 'battle without hope'.

All I may add is that Freeman took part in the Battle of Alam Halfa, though whether he fought at El Alamein, I do not know. After Alam Halfa, the 22nd Armoured Brigade, including the 1st Battalion of the Rifle Brigade, became a permanent part of the 7th Armoured Division; hence it lost its insignia of a rhinoceros and adopted the desert rat instead (after a sketch made of a jerboa in the Cairo zoo). The fame of the 'Desert Rats' preceded Freeman in Parliament in 1945.

For episode three of Freeman's desert war, we move forward six months to 29 March 1943, when he was promoted to DAQMG – a senior HQ staff officer – in the 22nd Armoured Brigade. From then on we know much more about his movements because he signed the weekly war diary in so far as one was written. During the preceding six months, the 22nd Armoured Brigade had been the leading formation of the Eighth Army, pursuing the remnants of the Afrika Korps and the Italian Army back west across the Western Desert.

The journalist Alan Moorehead accompanied that advance:

> Nine-tenths of desert warfare is the battle of supply. Whoever first gets up most water, food, fuel, guns and men, wins the campaign. Now Montgomery was given the means to plan his supply ahead so that he could hold what he had already won and eventually push on to Tripoli.[16]

Freeman must have been in his element. He was promoted to Staff Captain on 17 November, but then records show he was in hospital for most of December and January. By the time Freeman was out of hospital, the 1st Battalion had taken part in the victory parade through Tripoli on 31 January. 'His return to unit is particularly requested,' says his record. By then, the 22nd Armoured had moved out of the Middle East Theatre into Tunisia, which was classed as north Africa, and came to a halt at Medenine, near the old French Mareth Line (built before the war to keep French Tunisia from fascist Libya). It protected a bottleneck between the Matmata Hills and the coast, and the Axis forces had shored up the old defences with 100 kilometres of barbed wire, 100,000 anti-tank mines and 70,000 anti-personnel mines. Breaking through the Mareth Line at the end of March was one of Montgomery's biggest tactical achievements. On exactly that date, Acting Major Freeman took over as DAQMG. The final task of the Eighth Army was to link up with the Allied First Army that had landed in Algeria, and together they would capture Tunis – the last German-held city in north Africa.

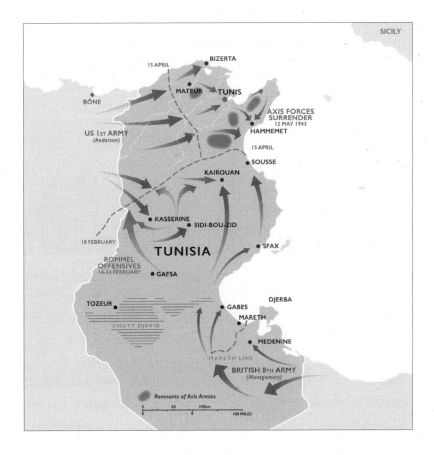

The advance of the Eighth Army – from the battles around Medenine to the capture of Tunis – took six weeks. This is the period covered by Freeman's citation for an MBE. It reads:

> Major Freeman had been the DAQMG of the 22nd Armoured Brigade during the period under review. During this time the brigade advanced from Medenine to Tunis and a heavy responsibility fell to Major Freeman.
>
> At no time was the brigade ever held up or delayed by shortage of supply and, in fact, everything ran with perfect efficiency and smoothness.

For this, Major Freeman is deserving of the highest praise; indeed, his energy, devotion to duty and attention to detail were of the first order. In particular, during the final stages of the advance to Tunis, when he accompanied the tactical brigade HQ in a tank in order to be in immediate touch with the situation.

Although at times under considerable shellfire, he handled the situation with cool and sure judgement, so that the brigade went short of nothing, while the echelons suffered a minimum of casualties.[17]

Was this the occasion that was recalled after the war by a rifleman to Paul Johnson? 'To listen to John directing armour and artillery hour after hour on the brigade radio was a marvellous lesson in coolness under stress.' This was not the only recollection. When Freeman was a TV celebrity around 1960, a retired general was heard to say: 'You think he's good on *Face to Face*? You've never heard him on the R/T [radio transmitter] with armour.' In fact, Major Freeman was recommended for the Military Cross, but this was changed by General Brian Horrocks to an MBE (presumably because the Military Cross is usually awarded for individual feats of gallantry).

Entering Tunis must have been Freeman's hour of glory, though Paul Johnson's claim that he had a girl waiting for him there seems a bit far-fetched. After the exuberant greetings with flowers, fruit, wine and kisses – from the French more than from the Arabs – there was a huge haul of spoils in compensation for the losses at Tobruk the previous June: '200,000 prisoners were waiting to be collected and booty exceeding anything we had seen before or would see again. Whole regiments of artillery, whole parks of vehicles, infantry brigades, workshops, stores and the administrative machinery of the German and Italian armies.'[18]

Now it was time for Major Freeman to order ten days of R & R:

'Tunis, 10 May. Every man will be in possession of one clean suit of summer clothing. The Jerboa Club is opening and baths will be arranged. Bde comd [brigade command] looks to all ranks to respect feelings and rights of the civilian population.'[19]

The victory parade through Tunis on 23 May was witnessed by the future Prime Minister Harold Macmillan. He was inspired, indeed overwhelmed:

> Faint, strange and magnificent over the crest of the road came the skirl of bagpipes and then, at a slow and steady pace, the massed pipers of the British armies swung tremendously past the reviewing stand, followed by 14,000 bronze and cocky British veterans of the desert war, each division led by its general. These swinging, striding, out-stepping men, with their jolly, honest, sunburned, smiling English, Scottish or Irish faces, were, on that day, masters of the world and heirs of the future.[20]

Somewhere in the march was 28-year-old Major Freeman. At the expense of Rifle Brigade cool, he must have felt a deep sense of achievement for, as the *Rifle Brigade History* summed up:

> The 1st Battalion, in their battered vehicles, had been in contact with the enemy, except for a short rest for a week in Tripoli, since December 1941, covering an immense mileage and taking its part in every battle, every withdrawal, every advance. It had retreated from Agheila to Gazala and, by a more protracted process, from Gazala to Alamein; it had advanced from Alamein to Tunis.[21]

Freeman's north Africa war was over. Subsequently he very rarely talked about it, but reviewing *The Rommel Papers* in the *New*

Statesman in 1953, he referred to the Rommel myth that had hyp-
notised the Desert Rats:

> Finally, for this reviewer at least, the *Papers* do one thing more. They
> end an illusion. To those who opposed him in the desert, Rommel
> grew into a myth, which was more than a projection of the truth;
> it was a distortion. The chivalrous super-man, whose high repute
> added lustre to the profession of arms and its German exponents, did
> not exist. Montgomery was not big enough to destroy the legend:
> Rommel does. History will not cheat him of his triumphs; but,
> thanks to Rommel himself, it will not conceal his fallibility of judge-
> ment, his arrogant conceit, his narrow outlook and, above all, his
> sheer orgiastic exultation in the brutality of war. It was from this
> impious joy in battle that sprang the romantic illusion, which hyp-
> notised so many of Rommel's opponents. He was the smiler with
> the knife.[22]

In September, Major Freeman signed orders for the embarkation of
the 22nd Armoured Brigade from Tripoli to the Gulf of Salerno, just
south of Naples – the brigade's first move in the invasion of Italy. On
18 September, the convoy of men and vehicles sailed on a glassy, calm
sea and landed in the gulf four days later, without opposition. Luke
was lyrical about the change:

> Nobody who has not come from the desert to the *campagna* of
> Naples in the soft sunshine of September can know what the word
> autumn means. Everything that is ripe and good is here for the ask-
> ing. Clean water is here to bathe in, to wash in, to drink. Tomatoes
> are here for the picking, round red ones and little yellow pear-shaped
> ones, the sweetest of all. There are persimmons, large and opulently

yellow; green walnuts that peel white as teeth; grapes in extravagant abundance. Only girls are not quite so easily had, although there are opportunities.[23]

For the next two months, the 1st Battalion was in close contact with the German enemy (Mussolini had signed the Italian surrender in September) fighting up to the River Garigliano. It was not the sort of war Luke expected:

> Do not be deceived because death is everywhere. Death is at every bridge and every crossroads marked on a German map. Death is in every golden vineyard concealing in its bounty lethal German mines. Death is in every ochre villa set temptingly among tall cypress trees, with its lavatories booby-trapped to explode in the arse of the ignorant desert soldier.[24]

It was to be good training for the invasion of north-west Europe, for which the Desert Rats were soon to be held in readiness. In November, they were billeted in Sorrento, where Freeman was already based with the HQ. In fact, according to his records, he embarked at Naples for the UK on the 19 November. A month later, Luke (and the rest of the 1st Battalion) followed him on the *Cameronia*. They landed in 'blacked-out, wartime Glasgow on 5 January 1944. It was raining wet soot.'

Between 9 March and 6 July, Major Freeman attended a war course for officers at Camberley Joint Services Command and staff college. He was impressed. He told Driberg that the seventeen-week course gave him 'the most effective education since Westminster'. He expanded on this in an interview he gave to William Hardcastle for BBC Radio 4 in 1968:

I've found that passing through staff college was one of the most valuable educational experiences I've had at any time. I found then and I've always found since that the intellectual soldier's habit of arranging his problems in a certain sequence, and trying to appreciate them and arrive by a given methodology at a conclusion, has been terribly useful. I still use it to this day.[25]

The war left him with a deep respect for the army and a pleasure in the company of intelligent soldiers. The army, in turn, gave Freeman his military bearing and aloof manner. He always presented an immaculate front to the world – the civilian equivalent of being on the parade ground. Until old age, he walked as straight as a ramrod and was well groomed. Some found this obsessive. One of his future lovers became infuriated by his habit of folding his trousers precisely before getting into bed with her.

It was a political meeting at Camberley, however, that was to shape his future. One evening in the mess, he joined the group listening to Captain Raymond Blackburn – a peacetime solicitor with well-known left-wing views. Blackburn had already stood as a candidate for Common Wealth (a short-lived political party with views to the left of Labour on some issues) in a by-election, and now, 'with a full head of striking white hair, a Heathcliffe-handsome face and dark eyes alight with enthusiasm', he was haranguing his audience. Most left, fed up with his 'bolshie' talk, but one remained. Blackburn takes up the story:

I met John Freeman when he was at the staff college. He was the most characteristic staff officer one could hope to meet – with perfect manners, a smart and handsome appearance, a command of army clichés and a considerable experience as DAQMG in the 7th

Armoured Division in north Africa. That evening, after others had left for the bar, he remained seated and I was amazed to hear him say: 'I hardly expect you to believe me in view of my behaviour here, but I have been a convinced socialist ever since I was at Oxford and I am a more convinced socialist today than ever.'[26]

A year later, Blackburn secured the nominations of both Freeman and Woodrow Wyatt as Labour candidates in the 1945 general election.

After staff college, Freeman was sent out to liberated France, seconded from the Rifle Brigade to become Brigade Major of 131st Infantry. He took up his post on 25 July, seven weeks after D-Day. The 131st Lorried Infantry Brigade, part of the 7th Armoured Division, had fought alongside the Rifle Brigade in north Africa and Italy. Less glamorous than the Rifles, it was nevertheless a front-line Territorial Army formation, and comprised, when Freeman became brigade major, three battalions of the Queen's Royal Regiment (the 5th, 6th and 7th).

By mid-August, the German Army had been flushed out of the close countryside of the Norman *bocage* – its very high, thick hedgerows made it difficult for an attacking force to shoot and manoeuvre through – and was retreating through the Falaise Gap towards the River Seine, 75 miles away. Here the countryside was open and rolling, but rivers like the Orne, Vie and Laison were wide enough to provide good, defensive positions. For the British Army, there had been a high cost to pay for the advance from D-Day. The very high losses of men, the sheer slog of living rough, eating out of cans, sleeping in holes and every day expecting to batter away at another German defensive position was taking its toll on the front-line infantry. According to Freeman, after heavy fighting on Mount Pincon, the 131st Brigade rested 11–15 August – its first break since landing in Normandy. It was entertained by George Formby and his ukelele.

Then the 131st Brigade advanced to Liverot. The village was already in the hands of the Maquis (the resistance fighters of the Free French forces), so the brigade was welcomed with flowers and wine. Capturing Lisieux was far more difficult. Freeman writes that 'an ill-advised attack by 30 Infantry of 12 SS was dashed by the annihilation of the enemy and the "brewing up" of supporting tanks'. This was followed by 'heavy fighting, strong pockets of German resistance and stubborn German defence round Lisieux' led by Tiger tanks of the 12th SS Panzer Division. However, 'aided by the Free French forces, Lisieux was captured the next day [24 August].'

The cathedral history relates it was only the intervention of a major of the 6th Queen's Battalion that prevented the famous Basilica of St Thérèse from being bombed flat. For the next three days, the 7th Armoured Division pushed on across rolling, wooded countryside, reaching the Seine on 28 August. Freeman reported that the 131st spent the afternoon 'bathing in the sunshine'.[27]

In January 1945, Freeman was awarded the *Croix de guerre* (a French military decoration), receiving a *palme en vermeil* (vermillion palm) for his part in the events of August. Presumably this was for the combined operations with the Free French forces. The citation reads:

> Throughout this period (June–August) the brigade was fighting continuously, and the success it achieved was due in no small measure to the hard work, efficiency and drive of Major Freeman, the brigade major. His cheerfulness and confidence at all times was an inspiration to the staff who worked under him, but also to the many officers and men whom he visited in the heat of battle.[28]

In 1947, Freeman went to Buckingham Palace, with a former girl friend from Oxford, Sally Chilver, who had been a civil servant working with the Free French in the war, and collected his *Croix de guerre*.

For the whole of November through to the end of March 1945, the 131st Brigade was bogged down in the Limburg province of south Holland near the German border, north-west of Cologne. It just missed the 'Battle of the Bulge' – the German offensive through the Ardennes at the end of the year. The rush across France and Belgium had stopped. The supply routes stretched back over 200 miles to the beaches. Petrol and ammunition, hauled by truck from Normandy, were in short supply. The weather had broken too. At the front it rained a fine, cold drizzle so that fields turned to mud. Soon it began to snow, so Freeman ordered another pint of tea a day ('carried in any form of container available, e.g. cigarette tins') and half a cup of rum. Chains were fitted to all vehicles. The Queen's regiments settled down to the routine of the infantryman's life – a mixture of violent action (at Isenbruch, Bakenhoven, Susteren, Schilberg, Dieteren, Melick and Posterholt, for instance), hours of footslogging, or simply waiting for something to happen. They ate 'armoured cow' (spam and corned beef) and soya sausages bedded in fat. They yearned for 'zig-zag' (getting drunk) and 'jig-jig' (having sex) with local women. Morale was low; combat fatigue had set in. Losses were so high that each Queen's regiment had fewer than 100 men left, out of the 450 who had landed in Normandy. 'There's only one way out of the infantry, lads, and that's *feet* first' went the fatalistic refrain. That was not quite true because the 6th and 7th battalions were withdrawn on 3 December and replaced with the 2nd Battalion of the Devonshires and the 9th Battalion of the Durham Light Infantry.

The 131st Brigade knew it was in 'the most exclusive club in the world' – the front-line infantry. The squaddies were contemptuous of the men in the rear echelons – the clerks, cooks and 'admin wallahs' – whose lives were more comfortable and in less danger. Freeman was the brigade major, but presumably he too was an 'admin wallah'. He was billeted at brigade HQ behind the front at Diergaarde and then at Altweert. Perhaps this accounts for his self-deprecating remark to Driberg about his 'completely undistinguished war'. It wasn't undistinguished, of course, but he was obviously aware that he was behind those who were doing the fighting. The American war historian Paul Fussell, who was wounded in France as an infantryman, described the gap between the two:

> Those who actually fought in the line during the war, especially if they were wounded, constitute an in-group separate from those who did not. Praise or blame does not attach; rather there is the accidental possession of a special empirical knowledge, a feeling of shared ironic awareness manifesting itself in an instinctive scepticism about pretension, publicly enunciated truths and the pomp of authority. Those who fought know a secret about themselves.[29]

Between 10 and 24 February 1945, Freeman was on leave in England. Encouraged by Captain Blackburn, Freeman agreed to put his name forward for the Labour nomination as MP for Watford. 'I only did it because I was sure I had no chance of election,' he said later – the sort of casual understatement that would have gone down well in the Rifle Brigade mess. His pessimism is understandable, however. Watford was a safe Tory seat and nobody expected a Labour landslide. His other reason for standing was more self-serving: if elected, he would get out of the army early. This was the first time his wife Elizabeth had heard of his political ambition: ' The first time I knew anything of this was on John's leave in the middle of February. We spent the week rushing round Watford seeing important people. Then John went back to the war and I started having tonsillitis.'[30]

On 28 March, the 131st Brigade crossed the Rhine opposite Bis-lich, north of Dusseldorf, with Montgomery's 21st Army Group. Then it drove north-east towards Hamburg. The further it advanced into Germany, the more desperate the fighting became. Freeman's brigade war diary recalls it vividly:

1 April. Next target Ibbenburen. Enemy consisted of cadets and student NCOs in bn [battalion] strength, who had been ordered to defend to the last. Their tenacity was outstanding. They would stay in blazing houses firing weapons until they themselves were lost in the holocaust.

10 April. First task to clear Wildeshausen. Progress made but pockets of resistance with bazookas. Enemy a mixed bag with elites of 12 SS and bazooka teams forcing caution in our leading troops.

On 14 April, Freeman signed Operation Instruction No. 1, titled 'Secu-rity Measures in Forward Areas Inside Germany':

On arrival of the bde in a new area, a 24-hr curfew without excep-tion will be enforced. Farmers will be instructed that cattle will not be turned out to grass. All civs will be instructed that:

— They will exhibit within ONE hour on the outside of their street door a list containing full name, d.o.b, sex and employment of each person on the premises.

— They will hand over at an appointed place within ONE hour all arms and bicycles.

— They will infm the mil authority IMMEDIATELY of the presence of any member of the GERMAN armed forces in the area.

The min penalty for any disobedience will be removal immediately as pw [prisoner of war]; the max penalty death. In the event of disobedience by the populace as a whole, the able-bodied male population will be evacuated as pws and the houses burned down. All persons found in occupied territories are potential enemies. Obedience to any order must be enforced ruthlessly.[31]

The iron had entered Freeman's soul. About this time he entered Belsen concentration camp because it was in the way of the line of advance. After he returned home the following month, he told a reporter:

As far as I could see, all the guards at the camp were either perverts or insane. The women had heavy moustaches. The medical officer of the place, one Dr Klein, complained bitterly to us that he did not have adequate facilities for killing people. He said that it was unsatisfactory having to inject petrol into their veins, and he wanted more gas chambers.[32]

The advance continued at a rush, the infantry shocked and enraged by what they saw. Freeman wrote:

24 April. The bns [battalions] now started a policy of vigorous patrolling and aggressive action by day and night. The 2 Devons contacted the enemy in area 40413 and, after a fierce fight with brens [machine guns] engaged them with flame-throwers, destroying all enemy in sight.
  A Nazi 'Hall of Fame' at Buchholz 4328 was burned down by

flame-thrower on orders of bde comd. 500 civilians were ordered to be present at the 'ceremony' and the Burgermeister made a short speech explaining the symbolic act.[33]

Freeman told the reporter back home:

> The civilians behave correctly and servilely towards us, but they are still cocky, you can see that. There is a lot of distress in the towns but the countryside seems prosperous enough. Usually we would find a farmer and his wife on 100 acres or so of farm. Nearby you find a barbed-wire cage for the thirty or forty slave workers whom the Nazis put at the disposal of each farmer.[34]

A world away, in the dormitory town of Watford, Elizabeth was fighting John's other battle. It was 19 April and a reporter from the *West Herts & Watford Observer* was covering it:

> The Place – Watford, Herts.
> The Candidate – Major John Freeman, one of the Desert Rats. He fought at Alamein, Tripoli, Salerno and Caen.
> The Battle – Nomination of the Labour candidate.

> 'Last Saturday was zero hour and no sign of John,' said his wife Elizabeth Allen Freeman. 'Two days before nomination day, I had a letter from the Labour Party saying that in John's absence they supposed I would be speaking, would I turn up at three o'clock and that twenty minutes was the maximum time. At the meeting everything was a bit blurred. I got to the end of my speech and then I had to stand up for questions. Oh dear! After that I had to wait forty minutes while the other candidates spoke and then there was a tea interval.'

Freeman may have regarded his marriage as 'a joke' but his wife came to the rescue on this occasion. She was coached by Raymond Blackburn who encouraged her from the back of the hall: 'Then she was called back onto the platform and told, roughly speaking, that she could now go and have her tonsils out in peace, because her Major John had been adopted.'

About ten years before his death, John Freeman surprised his old friend Norman MacKenzie with a question so out of the blue that, coming from Freeman, he could not dismiss it: 'Did I ever tell you that I was the conducting officer who took the German generals to surrender to Monty at Luneberg Heath?'

MacKenzie told me: 'John may have refrained from telling the truth, but I don't think he told an outright lie in his life. That phrase "conducting officer" is such a precise, John-like phrase.'

The war diaries reveal that Freeman's statement was based on an actual incident, although the claim was much exaggerated. Freeman was not at Luneberg Heath on 4 May, when the German armies of the Netherlands, Denmark and north Germany surrendered to Field Marshal Montgomery, but he was in Hamburg on 29 April, when General Wolz (the Kamp Kommandant in Hamburg) sent a medical staff officer and a junior staff officer to Freeman's headquarters with a letter offering surrender, subject to negotiations. The envoys were 'conducted by 131st Brigade to HQ'. As brigade major at HQ, Freeman may well have received or conducted them himself. However, it was not until 3 May that General Wolz, with two staff officers, came through the lines of the 9th Durham Light Infantry to discussed unconditional surrender.

That evening in the Hamburg Rathaus (town hall), the conditions of surrender of the German Army of Hamburg were ratified – but Freeman was not there. Brigade records state: 'On 30 April, the brigade major went to England as candidate for the parliamentary constituency of Watford, Herts.' All orders from the brigade major from 30 April onwards were signed by his deputy. On 23 May, the return states categorically: 'Major R. Sellers, Middlesex Regt, arrived at bde HQ as BM to replace Major J. Freeman MBE, who had proceeded to England as election candidate in April.'[35]

On 8 May, VE Day was celebrated by the 131st Brigade with a double issue of rum. But Freeman was already back home. His 'completely undistinguished' war had ended.

Chapter 3

Government minister
– the rise

T HE LABOUR PARTY closed its conference at Blackpool on 25 May, 1945, by singing *Jerusalem* with evangelical fervour:

I will not cease from mental fight
Nor shall my sword sleep in my hand;
'Til we have built Jerusalem
In England's green and pleasant land.

A new spirit had taken over the party – it had won back its will to win. Its leader, Clement Attlee, said in 1940: 'The world that must emerge from this war must be a world attuned to our ideals.' Those 'ideals' were based on socialism.

Tom Driberg, who was now a Labour candidate, wrote: 'The next parliament could be epoch-making: it could inaugurate the socialist epoch in Britain.' He remembered the soldiers he had met on Charing Cross Road on the evening of VE Day. One held a red flag, another wrote on it in ink: 'We will now proceed to the establishment of socialism – Lenin, 1917.'

Freeman was a favoured son. At the Blackpool conference, chairman Ellen Wilkinson summoned him to the platform: 'I give you a Desert Rat, who has just received the German surrender of Hamburg.' Legend has it that this rousing call was followed by silence – as Freeman was in the bath sipping whisky and soda and reading *The New Yorker*. This legend needs a sprinkling of salt, because Freeman told exactly the same story in reference to the announcement of his victory at Watford in the general election of 1951. It is the kind of story he would have encouraged, of course, because it displayed his nonchalant behaviour and his dislike of publicity – that Rifle Brigade cool again. When Professor Harold Laski, the chairman of the Labour Party, spoke for Freeman at Watford on 29 June, he recalled Blackpool: 'No person attending the conference made a greater impression than Major Freeman. A few weeks ago I was passed a cheque to give to a young candidate most deserving of honour. Without a moment's hesitation, I passed the cheque to Major Freeman.'

Nevertheless, that summer Freeman felt sure he would lose the election at Watford. It had been a safe Tory seat and perhaps he did not really want to win. In any event, he travelled back to Germany and applied for a permanent job with the control commission, just in case. He told his family years later that he had been offered a senior post with the Allied control council in Berlin.

Freeman's electioneering followed the Attlee line, which blamed the Tories for wanting to bring back the past, while Labour promised to bring in the future. Freeman said that this had been clear before the war as well as after:

> It was not all roses in the political garden before the war – there was great strife in this country, only delayed when both sides came together to fight fascism. But we were fighting for different things. The Tories were fighting for their privileged position. We saw not a threat to our privileged position because, God help us, we hadn't got one. But we saw a direct threat to our standard of living.[1]

Freeman's opponent, Commodore W. Helman, displayed just such 'privileged behaviour' in his conduct at the hustings. He arrived late for the Conservative meeting in the town hall on the eve of the poll and then refused to answer any questions: 'It is not my policy during elections.' According to the *West Herts & Watford Observer*, the chairman then announced 'with deep regret that at Freeman's final meeting when Mr Churchill's name was mentioned it was greeted with boos and shouts of Vote for Freeman'. The Tory's right to rule was overturned the next day and a framed photo of Freeman hung on the wall in the Labour Party offices for many years.

In fact, despite the scent of glorious victory in the air, Freeman found the counting of votes so disagreeable that he vowed never to go through it again. He wrote in the *New Statesman* in May 1955, when he was on the verge of leaving Parliament:

> Keenly observed by the press, by their followers and by their enemies, they [the candidates] will force the sparkle of optimism into their eyes, which are red-rimmed and perhaps near to tears. They will

squeeze out encouraging quips in voices harsh with the laceration of
public speech. And they will feel simple fear; the fear that a career is
about to be destroyed, that security has gone, that the cause has been
betrayed. The fear, in fact, of failure. As the pile of their opponent's
papers will overgrow their own, anxiety will give way to the suspicion and then the certainty that they have lost, to the suspicion as
certainty, and finally to certainty itself, tolled out in the flat strokes
of a town clerk's tongue. They must adapt themselves as best they can
to private life – hindered by the slightly absurd label of 'failed MP'.[2]

When the general election results were announced on 26 July, Labour
had won by a landslide: a gain of 212 seats and a popular vote of
12 million. Raymond Blackburn won for Labour in his Birmingham
Kings Norton constituency and remembered 'the hall seemed to
be full of shining eyes aglow with the sight of the Promised Land'.
Woodrow Wyatt won in the next-door constituency of Birmingham Aston and John Freeman overturned a big majority at Watford
to win by 2,194 votes (he had predicted 2,000). The Manchester
Labour journal proclaimed: 'POWER! The *revolution* without a
single cracked skull! The pioneers' dream realised at last. Now there
is nothing to stand in the way of laying the *socialist* foundation of
the new social order.'

On 1 August, Labour MPs gathered in the House of Lords (the
Commons was closed because of war damage) to elect a new Speaker.
They included many first-time MPs who would govern Britain or
lead Labour in the years ahead: two future prime ministers (Harold
Wilson and James Callaghan) and two future leaders of the party
(Hugh Gaitskell and Michael Foot). Future deputy leaders Roy Jen-
kins and Dennis Healey had not yet been elected. In an atmosphere
of excitement and some belligerence, they sang *The Red Flag* – the

only time, wrote Woodrow Wyatt, that this 'bloodthirsty and ridiculous anthem' was sung in Parliament.

They were back again on 15 August to hear the new Prime Minister announce the terms of the Japanese surrender. Attlee ended by moving 'that this House do now attend at the Church of St Margaret's Westminster to give humble and reverent thanks to Almighty God on the victorious conclusion of the war'. When they returned to the House of Lords – the bells of St Margaret's still ringing victory peels – they listened to the King's speech, which laid the foundations for the New Jerusalem.

Parliament can rarely have witnessed such drama in its long history. The next day it was the turn of Major John Freeman MP to take centre stage. Far from avoiding the spotlight, this time Freeman rose to the occasion. The Prime Minister had invited him to give the traditional Humble Address of Thanks for the Most Gracious Speech – it was a definite honour and a hint of future promotion. Hansard records that Freeman spoke in military uniform – the black-buttoned uniform of the Rifle Brigade – indicating the change in the character of the Labour Party. Driberg witnessed the speech as the newly elected MP for Maldon:

> Slender, youthful, well-groomed, red-haired, the major stood ramrod-straight and delivered, in the impeccable upper-middle-class accent of Westminster School and Oxford, a speech that was a model of its kind – diffident yet proud, proud of his constituents and of the armed forces in which he served, paying tactful tribute to the trade unions whose homespun representatives, seated around him, might be eyeing with a dubious surmise this new-image Labour member.[3]

Freeman's conclusion echoes down the years:

The country is conscious of the seriousness of the years that lie ahead; but our people are not depressed by the outlook nor are they overwhelmed by their responsibilities. On the contrary, on every side is a spirit of high adventure, of gay determination, a readiness to experiment, to take reasonable risks, to stake high in this magnificent venture of rebuilding our civilisation, as we have staked high in the winning of the war. We have before us a battle for the peace, no less arduous and no less momentous than the battle we have lived through in the last six years. Today the strategy begins to unfold itself. Today we go into action. Today may rightly be regarded as 'D-Day' in the Battle of the New Britain.[4]

Barbara Castle, the new Labour MP for Blackburn, was another who witnessed this singularly dramatic maiden speech. She wrote in her memoirs: 'John was a charismatic figure who seemed to have a dazzling career in front of him. As he stood there in his uniform, erect, composed and competent, everyone felt his star quality.'[5]

The Leader of the Opposition, Winston Churchill, spoke third and congratulated Freeman and his seconder, Fred Willey (the newly elected Labour MP for Sunderland), for speaking with 'so much decorum and becoming taste. We hope they will shine in our debates and we trust that important political careers may await both of them.' Later in the day, Attlee introduced Freeman to Churchill in the smoking room and the great man broke down and wept: 'Now all the best men are on the other side.'[6]

John and Elizabeth Freeman rented a flat on Marsham Street, within five minutes' walk of Parliament. Despite the elegance of the address, it was a shabby property owned by Westminster city council, situated above a snack bar and surrounded by a bombsight overgrown with weeds. Next door was Roy Jenkins and his wife Jennifer. Jenkins described Freeman as 'the very model of a modern Labour major', but they seldom met.

At the end of July, Hugh Dalton had been made Chancellor of the Exchequer. After the new government was in place, he celebrated by hosting 'the young victors' dinner party' at St Ermin's Hotel in Victoria. John Freeman was there, together with Raymond Blackburn, Harold Wilson, George Brown, Hugh Gaitskell, Dick Crossman, Christopher Mayhew and a few others. As Mayhew observed, 'It seemed to be composed almost entirely of future ministers, with a few prime ministers thrown in.'

It was a dinner several attendees remembered years later for the mood of triumph, as they speculated who would be the first new MP to be appointed straight into government. The answer was the academic Harold Wilson, who immediately became parliamentary secretary to the Minister of Works. But Freeman was to follow shortly. In October 1946, he became financial secretary to the Minister for War, John Lawson.

Hugh Dalton became Freeman's patron. In *The Political Diary of Hugh Dalton, 1945–1960*, he refers many times to seeking preferment for Freeman, using his status as one of the 'Big Five' (the others were Attlee, Bevin, Morrison and Cripps) to lobby for his promotion. He found Freeman attractive, and noted this repetitiously: 'One of the most attractive younger members of the party'; 'I took John out to dinner – he is very attractive and intelligent'. He was another person star-struck by Freeman's parliamentary debut, as he told the Prime Minister on 20 February 1951 (when he was angling, once again, for Freeman's promotion): 'I recalled Freeman's magnificent first speech of the first day of the 1945 parliament. That was something I should never forget.'

Although Dalton was married, he was well known for his Hellenic

– chaste but homoerotic – fondness of brilliant and, it must be stressed, heterosexual young men like Freeman. 'My love', wrote Dalton in his diary, 'is the Labour movement and the best of the young men in it.'

Tom Driberg very soon became Freeman's closest friend on the Labour benches. He was boastfully homosexual, though not, again it must be stressed, in his relations with Freeman. As Driberg's biographer put it, 'Tom and Dalton fought for Freeman's hand like rival suitors.'[7] It was a tug of love with homoerotic undertones, at least on Dalton's part. He confided to his diary on 4 January 1951: 'Freeman, I fear, has had a great fall since the first wonderful summer day in the 1945 parliament. I am very grieved about this. But he's a bloody fool in his own interest, and what can he see in Driberg to justify *so much* public clinging?' Shortly after, Freeman was ignored in a government reshuffle. Dalton moaned: 'I fear John Freeman's stock is badly down, because of Driberg.'

There are two entwined themes of Freeman's life in this decade, particularly after the general election of 1950. These are: his gradual disenchantment with Westminster, as viewed in part through Dalton's diary; and the diversions of his private life with Driberg, sometimes louche, like all-night gambling, and occasionally outrageous, like Driberg's wedding in 1951 when Freeman was best man.

Dalton was an unlikely socialist. He was an Old Etonian and the son of a Canon of Windsor, who was also a tutor to the future George V. In the '30s he had become a socialist and anti-appeaser, all of which made him a class enemy to the Tories. Now, post-war, he was a radical Chancellor of the Exchequer (1945–48), using a policy of cheap money (low interest rates) and a progressive budget to make Britain a more equal society. His first achievement was to nationalise the Bank of England, a socialist essential that, Freeman told him, was the most popular of all Labour policies, judging by the reaction in his Watford constituency.

Dalton was high-handed with his civil servants – 'He shits for England in the Olympic Games,' said one in 1948. Conspiratorial and a gossip, he was not trusted, and there is a story of him entering the Cabinet room 'eyes blazing with insincerity'. He was a man of strong bias: miners, handsome young white men, socialists, and refugees from Nazi Germany were in; Germans, the rich or pompous, and Bloomsbury intellectuals were out. Freeman obviously liked this combination of public principles with private indiscretions. When the third volume of Dalton's diary was published in February 1962, Freeman reviewed it for the *New Statesman*. As Dalton died the following week, it became an obituary:

> Dalton is traditionally accused by his many enemies of insincerity, cynicism and malice. Look deeper and you will find a man of feeling, humanity and unshakeable loyalty, who never quite found an idea that matched his talent. In all walks of life are to be found a small army of friends who have been allowed to see beneath the surface of this many-sided, mercurial man. These people love him with all his faults. And I am one of them.[8]

Nevertheless, Freeman was also perceptive about his faults. In 1953 he reviewed another Dalton memoir, *Call Back Yesterday*:

> He has no real political philosophy. He is the arch-pragmatist of the party. You choose your party; you back it through thick and thin; you fight its battle for power; and when you have won you do your best to confound your enemies and reward your allies. Even the wide circle of Dalton's friends – and few men have the power

to inspire a stronger affection – have learned to look elsewhere for philosophical guidance.[9]

If Dalton divided opinion then Driberg polarised it. Norman Mac-Kenzie told me Driberg was the vilest man he had ever met, while Catherine Freeman 'liked him very, very much. He was just so worldly, so funny, so indiscreet, but also so intelligent and affectionate.' He was forty when he listened to Freeman's Humble Address that August afternoon, but unlike many others on the Labour benches, he had been a Member of Parliament for the previous three years, as an independent (in reality, a member of Common Wealth). He had not really wanted to transfer to the Labour Party – thinking it stuffy and bourgeois – and, after 1945, he felt let down by the Attlee government: 'There was no fundamental or lasting change in the economic or social structure of Britain.' Occasionally he worked up some enthusiasm – like on the second reading of the bill to nationalise the mines, when he saw MPs from mining constituencies trooping through the lobby in tears and singing *The Red Flag* – but most of the time he was detached; interested but not involved. 'The whole bloody business bored him,' said the Labour MP Ian Mikardo.[10]

Some thought he was a dilettante, and, according to John Freeman, he had few friends: 'He remained an ambiguous, largely isolated figure … seen, I judge, by his Labour colleagues as not one of us, but whose heart was probably in the right place, who was a bit of a character, even though a character to be disapproved of.'[11]

This then was Freeman's closest ally in Parliament – the friend with whom he spent many hours gossiping and drinking during parliamentary business.

One reason why Freeman saw so much of Driberg was because he found him entertaining. Driberg was a man of refined taste, who, after public school and Oxford, had considered becoming a poet. He was a socialite who loved gossip and indiscretion, a journalist with a curiosity that took him to the extremes of experience (like studying the satanist Aleister Crowley) and a foreign correspondent who courted danger when, for example, he was 'embedded' (in more senses than one) within the British troops in Normandy in 1944 and Korea in 1950. Colourful and mysterious, High Church with a lust for low life, no one could say that Driberg did not live life to the full.

Freeman enjoyed the house parties that Driberg held at his home, Bradwell Lodge in Essex. It was a beautiful former rectory of Tudor and Georgian architecture, with installed treasures like a Robert Adam fireplace inlaid with panels painted by Angelica Kauffman. Driberg liked Bradwell Lodge 'better than anything else in the world'. He delighted in bringing together disparate guests for weekend house parties, as might a madam in a high-class brothel, he said mischievously.

One weekend just after the war, for instance, Driberg mixed the Labour politician Aneurin Bevan with the modern composer Constant Lambert and his wife Isabel, who was recently divorced from the famous journalist Sefton Delmer. As an Essex neighbour, Isabel was a frequent visitor: 'There was always good wine and food, and conversation on all subjects, word games and Lena Horne singing in the evenings.'[12] Freeman was another frequent guest, remembering 'weekends spent in total tranquillity with a delightful host'. Driberg's parties had quite a notorious reputation, which he did nothing to dispel. Catherine recalls a conversation with him soon after her marriage to John in 1962:

Louche is the word to apply to Tom Driberg. He once said to me, 'I could tell you *such* stories about John, but I dare not, because one day you will lose your temper with him and you'll mention them and then I'll really be in hot water.' So that was very irritating of him, to tell me only what he *would* have told me. But I remember him rolling his eyes and saying, '*Such* wild goings-on there were!'

The Driberg papers in Christ Church, Oxford, and Driberg's diary for these years (published as *The Best of Both Worlds*), are silent on the matter.

Driberg may have been a 'Jekyll' at Bradwell Lodge most of the time, but in the lavatories of Russell Square, the House of Commons and elsewhere, he was a 'Hyde'. He was a flagrant, promiscuous gay who boasted of his adventures in the rough trade, although practising homosexuality was illegal until 1967. For instance, he recounts in *Ruling Passions* a nocturnal liaison in Edinburgh in 1943 when he was campaigning in a by-election for the Common Wealth candidate Tom Wintringham. In the dark of Princes Street, he 'bumped into a tall figure in a foreign naval uniform'. One thing led to another and they were in an air-raid shelter, Driberg on his knees:

> Concentrating on a long, uncircumcised, and tapering, but rock-hard erection ... Too concentrated, for the stillness of the shelter was broken by a terrifying sound – the crunching of boots on the gravelled floor. Instantly the blinding light of a torch shone full on us, and a deep Scottish voice was baying, in a tone of angry disgust: 'Och, ye bastards – ye dirty pair o' whoors.' It was a policeman...

In desperation, Driberg threw caution to the wind. He took out his visiting card that showed he was both an MP and the author of the William Hickey gossip column on the *Daily Express*:

> The policeman scrutinised the card gravely. Then he exploded. '*William Hickey!*' he said. 'Good God, man, *I've read you all of my life!*'

I swore I would never do such a thing again, and it worked. When we said goodnight we shook hands, and he even gave me a – not too formal – salute.[13]

Freeman delighted in these stories:

Much of the scandalous material now known about Tom he told me – and others – shamelessly and, for all I know, candidly. In the purgatorial boredom of the House of Commons he could be a lifesaver, and I for one enjoyed the entertainment that he was prepared to offer.[14]

Driberg was probably a spy when Freeman knew him. Although he was only 'outed' as such after his death in 1976, Freeman must have had his suspicions, because many others did. However, as with other supposed spies of this Cold War era, whose side Driberg was on and whether he was a real threat to security remain uncertain. He had been a member of the Communist Party until early in the war and he was an acquaintance of the traitor Guy Burgess, who he visited in Moscow after his defection in 1951.

In 1981, the veteran 'spy-catcher' Chapman Pincher wrote *Their Trade is Treachery*, in which he labelled Driberg as 'in the KGB's pay as a double agent'. Then the author Nigel West twisted the screw by claiming that Driberg had, for many years, been a double agent working for MI5 – secretly reporting on the British and Russian communist parties, while also serving as a spy for Russia. Some said that Driberg's homosexuality made him vulnerable to blackmail; others that he was far too indiscreet to be a spy. Freeman and Wyatt discussed their old friend's spying over the dinner table in 1986. Wyatt recorded:

> John thinks, from some of the observations he [Driberg] made to
> John, he was definitely a Russian agent and was almost certainly then
> turned by the British, so must have worked for both sides. He said a
> significant moment in his life was when he was going bankrupt: he
> got £50,000 from somewhere, which was never explained.[15]

Whatever the truth, Freeman seems to have been drawn to the mysterious double life of the spy. In the 1950s he was also a friend – and Freeman made few friends – of the *New Statesman* journalist and spy Aylmer Vallance (see Chapter 7). Was it the enigma of the spy that appealed to Freeman – the chameleon quality of appearing all things to all men, while keeping your own counsel?

One night in the 1960s, Catherine and John Freeman were reading in bed. Her book was *The Portrait of a Lady* and his, she noticed, was *A Double Life*.

Michael Foot, a fellow Bevanite MP in the post-war Labour governments, who worked closely with Freeman, said to me: 'John had a cold manner but undoubtedly he had another side, as his friendships with Driberg and Boothby showed. He liked rough company.'

At this time, Robert Boothby was a Conservative MP, until, in 1958, he was given a peerage. He was rumoured to have fathered three children by the wives of other men, one of them with Lady Dorothy Macmillan, whose husband was later Prime Minister (1957–63). Boothby was also a bisexual and, like Driberg, he flaunted his homosexuality at a time when it was illegal. Together in the 1960s they visited East End clubs where, in return for protecting from the law the sinister crooks, the Kray Twins, 'rough but compliant East End lads were served to them like so many canapés'.[16]

In August 1960, Lord Boothby was John Freeman's guest on *Face to Face*. This is how Freeman introduced him:

He is a personal friend of long standing. I'll tell you how I see him: I think he is one of the most gifted and idealistic and truthful men in public life. I also think he is lazy, self-indulgent and over-generous. They have led to the failure of his public career but the total success of his personal friendships. He's either in disgrace for having blurted out something indiscreet or else he's playing baccarat at Deauville. From time to time he denies these charges. You'll be able to judge if he does so in this programme.

What are we to make of this? Freeman liked 'rough company' all through his life, but there is no suggestion that there was anything sexual to this. He liked people who crossed the boundaries with impunity and entertained him; moral judgements about sexual behaviour were not among his principles.

Driberg's diary of these years was published at the same time as the first volume of Dalton's *Memoirs* in 1953. This left the reviewer of *Truth* magazine in a quandary:

Or instead, shall I read Mr Driberg,
Whose bright, chatty diary extends
To back stage accounts of the Commons
And his cultured impeccable friends?
Shall I read of his mansion in Essex,
Of his views on the church (which are high)
Will he drop me some Bevanite tit-bits
On the personal habits of Nye?
About halfway through in a footnote
I expect he will coyly confess,
In the gay unregenerate '30s
That he wrote for the Daily Express?

Well, whom shall I go to this evening,
To seek some enlightenment from?
Shall I plunge into history with Hughie,
Or go for a gossip with Tom?
The more I consider the problem
The more with this knowledge I'm faced –
That the journalist's book, and the doctor's
Both fill me with equal distaste!
Hurray then for personal freedom,
Which is the Englishman's right!
Away with both Driberg and Dalton –
And would somebody turn off the light?[17]

Freeman's contribution to the transforming legislation enacted by the first Labour government of 1945–50 was slight. During its first two years he was at the War Office – first as parliamentary secretary, then financial secretary and then under-secretary of state to Fred Bellinger, a kindly but ineffective minister who had been an army officer and then an estate agent before entering Parliament. The story of Bellinger's dismissal by the Prime Minister in 1947 is often quoted as an example of Attlee's terse, gauche personal relations, here related by Woodrow Wyatt:

'Bellinger, I want your resignation.'

Poor Fred was aghast. He was not brilliant but there were worse ministers.

'I'm very sorry to hear that, Prime Minister. I thought I'd been doing rather well. Could you give me any reason?'

'No good. That's all. No good.'

End of interview.[18]

In November 1946, Freeman flew off to the Far East on a tour of overseas commands. He had already, according to Dalton, 'made a most excellent front-bench beginning, both answering questions and speaking on adjournments … an exceptionally promising parliamentarian'. His first stop was the British Commonwealth occupation zone in Japan, where he met General MacArthur and visited the British troops. There was no chance, he told the press, of either bringing the troops home or reducing their numbers. He spent Christmas at the commander-in-chief's house in Delhi, from where he wrote to Tom Driberg. The flight from Tokyo to Calcutta had been alarming because 'the flight pilot developed appendicitis in mid-air and damaged the undercarriage when landing'. This must have been the origin of the story Freeman told his children in the 1960s about how he had helped land an aircraft by taking over the controls and preventing a crash.

In his letter, Freeman told Driberg that, in his private view, the Burmese had to be granted independence after elections, otherwise 'we should be gradually and ignominiously expelled, probably with casualties. From the soldiers' point of view, the politician must avoid an anti-British crisis.'[19] This comment was obviously an answer to Churchill's speech in the Commons earlier in December. In response to the Labour government's plans to make Burma the first independent ex-colony, he had exploded: 'This haste is appalling; "scuttle" is the only word that can be applied.'

Driberg and Freeman shared a belief in Burmese independence that was vindicated the next year when power was successfully transferred. It became a model for policies elsewhere and was one of Attlee's proudest achievements. In fact, Freeman played an important part in this. In August 1947, he led a defence mission to Burma, which agreed, after much argument, to send a combined task force from all three armed services to build up an adequate army, navy and air force. Freeman described the mission in an article for the *New States-man* seven years later:

> We were lent a heavily guarded house, surrounded by a 10 ft wire fence, observed in almost every moment by soft-footed guards, battered and deafened by the monsoon.
>
> As we bargained it became clear that what troubled the suspicious Burmese revolutionaries was the fear that a military mission would infringe Burmese sovereignty, and might even become a centre for insurrection.
>
> The most formidable of the Burmese delegates was the Finance Minister, U Tin Tut, later, to my great sorrow, assassinated. One afternoon, as we broke off discussions, he invited me to join him for his daily swim the following morning.
>
> At six o'clock, in the grey dawn of a Burmese monsoon, Tin Tut and I slithered down a grassy bank, through a ring of silent tommy-gunners, and waded into the opaque and stinking water.

Out of earshot of the shore, Tin Tut explained the Burmese suspicion of the colonial British, and Freeman, panting and spluttering, advanced the true cause of Clement Attlee and his socialists. They attained a degree of candour and from then on the talks changed for the better: 'This episode must, I should think, rank as one of the more bizarre diplomatic occasions. Certainly, what with shortage of breath, a near certainty of typhoid, and my dark suspicion that there were crocodiles in the lake, I still reckon it among my most hazardous public duties.'[20]

Freeman's mission was judged 'an important practical step' in a *Times* leader. The transfer of power officially took place three months later. It is now, wrote the historian Peter Hennessy, 'a long-forgotten but highly significant imperial disposal'.

Two months before, in June, Freeman and several other government ministers had been sent letter bombs by the Stern Gang, an Israeli terrorist organisation. The number one target was Foreign Secretary Ernest Bevin, whose policy to block the creation of an independent Jewish state in Palestine – to be called Israel – was considered anti-Semitic by many Jews. The mini bombs were intended as the first of a huge strike of twenty-one bombs to be sent to every member of the Cabinet, and others. Chancellor of the Exchequer, Sir Stafford Cripps, was only saved when his secretary threw the fizzing parcel into a bucket of water. Years later, Freeman came face to face with his assailant. He told Catherine at the time: 'I bumped into a former member of the Stern Gang recently who told me that he had been deputed to kill me. He had red hair too.'

In 1947, Freeman was appointed vice-president of the army council, of which Field Marshal Montgomery of Alamein, Chief of the Imperial General Staff (CIGS), was a member. No respecter of politicians, and increasingly out of sorts with peacetime Britain, Montgomery accused Freeman of being rude to a senior officer when visiting a regiment, and undermining discipline by discussing policy with other ranks. Freeman denied this vehemently. It obviously did him no political harm though, because the next year Attlee consulted him about Montgomery's successor as CIGS. He suggested Field Marshal Slim, and this was acted on.

Freeman did not forget. Monty may have called him 'the best brigade major in the Eighth Army' but this cut no ice. In the 1960s, Freeman used Monty's opposition to the common market to put in the military boot:

> It is sad to see how this justly honoured soldier has declined in public esteem – and all for being unable to shut up about subjects he

does not understand. Monty was respected and trusted by those who served under him in the war. He seems to have found it more difficult than most of them to resettle in civilian life.[21]

In 1947, John Freeman and his wife Elizabeth separated. She remained at Marsham Street and he moved into a flatlet in Threeways – a substantial house on Wellgarth Road at the edge of Hampstead Heath. This was the lively and chaotic home of the remarkable Hubback family. David Hubback had been at Westminster School with Freeman. In fact, David and his mother Eva had visited Russia in 1932 with a party of Fabians, including the headmaster of Westminster, Hugh Dalton and Naomi Mitchison. David went on to fight in the Western Desert before joining the civil service in 1946, where he helped to shape the New Britain. It was Eva, however, living with her son and his family, who had an inspiring effect on Freeman. Now her plaque in mosaic is outside Morley College in south London, where she was principal in the 1920s. She was a member of London county council and an ardent believer in citizenship. Prior to that, she had been a suffragette, a feminist, a eugenicist and the founder of the Townswomen's Guild. According to Eva's daughter, Diana Hopkinson, in her last years after the war (when John was living with the Hubbacks) 'she habitually woke at 6 a.m. and sat outside, even on chilly mornings, considering the philosophical and religious interpretations of existence. She suffered from all the uncertainties about life and death which can beset the bravest of agnostics.'[22] I see Eva's spirit hovering over Freeman's shoulder in the BBC studios while he conducted his many interviews on those same subjects.

Before the end of the war Freeman had met Mima Kerr, a journalist writing for *Le Figaro* and a Free French publication based in Whitehall. She was married with a daughter (Lizi, born in 1942), but had separated from her husband soon after Lizi's birth. During the war and after, Lizi lived with a nanny in Hove, while Mima remained in London and began a love affair with John. After the war, Mima was appointed royal reporter for *Picture Post* magazine. She continued to visit Paris frequently, as she always had done since she had been to finishing school there, and enjoyed skiing in Switzerland.

Lizi remembers her first meeting with her future stepfather: 'John and Woodrow [Wyatt] came down to Hove. I remember them taking me to the beach and I remember asking myself, "Is one of these men going to be my dad?" And I was very relieved that it was John.'[23] Elizabeth Freeman sued for divorce, and Lizi recalls the secretary John shared with Mima, Joan Harper, arranging for him to spend the necessary night in Brighton to provide evidence of adultery: 'He was somewhere completely different the night before and had to get over there. He said, "I couldn't be more displeased."' Elizabeth was granted a divorce on 19 January 1948 on the grounds of John's adultery.

John and Mima (an acronym for her maiden name, Margaret Ista Mabel Abbott) were married at Folkestone registry office on 23 March 1948. The certificate states that she had obtained a divorce from her first husband and John was a 'journalist and advertising copywriter' – a curious deceit. Did he want to put off press interest or was it second nature to avoid giving away more about himself than absolutely necessary? After all, he was an under-secretary of state in the Labour government. After the wedding, the Freemans and Lizi moved briefly into a small flat in Spanish Mansions off Marylebone High Street, before moving back to the Hubbacks'. Not long afterwards, they set up home at 8 Heath Mansions in Hampstead, where John would live for seventeen years.

Mima was a tall, stylish 31-year-old, with a taste for hats and elegant clothes: 'My God, she knew how to shop for clothes,' says Lizi.

'A wardrobe of black, navy and camel would suggest best quality, and all one needed was a simple, elegant line. She would buy a new hat before it appeared in *Vogue*.' But she was a hopeless mother:

> John realised that. He said to me, 'I knew your mother was completely hopeless and I'd have to do something about it.' So I used to say, 'Please can Daddy wash my hair because he doesn't get soap in my eyes?' And he would pretend to play the piano with me; and he would make tents if I had a cold, to inhale in. I was always impressed at how caring he was with this ready-made child. I've always referred to him as my 'mummy-daddy'.[24]

An unexpected perspective.

On 7 October 1947, Freeman was appointed parliamentary secretary at the Ministry of Supply – a post he was to hold for the next four years, working for the minister George Strauss. Strauss was a Jewish intellectual, a founder of *Tribune* magazine in the 1930s. He was on the left of the Labour Party in government and was also a friend of Tom Driberg – all of which ought to have commended him to Freeman. Nevertheless, for Freeman this was an increasingly frustrating appointment, because Strauss would not delegate but left him with the rubbish – almost literally. A search of Hansard 1947–50 reveals eloquently how excruciatingly boring Freeman's work at the Ministry of Supply must have been. In 1948, he made three speeches in the Chamber – on conveyor belting; dumped radio equipment; and disabled ex-servicemen's cars. He provided a large number of written answers on such topics as: electric light bulbs; bicycle rear lamps; pig iron; zinc prices; and the aircraft establishment at Farnborough. The next year his speeches were up to eleven – aircraft sales (abroad); surplus equipment (handling); stores disposal in Egypt – while his written answers continued in the same vein – hearing aids; Tudor aircraft [?!]; flying boats. No wonder he sought the company of Tom Driberg! Was this what the 'Battle of the New Britain' was all about?

In February 1950, the Labour Party was returned to power after the general election, and Freeman retained his position at the Ministry of Supply. His work continued to be deeply unsatisfying. The following January, he unburdened himself to Dalton on a Sunday afternoon walk in Battersea Park:

> He said he would be quite willing – and, from the constituency point of view, would prefer – to go back to the back benches. Strauss, he admitted, had given him no show at all, not even *one* parliamentary question to answer during three years. But, very generously, he did not speak ill of Strauss … I like Freeman a lot, and would like to see him climbing. I'll try again at a good moment.[25]

In fact, only weeks later Strauss *did* give Freeman his opportunity. He asked him to 'wind up' the iron and steel nationalisation debate that would bring into effect the bill that had been passed, in principle, in November 1949 (although its implementation had been postponed until after the general election). The Conservative Party decided to make a rearguard fight of it, and the result was a cliffhanger – Labour won by only ten votes. By all accounts, Freeman made up for lost opportunities: 'Mr Freeman made one of the outstanding speeches of recent years. Labour MPs roared with delight at the spectacle of this red-headed, pink cheeked young minister infuriating the Tories with a stream of brilliant but barbed shafts.'[26]

'I thought we might easily lose,' said Dalton. 'John Freeman wound up very well, and I hope this has renewed a little of his personal reputation.' (7 February 1951)

Chapter 4

Government minister – the fall

I T WAS 1950 and the fag end of a revolution. The first post-war Labour government – the strongest in Britain's history – had come to an end. At the general election in February, Labour was returned again, but with a majority of only five. Labour's programme of social and economic reform, for which it had campaigned for a generation, had largely been carried out. Its 'shopping list' for the next round of nationalisations showed that it had run out of steam on public ownership; only the incomplete nationalisation of iron and steel remained among the big manifesto intentions. Labour voters had run out of steam too. The historian Peter Hennessy wrote:

The electoral shift was a reaction to a decade of rationing and constant exhortation to personal sacrifice for the public good. It was an example of Galbraith's Law that centre-left parties do themselves out of a job by making more and more people comfortable, secure and therefore conservative.[1]

There was also a redrawing of boundaries, particularly in the London area, that favoured the Tories. All of this accounted for the loss of votes for Freeman in Watford, but nevertheless he won again, assisted by a visit to the constituency from Prime Minister Attlee. Freeman did not attend the count.

Labour's campaign had been lacklustre. The Big Five were exhausted. Foreign Secretary Ernie Bevin was seriously ill, often away or falling asleep in meetings. Chancellor of the Exchequer Sir Stafford Cripps was failing fast, with a gastric illness that deprived him of food and sleep. Prime Minister Attlee suffered from gastric problems too, so he was in and out of hospital. That left Hugh Dalton, whose power – though not influence – was much reduced after he had resigned from the chancellorship in 1947, after inadvertently leaking Budget changes to a journalist. He was back in the Cabinet, but with a relatively minor post as Minister of Town and Country Planning.

That left Aneurin (Nye) Bevan, but he too was a spent force as Minister for Health – a post he had held since 1945. He was ambitious for one of the top two posts, but Attlee preferred Hugh Gaitskell as Chancellor when Cripps resigned in October 1950, and he preferred Herbert Morrison as Foreign Secretary when Ernie Bevin had to retire six months later in March 1951. Bevan was humiliated and intent on revenge. That January, he had agreed to move sideways to become Minister of Labour; his successor as Minister of Health, Hilary Marquand, did not have a seat in the Cabinet.

The stage was now set for the split in the Labour Party that contributed to the loss of the next general election, banished it to the
political wilderness for the next thirteen years, and caused an inter-
party civil war of a ferocity Labour was not to experience again until
the early 1980s. It was, said Gaitskell to Dalton, 'a fight for the soul
of the Labour Party'. It was a fight that cost Freeman his promising
political career – one that some people thought might have taken him
to party leadership and even beyond.

A year into the second Labour government, shortly after Freeman
had steered through the iron and steel debate, Dalton spoke to Attlee
again about him:

> I then returned to John Freeman, recalling his very remarkable speech
> last week; how he had been completely wasted at [the Ministry of]
> Supply; how Strauss had given him no show at all. Attlee seemed
> shocked to hear this. Then Attlee said he would like to put Freeman
> [as a minister] at the War Office. 'That,' he said, 'would be a bold
> stroke, wouldn't it?'[2]

Dalton reported this to Freeman, who agreed he would accept the job
if it were offered. Promotion was in the air. Michael Foot concurred
with this: 'Thanks to his extreme competence at the despatch box and
elsewhere, he was clearly destined for early promotion.'[3] As it turned
out, this was the apex of Freeman's political career. Only two months
later, on 23 April 1951, he resigned from the government. He did so
with Nye Bevan and Harold Wilson, and this precipitated the split
of the Labour Party.

The row had been simmering for several weeks. The presenting
issue was whether or not Bevan, spoiling for a fight, would resign
over the government's decision to impose charges on his precious

health service. If so, would his resignation, as Freeman believed, bring down the Labour government within weeks? Throughout this period – 'this odious war of nerves, which is becoming totally intolerable' is how Dalton described it in his diary on 20 April – Dalton was both mediator and counsellor to Freeman, taking his task very personally. He begged Freeman to stay in the government like a forlorn lover:

> I say as we part: 'I shall be *très déchiré* [heartbroken] if you break.'
> He [Freeman] says: 'Don't let's discuss it again out here.'
> I say: 'No one will know what *déchiré* means. But your going would serve no useful purpose whatsoever.'[4]

In the event, this was true. What is more, the Labour establishment from Attlee downwards tried harder to keep Freeman than it did either Bevan or Wilson. He was offered a choice of jobs. So why did Freeman resign? Didn't he really want the seat in the Cabinet that was his for the taking?

Ten years ago, when I began writing this biography, I asked Norman MacKenzie to pose these questions to Freeman. Freeman replied that he resigned because he had given his word that if Bevan went, 'so would I, and I didn't want to renege on my promise as others had done'. Personal principles were more important to Freeman than political ones – and once he made up his mind he never changed it.

One external event had brought about the split. This was the Korean War that Britain had engaged in since July 1950, fearing that a victory for Stalin and North Korea might well heat up the Cold War in Europe. The fear led to a massive re-armament programme in the United States and Britain. In January 1951, the new Chancellor, Hugh Gaitskell, proposed in Cabinet a colossal increase in the defence budget of 30 per cent, to total £4.7 billion spending over the following three years. He acknowledged that this would divert over half a million workers into defence production, and adversely affect house building, investments and consumer spending. What is more, he volunteered that there was no certainty Britain would be able to obtain the additional raw materials or machine tools necessary to achieve this target: 'There is a danger that the increased defence programme might, in practice, yield less and not more production within the next two years.'[5] Nevertheless, the Cabinet agreed to the programme. It remained to be seen how the government intended to pay for it, and that was a matter for Gaitskell's Budget two months later. For Freeman, as an under-secretary at the Ministry of Supply, and therefore closely involved in the process, it was the re-armament proposals that became his resignation issue.

Gaitskell knew that the only way he could meet the costs of re-armament would be to curb expenditure on social services, particularly health, which had been protected under Bevan like a sacred cow. On 9 April, he informed the Cabinet of his Budget proposals. These included capping the National Health Service expenditure at £400 million and imposing charges for glasses and false teeth, which would produce £13 million. Bevan retorted that these savings were a serious betrayal of socialist principles and threatened that he would be obliged to resign if they were announced in the Budget the following day.

In the circumstances, the savings were very modest, but a personality clash inflamed the row. Bevan was the son of a Welsh miner. He had left school at thirteen and was propelled to greatness by a passionate belief in socialism. Gaitskell was the son of a civil servant. He had been educated at Winchester and Oxford University and lived in Hampstead. Bevan called him a 'dessicated calculating machine'. What is more, this new-school Labourite had got the job Bevan had coveted after a lifetime of service. The social divide ran through the party, though there were some like Freeman – a 'Nye-ite' and member of the 'Keep Left' group – who had crossed it. This is not to say there was no policy issue. For the Bevanites, it was a matter of socialist principle: for the Gaitskellites, it was good economic housekeeping.

Gaitskell refused to back down, threatened to resign himself, and was only given the go ahead by Attlee to announce the Budget on the morning of the announcement itself. 'I'm afraid they will have to go,' said the Prime Minister, referring to Bevan and his supporters.[6]

Shortly before, Gaitskell and his wife Dora had been staying with the royal family at Windsor. The King had waggled his foot at his Chancellor and said: 'I really don't see why people should have false teeth free any more than they should have a pair of shoes free.'[7]

Dalton provides in his diary an intimate account of the splitting apart of his party. He writes how his friend John Freeman twisted and turned in reaction to events – but, at the end of the drama, stayed loyal to Bevan:

> *Friday 6 April.* Freeman thinks that on the narrow issue – teeth and spectacles – Nye would have very little support. But on the wider issue of finance and re-armament he would have a lot, and Freeman himself would have to consider his position very carefully. He was sure our re-armament was excessive, could not be carried out and would cause great dislocation. If Nye went, he said, the government could not last more than eight or ten weeks.

That Sunday, 8 April, Wilson and Freeman spent a long evening at Bevan's home in Cliveden Place, persuading him to broaden his opposition from simply health cutbacks, hence Freeman's later remark: 'When Nye had finally determined his course of action, Harold and I made up Bevanism to give him a justification for it.'[8] Freeman's claim is an exaggeration because Nye had resisted the colossal re-armament policy from the beginning, but it was the health issue that stirred him emotionally. Dalton's diary continues:

> *Monday 9 April.* I saw Freeman later this evening. He said all Nye's friends were trying to persuade him not to resign before the party meeting on Wednesday, but if he goes he must go with him. He hopes that, if we are on opposite sides of the gulf, it won't end our friendship.

> *Tuesday 10 April.* Freeman came to see me in my room. He has been working hard on Nye. He still thinks that if Nye goes he must go too. But he won't decide yet. I am trying to make him think less idolatrously of his idol!

In fact, on that day, 10 April, Freeman wrote what Michael Foot MP (Bevan's biographer) called 'a very powerful letter' to Bevan. His point was that Attlee intended to call a general election in the near future to increase the size of the Labour majority. If Bevan resigned in April, it would cause a split in the party that would lead to an election debacle 'of 1931 proportions', whereas if Bevan campaigned during the election on the reasons for his threatened resignation, 'three-quarters of the Labour movement would rally to you':

> If you could find some way of not making your resignation public at the moment on this issue, you would not lack the opportunity in the coming weeks to go out on an issue to which millions of Labour supporters would rally enthusiastically – [your opposition to] the drive towards war, the absence of any coherent foreign policy, the inflationary and anti-working-class character of our re-armament economies.

We would still probably lose the election but you would hold the initiative and have a good chance of capturing the machine.

He ended, however, with the promise to stand by Nye whatever his choice: 'The assurances I gave you this afternoon are in no way modified or withdrawn; but they do give me the right to address this last appeal to you.'[9]

To Freeman, then, personal loyalty was everything. True to his nature, however, he showed no apparent warmth or intimacy towards Bevan. Michael Foot, who was a witness to these events, makes that same point in his biography. Bevan, he writes, described Freeman as the most inscrutable of his Bevanite colleagues, calling him 'the man from Saturn' (i.e. a man of mystery).

Bevan did agree, however, to postpone his resignation until the third reading of the Health Charges Bill on 23 April, should that come to pass. Back to Dalton's diary:

Tuesday 17 April. Freeman says he would give anything to leave his present post. He thinks he must tell Clem, if he offers him the War Office, that he would have gone with Nye if Nye had resigned. I ask how far Freeman will follow Nye like a dog? Won't he in future recover his own judgement? He says yes, certainly, and if Nye were just to resign on the Charges Bill, he thinks he wouldn't go with him.

Friday 20 April. What, asked Hugh [Gaitskell], did I think of Freeman? I said I thought he was by far the most talented of the under-secretaries. Hugh said he liked him very much and Dora liked his wife [Mima]. Hugh would quite like him as financial secretary to the Treasury. He said he had been much moved by a letter from Freeman. He hoped there was no fear of his resigning.

Freeman's letter to Gaitskell said that breaking up the government on such a narrow issue as 'teeth and spectacles' was the height of folly and he was working to prevent it happening. He hoped their good relations would continue and he was 'delighted to see how clearly the mark of greatness sits upon you'.[10] The strength of Freeman's position as a junior minister was that he was valued highly by both sides – the Bevanites and the Gaitskellites – and his charm and conciliatory manner therefore might have brought them together. Presumably Attlee thought so, which is why Freeman's future looked so bright. Dalton's diary continues:

> *Sunday 22 April.* I go walking with John Freeman on Hampstead Heath. I say I feel as if I am taking him to a high place and tempting him, as they tempted Christ, by showing him all the kingdoms of the earth. I tell him his stock is quite high and there are various ministerial changes that might interest him apart from the War Office. He agrees to see Hugh and tells me he is *not* now committed to follow Nye.

The following day, events everyone had dreaded unfolded. During the debate on the third reading of the Health Charges Bill, Bevan resigned from the government. Dalton's diary drips with despair:

> *Monday 23 April.* Nye flopped today in resignation speech. It was most vicious. I saw John Freeman standing at the Bar listening. I tried to find him. I was very much agitated. Later I went to see Willy Whiteley [the Chief Whip]. Willy had asked John if he could tell the PM that John would accept promotion. He had asked for an hour to think it over. [Then Freeman had written Whiteley a note informing him of his intention to resign.] Willy told me John was out of the government.

Then I saw John in the passage and brought him to my room and was very sad. Then the phone rang from No. 10 and the secretary asked John to go see the PM in hospital [where he was receiving treatment for ulcers]. I gave him my car. I said, 'Think again. Be prepared to change your mind.' But later that night he wrote me another note. 'No change. So sorry!'

Oh, hell!

Dalton concludes his account of Freeman's resignation in his memoirs:

The next day I talked to Freeman on Hampstead Heath. He told me that Attlee had been 'most kind and friendly' but that his own mind remained unchanged. I told him, with Attlee's authority, that if he stayed Attlee had the possibility of promoting him to be either Secretary of State for War or president of the Board of Trade [both Cabinet posts]. I asked him to reconsider his opinion, but he made it clear he had finally decided to resign. I deeply regretted this. As a junior minister, he had not been fully used, not given a chance, and he had become browned off. If he had been my junior minister, things might have been different. I liked him and thought highly of his political intelligence.[11]

Freeman was not susceptible to flattery and, in his mind, Dalton had gone too far. He said in the 1970s that this 'clumsy talk of promotion' had made him more determined not to change his mind, for he had interpreted it as simply a bribe to keep him without any commitment attached.

Unlike Nye Bevan and Harold Wilson, John Freeman did not make a resignation speech. Instead, he wrote to Attlee. He did not give as a reason for resigning the 'teeth and spectacles' charges (although he did oppose the 'real reduction in our social services'), but instead cited his opposition to the re-armament programme – it was neither practical nor necessary and it would 'rob us of our vitality as a nation'. He said he had hoped these difficulties would be resolved by internal discussion, given time, but that the government had forced the issue with the Budget. He felt honour-bound to resign from a post that, although minor, carried the responsibility for administering a policy of which he did not approve. The Prime Minister replied that he did not agree with Freeman's reasons and was sorry to lose him, but he accepted the resignation.[12]

All three men majored on re-armament as the main reason for resignation, but this was only the presenting reason. It was a common assumption that Bevan resigned out of pique, Wilson out of opportunism, and only Freeman out of principle.

Bevan certainly resigned out of pique, as his resignation speech made very clear. He did put across his central argument, but he did so with a Welsh *hwyl* (emotional fervour) that many found excessive. The American re-armament programme was a greater threat to the West, he blustered, than the Russians were, for if Britain followed it, the programme would imperil 'the foundations of political liberty and parliamentary democracy'. Much of the rest of the speech was an attack on Gaitskell for his incompetence as Chancellor. Freeman dropped a regretful note to Dalton: 'Nothing could have done more to influence me the other way than Nye's outburst this afternoon.'[13]

Meanwhile, Dalton was sure Wilson's motives had been opportunistic throughout. He referred to him dismissively as 'Nye's Dog' and wrote: 'I made no effort to persuade Harold Wilson from resigning. In contrast with the other two, he did not have much strength of character.' Wilson made little secret of his tactical resignation, telling Woodrow Wyatt at the time:

He feared he would be blamed as president of the Board of Trade
for the adverse balance of trade arising from the Korean War, to the
detriment of his career. He thought a resignation at this stage would
do his long-term career good. It would win him backing from the
Labour Party activists, among whom he would be able to work, and
with whom he had had no contact.[14]

Wyatt felt so 'shocked and disappointed' to hear this that he did
not talk to Wilson for the next eight years. Freeman's own view was
that 'at first [Wilson's resignation] seemed public-spirited, but later
I thought that it was his best chance of getting to the top: if Wilson
backed Bevan, and Bevan won, then the succession was his'.

In retrospect, Freeman was right to oppose re-armament. The huge
programme changed the £307 million surplus balance of payments
in 1950 to a deficit of £369 million in 1951 – a dramatic turnaround.
Lord Croham, who was in the Treasury then and became head of the
civil service, wrote after his retirement: 'It may be too much to claim
that, but for the headlong rush into defence in 1950, the UK would
have enjoyed an economic miracle, but there would certainly have
been much less stop-go and a much better balanced economy.'

Did Freeman have other reasons for throwing in the towel? He was
'browned off', as Dalton wrote. Tony Crosland said John Freeman
resigned because he was 'a *New Statesman* leftist, happiest in opposition'. In fact, during those same weeks, he was offered a job with the
New Statesman.

These views are all speculation though, for Freeman never discussed in a public forum why he resigned. At the general election
in October, he did not follow his advice to Bevan to make the huge
cost of re-armament, with its welfare implications, a matter of principle. This extraordinary reluctance to defend his resignation (which

had cost him his career) disappointed his fellow Bevanites. Barbara Castle wrote:

> Now he had resigned, we all waited expectantly for him to carry the debate on to the high intellectual level of which we knew he was capable. Instead, he made no personal statement at all, either in the House or in the press. In one stormy meeting after another he stood against the wall, almost hiding himself behind the window curtains, but did not speak.

She gave a partial reason for this, and, as she was soon to become his lover, she ought to have known: 'After years of studying his complex personality I decided he was afraid of giving himself too fully to anything or anyone. I once told him his motto ought to be: *Je me sauve* [I protect myself].'[15]

This brings to mind what other friends have said, including Paul Johnson ('He is exceptionally hard of access') and Norman MacKenzie ('John has the capacity to put up the shutters that is excelled by nobody except a shopkeeper during riots'). Freeman was very private, self-protective and coldly distant when he wanted to be, but the question that remains unanswered is why?

It is clear that Freeman actually disliked power. He said so himself, in no uncertain terms: 'I personally find the pursuit and exercise of power arid, unsatisfying and distasteful.' What is more, according to John Birt, who worked under Freeman in the 1970s at London Weekend Television, he also disliked proselytising: 'He did not want to impose himself on the world, and that was the theme of his career. He did not want to stand on a platform and parade his views or ask to be loved. He was not self-regarding and he was without ambition.'

So why was Freeman's career a case of moving from one powerful job to another? He gave a convincing answer to William Hardcastle in an interview for Radio 4 in 1968:

> If you mean by power merely the responsibility of running something that you think is worthwhile – well, I enjoy that very much. But this, I think, is rather different from the whole apparatus of soliciting other people's votes, and of governing and instructing them, which is something that I find psychologically unsatisfying.

To which the next question must be why did Freeman go into politics in the first place? What, in particular, was his approach to socialism? Anthony Howard worked with Freeman closely at the *New Statesman* and wrote an insightful portrait of him in 1961:

> If his original conversion [at school when he met Gandhi and watched the hunger marchers] was emotional, it very rapidly became entirely intellectual. A deliberate decision seems to have been taken to root out feeling, like a cancer, and to put in its place the radium of the intellect.[16]

Politics without a gut feeling, without tears and wounds, must be rooted in shallow soil. Freeman's 'Keep Left' and then Bevanite politics ('almost Trotskyite' was a verdict at the time) were superficial compared to those of the working-class Bevanites he knew or the eastern European intellectuals he was about to meet on his next seminal journey. It was their lives that were at issue, whereas for Freeman it was only a matter of lifestyle. The gap between poor and rich was so wide, so socially unjust, that the poor seemed to belong to another world.

This is how Freeman put it in 1964:

Thirty years ago, when my own political prejudices were formed, up to 15 per cent of our population was unemployed. Real poverty and malnutrition were commonplace. The main anxiety for two or three million families was how to eat. In the case of injustice and cruelty on that scale, the course of political action seemed plain: get the Tories out so that the people of Britain can inherit their own country. The need was so great, the abuse so evident, the cause so simple, that it would have been accepted as axiomatic by even a tribe of South Sea Islanders.

This being the case, any sacrifice to Freeman's own lifestyle would be as irrelevant as it would be unexpected. Freeman could live comfortably in a democratic state, secure behind a set of rational assumptions that he considered self-evident.

This was just as well because, as Tony Howard wrote, 'The most common, concerted criticism of John Freeman, made by his friends and enemies alike, is that he is the greatest establishment figure of them all.'

'I have the faults of an English gentleman,' Freeman once said, although Tony Benn (who entered Parliament in the 1950 election), put it another way.[17] Freeman, he said in his diary, is as 'pompous, smug and urbane as ever'.

When Catherine Dove met Freeman a few years later, she did not find someone with strong political convictions so much as someone who was above politics. She quoted Walter Landor: 'I strove with none, for none was worth my strife.'

Marghanita Laski, who had been at Oxford with Freeman and also wrote for *Cherwell,* said much the same thing: 'John is incorruptible because he is too grand to be ambitious. He cannot be bought.'

Richard Crossman, however, who had clashed with Freeman in journalism and politics, took a more cynical view, simply saying: 'John is a complete nihilist.'

However, in April 1951, Freeman had no intention of leaving politics. He had resigned from government but not from Parliament. He was shortly to fight, and win, Watford for the third time, in a bruising election. He would stay in Parliament for another four years.

On 30 June 1951, Tom Driberg married Ena Binfield at St Mary's Church near Sloane Square, London. John Freeman had arranged the marriage, was best man and, it was rumoured, a former lover of the bride. Lizi has no doubts that her stepfather married off his rampantly homosexual friend on purpose: 'He engineered the wedding, of course. She was a friend of ours, a lovely widowed Jewish lady. It was a cover-up to conceal Tom's sexuality. I don't know why she agreed to it.'

Freeman provides an answer to that:

> Ena discussed with me at length the pros and cons of marrying such a hopeless case. I don't think she expected to reform Tom, but she probably did expect that if she could provide him with a comfortable and stable background, his behaviour might become less promiscuous and self-destructive.[18]

There was little sign that this happened. In some ways, however, the couple was well matched. She was gregarious, witty, and popular in left-wing Labour circles. In fact, they met at a party hosted by George Strauss. She needed companionship, too, and, according to her son by a previous spouse, accepted that the marriage would probably not be consummated.

The wedding was a charade. A large number of Tom's constituents came up by charabanc and arrived early so that, according to Roy Jenkins (one of the ushers), they packed into the front pews leaving the 'po-faced diplomats' and 'high literary society' (such as John

Betjeman, Constant Lambert, Osbert Lancaster and Osbert Sitwell) standing at the back. Alongside them were the leaders of the Bevanites, including Nye himself, his wife Jennie Lee, and the editor of the *New Statesman*, Kingsley Martin. Most of them were secularists, so the high nuptial mass that lasted over an hour was a trial. According to Driberg, Kingsley Martin sat looking 'quite shocked', Bevan growled that his 'Calvinist blood was roused' and the communist scientist J. B. S. Haldane filled his pipe to register his disapproval. Driberg wrote afterwards in his diary that all this had given him 'a twinge of naughty amusement'.

Lizi and her mother were in the congregation and she remembers that Driberg chewed gum throughout. He wrote later that he was very nervous, though fortified before by one or two brandies supplied by his best man. He gasped a loud 'phew' after silence followed the obligatory announcement by the bishop of 'if any man can show any just cause why they may not be joined together in holy matrimony, let him now speak, or else hereafter hold his peace'.[19] Afterwards there was a champagne reception at the House of Commons and then a honeymoon in Brighton. 'Thank goodness it's over anyway,' wrote Driberg in his diary. 'This evening I am still dazed – but much happier than when I woke up this morning.'

John Freeman's wedding present was a cheque for £12. As far as is known, he kept a straight face throughout.

Attlee called for a general election on 25 October 1951 after twenty months in office, in order to increase the Labour majority. The result was that Labour polled more votes than any previous political party at a general election (13,948,605), but still won twenty-six fewer seats than the Conservatives. As the Liberal Party was reduced to six seats, this meant any coalition was impossible and Labour was out of power. Churchill had sneaked back but Dalton, for one, was not depressed.

He said the result was 'wonderful' and reported that Attlee told him he expected to be Prime Minister again in two years. In fact, Labour was out of office for thirteen years, by which time Attlee had retired to be succeeded by Harold Wilson.

Freeman's election in Watford was a rough experience. His political organiser, the secretary of the Watford Socialist Party, had resigned, saying: 'The Labour Party does not believe in itself or its principles.' According to the *Daily Mail*, when Nye Bevan came to speak there on 10 October, a bearded man brandishing a crucifix and shouting 'Vermin!' and 'Rubbish!' gave him a 'lively reception'. This seems an understatement: 'The orchestra platform behind the stage on which Mr Bevan was speaking became a battleground at one time for hecklers and supporters, with women members of the audience noisily trying to keep the peace.' Nevertheless, Bevan sat down to 'thunderous applause'.

Freeman looked thin and pale in his election brochure 'John Freeman: A Man You Can Trust'. The pamphlet did not refer to his resignation from government, but it did stress, in general terms, the Bevanite line of negotiation rather than re-armament being the answer to communist aggression. In the end, Freeman scraped home by 508 votes (after a recount) out of over 43,000 cast – a very large turnout of 87 per cent.

This was the occasion, so he wrote in the *New Statesman*, that he was lying in the bath as the returning officer made the announcement. When the press asked him later what he intended to do next, he replied: 'Go home and have a whisky and soda.'

In 1953, he announced that he would not stand for the constituency again. He was feeling ill. On 19 September, Dalton had recorded in his diary:

> Back to flat to receive Freeman at 10.45. Rather ill, and overwrought
> – pain in his ears and very tired, going off for ten days' rest before

the election. Tony [Crosland] thinks he has become more and more emotional (a word of discredit in Tony's vocabulary) and confused about politics.

Not that his rest did him much good. Dalton wrote a month later: 'Freeman is still having great trouble with his ears (daily treatment at hospital) and with his sinus (very painful weekly wash out). He is below par.' Was this a psychosomatic reaction to the traumas of the previous few months?

His time in Parliament was taken up with the 'Keep Left' group, later known as the Bevanites, the aim of which was to push left-wing views and get Bevan back in power. Straight after the general election it instituted weekly meetings and appointed a chairman – Harold Wilson. One of its members, Ian Mikardo MP, was proud of the punch that it packed:

> Out of the forty-nine members [in 1952] forty-seven were MPs. We included five ex-ministers, fourteen future ministers, nine current or future members of the party executive. We had among us six distinguished writers and nine members who were in the front rank of parliamentary orators.[20]

Freeman was one of the 'distinguished writers'. The worry within the Labour establishment was that the Bevanites might become a caucus within a caucus, a group within a party, which was not what Freeman wanted. Tom Driberg found the composition of mainly middle-class intellectuals and journalists – who were good talkers and equally good drinkers – very congenial. He called it 'the smoking room within the smoking room'.

Freeman was not 'a joiner', but he was part of the inner group as he was one of the foremost writers. Already, in July 1951, he had been a named writer in the *Tribune* pamphlet 'One Way Only', which quickly sold 100,000 copies. The main theme of 'One Way Only' was that all the resources being poured into re-armament to meet an exaggerated threat from the Soviet Union should be diverted to social services and to support the 'social revolution in Asia, Africa and the Middle East', where millions were still dying from famine. He made a speech at the Fabian Society summer conference saying much the same thing, and this was printed up as 'Re-armament – how far?'. This message went down well with the working class particularly, who still admired the socialism of the Soviet Union and its contribution to the defeat of fascism.

The strength of the Bevanites became clear in March 1952, when Bevan led fifty-seven Labour MPs to vote against the party's support of the government's defence White Paper increasing re-armament expenditure yet again. Freeman was one of them. The *Daily Herald* was furious – a clear sign that the Labour leadership was worried: 'Bevan and his supporters are challenging the democratic decisions of the Parliamentary Labour Party. There must be an end to this minority's egotism.'

While most of the Bevanite work was researching, writing and publishing policy papers, the group kept contact with the public through its Brains Trust – copied from the BBC radio version and organised by *Tribune*. These meetings, said Ian Mikardo (who was usually the question master), were a 'runaway success'. He remembered an audience of 900 in Worthing, despite it being 'scarcely the most fertile soil for the seeds of socialism'.

John Freeman and Barbara Castle travelled the country together and it was then that they began an affair, Michael Foot told me. On one occasion, at Lowestoft in 1953, they were asked what the attitude of a socialist ought to be to the coronation. Realising the huge popularity of the new Queen, Castle was considering a careful answer when Freeman said tersely: 'Deplore it!' He said the coronation was 'a shocking waste of money' and, true to his view, on the day of the coronation (2 June 1952) he gave up his seat in front of the TV rather than watch it.

Driberg had no such reluctance, reporting from inside Westminster Abbey for a big spread in *Picture Post*. Presumably, as a royal reporter for the magazine, Mima was on duty too, though she has no article printed under the Mima Kerr byline. She had already done her royal duty, with an article a year earlier on the Queen's first official visit to Scotland entitled 'Scots welcome their Queen', and another in December 1952 on the Queen's first portrait painter, Douglas Chandor.[21]

That same year, Barbara Castle and John Freeman found themselves on a private tour of the Middle East organised by a Lebanese businessman – Emile Bustani. There were four other MPs too. 'By common consent,' Castle wrote, 'We gave John Freeman the job of conducting our press conferences, which he did with consummate skill, keeping the nervy Arab journalists happy while not giving anything away.'

At the Labour Party annual conference, held in Morecambe in September 1952, the Bevanites won six out of the seven national executive seats up for election, including one for Driberg. This was 'the worst Labour conference for bad temper and hatred since 1926' wrote Dalton, who was incensed by Driberg's election. He moaned to Freeman (who had not put himself forward for election) about Driberg's dilettante behaviour.

This, however, was the high-water mark of the Bevanites. Attlee realised they needed cutting down to size, and in October he made an unequivocal speech. He found 'the existence of a party within a party quite intolerable. I say work with the team. Turn your guns on the enemy, not on your own friends.'[22] This struck home. Bevan announced that he was ready to rejoin the shadow Cabinet and wished to throw open the Bevanite group to the whole party. This was not enough for Attlee, who demanded a vote among Labour Party MPs on whether or not the Bevanites should be disbanded. He won and they were.

A much smaller, inner group continued to meet every week for a working lunch in Richard Crossman's house in Vincent Square. This consisted of six members of the NEC – Bevan himself, Driberg, Castle, Mikardo, Wilson and Crossman – plus the journalists' group, including John Freeman.

In 1954, the Vincent Square meetings became the focus of a row that, in Freeman's view, could have broken the rump of Bevanites. Bevan had rejoined the shadow Cabinet but resigned again in May over a foreign policy issue. To the amazement of his fellow Bevanites, Harold Wilson accepted Attlee's invitation to take his place. They regarded this as an act of betrayal. Once again, out of pique, Bevan threatened to resign from the inner group; once again, Freeman wrote him a persuasive letter attempting to change his mind: 'I hope you will come to lunch at Dick's tomorrow. If you don't come I fear the inner circle of your following may be broken – perhaps irreparably. Harold's ambition has created a disastrous situation.'[23]

In fact, Freeman had never considered Wilson a sincere member of the group: 'He wore the label of Bevanite like a poppy on Remembrance Day – for form's sake.'[24] In the end, this squabble was patched up, but its legacy was Freeman's dislike of Wilson. He had no time for the placement of personal ambition above loyalty. The Bevanites continued but often without Bevan himself, for he was not a team player. Freeman, though conscientious, was losing interest.

He was finding parliamentary life increasingly tedious. Time was heavy on his hands, particularly in the evenings when MPs had to hang around to vote, sometimes until dawn. He wiled away the hours gambling at canasta, although it was illegal in Parliament. He had hosted the card table since his time as junior minister, because the rank qualified him for his own small room in the House of Commons. Driberg was the croupier and sat with his back to the door, preventing the policeman – who came around opening doors and shouting 'Division!' (the call to vote) – from seeing what was going on inside. The other members of the canasta school were Woodrow Wyatt, Tony Crosland and Roy Jenkins.

The Bevanite split had not isolated Freeman. 'He was of such apparently controlled and ice-cold a temperament,' wrote Jenkins, 'that it did not make much difference to relations whether one agreed with him or not.'[25] Idleness brought out the hedonist in Freeman. He admitted to being 'self-indulgent and lazy'. Given the chance, he said, he surrendered to 'wine, Dr Castro cigars and warm-hearted women'.[26]

He was not a natural House of Commons man and this contributed to his dislike of the institution. On his frequent social visits to Woodrow Wyatt's home, the two 'spirit of 1945' MPs discussed why their ambitions to change the world appeared to have stalled.

'But the House of Commons is such fun, such an education in human nature, such a good club,' said Wyatt.

'That,' said Freeman, 'is just what I hate.'

He confessed to doodling during 'unspeakable committee meetings', demonstrating a small repertoire that might well interest a graphologist looking for psychological insights. First, there was a 'very freehand map of the British Isles'; then a fancy arrangement of swallows in flight; then 'a mouse *couchant*'; and also a pictorial presentation of the Pythagorean theorem. 'In this last, incidentally, one can pass a pleasant enough fifteen minutes variously shading the resultant network of triangles,' he wrote in the *New Statesman*. He also tested his memory through mental arithmetic: 'Simple multiplication and division – nothing tricky. But oh, what joy awaited me! What could be more natural than to start multiplying 123,456,789 by various figures? And what more rewarding than to find that if you multiply it by 8, the answer is 987,654,312?'[27]

Freeman obviously possessed a very retentive memory and enjoyed testing it, which might account for his appearances on the *Chan Canasta* TV show a few years later. Chan Canasta was described as a 'pioneer of mental magic'.

The Freemans spent much of their leisure time at Bradwell Lodge. Lizi slept above the library and remembers being kept awake late into the night by canasta. On one occasion, Driberg, Freeman and others played all night and through breakfast, until 11 a.m.: 'I thought this was very wrong, very naughty!'

Lizi made friends with the live-in couple – Hilda the cook and Joe the gardener. She breakfasted with them while the grown-ups had breakfast in bed. They were all sorry for Ena, who was often 'very unhappy', because, said Lizi, 'she had to rescue young men whom Tom had picked up in the pub or railway station and brought home. Then they would suddenly find they were in a house party they weren't expecting. We would find a stranger in our midst!'

From the start of their marriage, Driberg had treated Ena 'abominably', said Freeman. The first Christmas after the wedding, he had gone off to the Sudan leaving her on her own. She spent Christmas Day with the Freemans at their flat in Heath Mansions, where they had lived with Lizi since about 1948. 'John was being fairly intolerable,' Ena wrote. 'He slept during the afternoon and Mima took down her back hair and I comforted.'

Since that Christmas, Ena's relationship with Driberg had gone from bad to worse. Weekends alone at Bradwell Lodge were spent in moody silence. He insisted that she slept at the other end of the house, while he played endless games of solo canasta and communicated with her by notes. She felt lonely, humiliated and prepared to separate. It was Freeman who dissuaded her, by pointing out what a bad effect separation would have on Tom 'professionally and socially'. So she agreed to stay, on the following conditions:

> I will be with you occasionally at Bradwell – say one weekend a month, the first Sunday if you like, so that we can go to church together. I will go with you to such functions in London and elsewhere as will serve to keep up the façade of friendly relations between us ... I am very sorry our marriage has turned out so badly, but you have so consistently undermined my self-confidence by your behaviour to me that I cannot let it continue.[28]

The Freemans spent other weekends with Lord Faringdon, a leading member of the Fabian Society. He was a gay friend of Tom Driberg's, known for his effeminate ways such as opening a speech in the House of Lords with 'My dears' instead of 'My Lords'. He was also a supporter of left-wing causes. At his country estate Buscot Park, prominent refugees from Franco's Spain could find themselves with the Bevanite group holding a policy weekend. 'During this time, Freeman cultivated his taste for fine wines, which he'd established at Oxford and continued in the Driberg cellar. In September 1952, he sent his host a postcard from Bordeaux:

> I have visited and drunk in the cellars of the Chateaux Olivier, Haut Brion, La Mission Haut Brion, Pichon Longueville, Mouton-Rothschild, Hautellan, Cissal, and several smaller ones; also in the enormous cellars of Calvet and Erchenauer and Kressman. The '47s are excellent

for both Medoc and Graves; '49 very good for Graves; '49 and '50 and '51 promise quite a good average for the Medocs. '52 looks – the harvest is next week – as if it will be outstanding; the best, certainly, since '47, perhaps since '34.[29]

This particular visit led to a series of articles for the *New Statesman*. When Freeman became editor he would bring in wine corks after a particularly fine meal and invite his team to enjoy the fragrance.

By the time of the general election in May 1955, Freeman had had enough. He had made his intention clear not to stand again at Watford and he turned down a last-minute invitation to become Labour MP for Durham. Apart from disliking the job, he had a political reason for leaving Parliament. The phrase of 1954 was 'Butskellism', meaning a convergence of middle-of-the-road policies by the two Chancellors of the Exchequer, the Conservative Rab Butler and Labour's Hugh Gaitskell. This amounted to bi-party approval for a Keynesian mixed economy, with moderate state intervention to promote social goals, particularly in health and education. It was debated at the Labour Party conference in Scarborough and Freeman was strongly opposed to it:

> While it can be argued that a policy of Butskellism might be the easiest way of winning an election, it seems to me the surest way of destroying the Labour Party. Labour has never been a tightly organised party of disciplined militants, but it has always been a party held together by a belief in socialist economics and socialist ethics. Its rank and file has always been deeply rooted in the class-conscious working class. These two characteristics are intimately connected, and they are the strength of the party. It is the socialist content of its idealism that has distinguished it from other progressive groups and cemented

the loyalty of the working class. It is working-class loyalty to a non-communist Labour Party that has kept strong in Britain the flame of democratic socialism, at a time when it burns so low in the rest of the world. I would rather lose an election than betray the hopes of Labour supporters.[30]

A powerful statement and a political epitaph.

Just before the election, Freeman vented his frustration in an article for the *New Statesman* called 'Night Thoughts of an Ex-MP'. He began: 'My principal thought at this time is one of thankful relief.' There follows a carefully balanced article, in which the reader is left waiting for the sting in the tail. He said he would miss his daily companions, who would change into distant friends, and, above all, he would miss his sense of being at the centre of things: 'It is the community of interest in power and responsibility, which pervades the Commons, that makes it, outside the formalities of the debating chamber, the very best of talking shops.'

Then comes the sting – Freeman's vision of his future if he stayed:

I have in my mind a disenchanted vision of parliamentary man at his worst: at forty-five [he was forty] he is pallid, bald and ulcerated; arrogant, narrow-minded and periphrastic. And worse, he is complacent about it all. Too many MPs cease to look outside. They perceive one another with the vapid intensity of a goldfish. If he understands at all that he has deteriorated, he claims he has sacrificed himself to his cause. This is true in a few cases; but more often he has sacrificed himself to the sheer self-indulgence of being a public man.[31]

Freeman told Edward Hyams, a colleague at the *New Statesman*, that he had detested parliamentary life. He considered his ten years as an

MP to have been worse than his five years as a soldier. Freeman had done his best, but ultimately ended his career because Parliament had not been to his taste.

In 1964, when Labour was planning its return to power after thirteen years in the wilderness, Freeman was asked by his old friends Barbara Castle and Richard Crossman, who would both become Cabinet ministers, if he would consider standing for Parliament again, if he was guaranteed a place in the Cabinet. He refused.

Could Freeman have become Prime Minister? This, of course, is impossible to answer. He did, in my view, fulfil most of his own prescription: 'The great political leader requires not only the courage, ability and integrity of the statesman; he must also understand intuitively the emotions, prejudices and ambitions of fools and rascals. Paradoxically, he must contain in himself something of the rascal and something of the fool.'[32] No one could call Freeman a fool, but nor did he tolerate fools. Nor would he have enjoyed the scheming, public performances and confrontation that the Prime Minister's role required. He was, nevertheless, an outstanding leader – in the army, in politics, in diplomacy and in business.

Endorsements for the top job came from an impressive variety of those who knew him well, from the elder statesman Dr Henry Kissinger ('He would have made a great Prime Minister') to a fellow government minister at the time, Woodrow Wyatt ('He could have been Prime Minister but he disdained the grubby atmosphere of political life') to the comedian Tony Hancock, who gave him the vote of the man in the street ('He should have been Prime Minister'). Paul Johnson, who succeeded Freeman as editor of the *New Statesman*, told me:

He could have become leader of the Labour Party and then Prime Minister – a great Prime Minister. He was in the mould of Attlee, essentially a staff officer, a major who led with quiet authority. In the Cold War tensions, he would have been a calm – cold, perhaps – hand at the helm: unflappable, reasoned and authoritative.[33]

Had he not resigned, it is very easy to see him as a senior member of Wilson's Cabinet, perhaps as Foreign Secretary, on a par with his friend Tony Crosland. After that, there is no point in speculation: I was told with certainty that he did not vote Labour again after 1966.

In fact, much later in his life when he was teaching at UC Davis in California (see Chapter 12), he said he regretted the radical left views of his earlier years – 'they did a lot of harm'. This is an admission to ponder.

Chapter 5

Television interviewer
– *Panorama*

WHEN FREEMAN WAS asked by Nigel Lawson in the 1990s why he had not written his autobiography, he replied that he would have been too rude about too many people. However, if there was one person Freeman admired and praised without qualification it was Grace Wyndham Goldie. She was the founder of the new-look BBC TV programme *Panorama*, which came on air on 19 September 1955. In his biography of her, *The First Lady of Television*, John Grist writes:

> John Freeman, by any reckoning an outstanding man of his generation, said that, in retrospect, his education, St Pauls [*sic*] and then

Oxford, was outshone by two other periods, army staff college and working with Grace Wyndham Goldie. He thought her classical values represented the finest liberal approach to life and duty. He thought she was outstanding compared to the grey-suited men who ran the BBC. She should have been director-general.[1]

Grace Wyndham Goldie was fifty-five in 1955. Her civil service type title (assistant head of talks television) was evidence of how fundamentally un-visual factual television was in those days – a radio-led, outmoded practice she was determined to change. It was a misleading title, too, because Grace was assistant to nobody. She had to be in charge of any activity she was engaged in, so her boss Leonard Miall wisely gave her the task of launching new projects. First and foremost was *Panorama*.

Wyndham Goldie was fearsome. A future director-general, Sir Ian Trethowan, wrote: 'Her sharp tongue and angry snapping eyes were feared and disliked by newer and more junior members of her staff, but older hands held her in deep respect, even awe.'[2] She was a workaholic who demanded total commitment – 'If you don't dream about television every night you are no use to me!' – and her moods were so unpredictable that she was said to rule 'with a whim of iron'.

Her biographer, John Grist, who also worked with her in the 1950s, gives an insider's picture of Grace Wyndham Goldie at an editorial meeting (a BBC institution that anyone who has worked there knows may determine success or failure):

She carried an aura, and senior men shuffled their papers when she came into a meeting and moved their bottoms in their chairs when she interjected some comment, looking uneasy. She talked very well and laughed a lot with her young men. She was immensely proud of 'her boys' and would defend them against all comers, but would box their ears, figuratively, and glare in a steely way. I confess I did not like her, but, like everyone else except perhaps Huw Wheldon, I was frightened of her.[3]

Catherine Dove (later Freeman), then a young producer in her department, remembers Grace as:

A colourful small bird, with bright eyes always darting about the room and a thin mouth. She dressed elegantly but conservatively, neatly nipped-in jacket, always a brooch in her lapel. I respected her totally, and had every reason to like her, because she was always very kind and supportive of me.

Pre-eminent among 'Goldie's boys' were a handful of former junior ministers from the post-war Labour governments, who had left Parliament between 1950–55, just when television factual programmes were on the cusp of change and needing new-look reporters and interviewers. John Freeman was one of them. Now forty, and despite his record of high achievement in both the army and politics, he was probably not averse to being a Goldie boy.

Others Goldie boys were Christopher Mayhew (once under-secretary of Foreign Affairs), Aidan Crawley (Air) and Woodrow Wyatt (who had been given Freeman's post of under-secretary in the War Office after Freeman had moved to the Ministry of Supply). The difference between Freeman and the others was that, while they returned to politics in the 1960s, he never went back. However, what they all shared, in Grace Wyndham Goldie's view, was 'a cross-bench mind'. Mayhew moved from the Labour to the Liberal Party; Crawley crossed the floor and became a Conservative MP (before leaving politics and becoming chairman of London Weekend Television); and Wyatt became a thorn in the side of the Labour Party, with very right-wing views. Freeman, in her words, 'abandoned the party political scene, became editor of the *New Statesman* and, in the television series *Face to Face*, showed interviewing skills comparable to Edward R. Murrow in the United States'. None had any problem being fair and impartial. She sensed in all of them disillusionment with party politics:

> They had joined the Labour government in 1945 with a burning enthu-
> siasm, but, after five years in power, the millennium had not arrived.
> The split in the party, which had helped to bring it down in 1951,
> still existed. Now television offered a new form of expression, not of
> party politics, but of the driving force that had sent them into poli-
> tics in the first place. They delighted in its technicalities and wanted
> to explore its possibilities. They found no problem working long
> hours, travelling abroad and contributing generously as part of a
> team. They were informed about current affairs, showed an under-
> standing of the difficulties of government and were more interested
> in elucidation than dispute.[4]

All in all, Grace Wyndham Goldie was delighted. They were superior in every way to the 'dirty-mac brigade' of journalists, which she despised. The problem, of course, was of perceived political bias. Where were the former leading lights of the Conservative Party?

Winston Churchill, for one, asked this question in May 1953, when Aidan Crawley was in India with his wife Virginia Cowles, filming what became the six-part television series *India's Challenge*. Grace Wyndham Goldie was able to report that Crawley was no longer a Labour MP, nor was he a prospective Labour candidate, so the obli-gation for 'balance' did not apply.

However, Conservative pressure mounted and Grace shared the BBC's anxiety. The trouble, she reported, was that 'television in itself did not interest the Conservatives'. Many former Tory MPs were businessmen who earned much higher salaries than the BBC could ever offer. Furthermore, while they were prepared to air their views, they did not seem to be interested in the role of expositor or moderator. One Conservative councillor (on the London county council for Lewisham) did present himself: Christopher Chataway spent three years as a Goldie boy before becoming a Conservative MP.

The first reporter for the new-look *Panorama* (one or two models had failed before) was Woodrow Wyatt. His film test had been a disaster: 'I looked like a stuffed pig and recoiled from this revelation of myself as someone I should hate to hear or see.' Catherine Dove, the first woman on the *Panorama* production team, said he reminded her more of Toad of Toad Hall. However, he persisted and filmed a twenty-minute report on Malta for the opening edition, although he was not sure what to do when he got to Malta:

> Ignorant of television, I decided on a direct approach. I stood on a promontory with the sea behind me. 'To my right,' I yelled, 'are Africa and Egypt. On my left are Sicily and Italy. In front of me is Cyprus. Behind me is Gibraltar. That is why, for centuries, Malta has been of strategic importance to anyone who wants to control the Mediterranean.'[5]

So began the longest-running and most prestigious of TV factual programmes. It was not, strictly speaking, 'current affairs'; more, in the words of its first producer Michael Peacock, 'a reflection of everyday life – ships, jazz, people, ploughing, theatre, industry, art, books, buildings, or bulldozers'. A 'window on the world', as it called itself in those early days, its mission was to introduce serious subjects to a popular audience – the heart of public service broadcasting.

Wyatt's 'piece to camera' in Malta was, surprisingly, a bit of a breakthrough, because most foreign factual coverage on television in the early 1950s had been confined to the programme *Newsreel* – and that had consisted mostly of silent film shot by a cameraman, to which a commentary would be added back home and then voiced out of vision, rather like a TV version of the cinema's *Look at Life*. Grace Wyndham Goldie said that in those early days of *Newsreel* she used to throw onto the cutting-room floor chocolate-box pictures of cherry orchards in flower, or girls in local costume, or flocks of bleating lambs, because they offered nothing 'to a study, say, of the relationship between Yugoslavia and the USSR'. The cameraman might not have been briefed at all on the story – if one had even been decided – before he set out for foreign parts. No doubt this is partly why Grace was experimenting at the time with *Viewfinder*, which saw Aidan Crawley and Christopher Mayhew send back 'illustrated reports on world affairs'. Meanwhile, *Newsreel* passed from the film department to the TV and radio news department – from the former, which knew nothing about content, to the latter, which knew nothing about the visual requirements of television. The news department – dubbed by the next director-general, Hugh Carleton Greene, as 'the Kremlin of the BBC' – was under the reactionary 'dictatorship' of Tahu Hole, the head of news. His enemy was the visual, so on BBC television news, nothing moved. The only things television news was allowed to add to a radio broadcast were a clock, the BBC coat of arms, a few captions and some still photographs. Such was the dread of the cult of personality that, up until September 1955 (three weeks before ITV began), TV newsreaders like Richard Baker and Kenneth Kendall were neither seen nor identified. In 1954, the

Star newspaper called TV news 'about as impressive visually as the fatstock prices'.

All this is one way of saying that Grace Wyndham Goldie and *Panorama* were kicking against an open door. In the mid-1950s, broadcasting was still in the age of radio. The night ITV began transmitting, just three days after Woodrow Wyatt's *Panorama*, the BBC Light Programme station scooped an audience of eight million, with the death of Grace Archer on, of course, the ever-running soap opera *The Archers*. The radio reviewer of *The Guardian* summed it up the next morning:

> She dwelt unseen amid the Light
> Among the Archer clan,
> And breathed her last the very night
> That ITV began.
> She was well loved and millions knew
> That Grace had ceased to be.
> Now she is in her grave, but oh,
> She's scooped the ITV.

One of *Panorama*'s most important running stories in those early days was the exposure by Woodrow Wyatt of communist vote rigging, first in the Amalgamated Engineering Union (AEU) and then in the Electrical Trades Union (ETU). John Freeman took over from Wyatt and it was his interview with the communist president of the ETU in 1960 that became one of the most controversial in the history of *Panorama*.

In 1957, Wyatt obtained masses of confidential documents from the one remaining full-time, non-communist official in the ETU, Jock Byrne, which proved that, since the war, the communist membership had falsified election returns. By December 1957, he had compiled a devastating report, with the help of Norman MacKenzie. The director-general of the BBC gave his approval for the exposure on *Panorama*. This was a brave move, because the TV studios depended on the ETU to get their programmes on air. Wyatt had to resort to what has now become accepted practice:

> I had no alternative but to talk to a number of witnesses from the ETU with their faces hidden from the cameras. The fear in their voices made the more convincing their description of how they had watched communist officials falsifying the election returns and disqualifying votes for Les Cannon [the non-communist candidate]. I invited the ETU communist leaders Foulkes and Haxell to come to answer the charges. They refused.[6]

'In last week's sizzling *Panorama*,' wrote Maurice Wiggins in the *Sunday Times*:

> Mr Woodrow Wyatt's interviews gained a huge increment of drama from the fact that several of them were not seen. In its strange, chilling way, this was one of the most dramatic things I have ever seen. In your quiet, insulated room you felt the weight and swirl of:

> *The dangerous flood*
> *Of history, that never sleeps nor dies,*
> *And, held one moment, burns the hand.*

The next year Wyatt left *Panorama* to return to politics. It fell to John Freeman to complete what Wyatt had begun. Following another *Panorama* report, in which non-communist local officials made further allegations about ETU vote rigging, on 22 February 1960, Frank

Foulkes, the communist president, finally came in to the *Panorama* studio. The interviewer was John Freeman.

It almost didn't happen. Four days before the live transmission, Freeman and Peacock met with Foulkes in Broadcasting House to discuss the terms of the interview. Foulkes refuted the allegations of the previous Monday's *Panorama* and demanded a 'conversation' rather than a 'cross examination' in the studio follow-up, otherwise he would not appear. Freeman insisted that 'on no account must he be placed in a position of being unable to ask the questions he wanted to put to Mr Foulkes', as Peacock reported to Leonard Miall. He added that Foulkes would not accept Freeman's terms because 'he would have everything to lose and nothing to gain'. It had been 'a difficult and sticky meeting'.[7]

Eventually, to the surprise of the *Panorama* office, Foulkes did agree 'to unrestricted questioning and answering'. The result was embarrassing to watch:

> FREEMAN: You do realise, don't you, that these charges concern you personally? If they are not charges of administrative inefficiency then they amount to charges of fraud, perhaps of criminal conspiracy. What do you feel about that?
> FOULKES: I don't want anybody to … I don't want anybody to … prove my innocence. I am quite able to stand up to any charge of criminal conspiracy.
> FREEMAN: You have a very simple remedy. You can go to the courts tomorrow morning and issue writs for libel against me, against the BBC, against all the papers that have attacked you and against the four gentlemen who appeared in last week's programme.[8]

Peacock saw it unfold from the gallery:

I almost felt sorry for Frank Foulkes because he was destroyed. John was supremely hard. There was no playing about. He went straight in. In theory the interview was to enable Foulkes to deny the allegations, but actually he ended up un-denying. He just gave in.

Any really competent, heavyweight interviewer could have done the interview. But John, well, he wasn't cold so much as impersonal and with this authority, this charisma. You couldn't actually *deny* his voice.[9]

Mary Crozier of *The Guardian* was mesmerised:

Freeman's inquisitorial manner was necessary to the occasion. This had to be a hard interview, and it was. Freeman kept hammering his nails on the head. Foulkes's melancholy eyes and worried expression gave the viewer a portrait to engage the eye as fully as the mind. Rarely has television done an interview of such interest.[10]

The next day, the interview made headlines in the *Daily Mail*: 'ETU in the dock: *Why don't you sue us all?* Challenge on television to union chief Foulkes.'

It instantly became a cause célèbre. A group of Labour MPs wrote to *The Times* accusing Freeman of being 'a self-appointed prosecutor coercing Foulkes by challenge to prove his innocence'. A counter-group of eminent journalists and politicians, like Malcolm Muggeridge, Francis Williams, Woodrow Wyatt, Christopher Chataway and Lord Boothby, retaliated:

To deny to the TV interviewer the right of questioning, which, subject to the laws of libel and contempt, is conceded almost without query by the newspaper journalist, is unnaturally to limit the freedom of television to serve the public, whether as a purveyor of news and ideas, or as a watchdog.[11]

Strictly speaking, it was not trial by television, for television has no legal authority. It took high-court action before the ballot rigging in the ETU was confirmed, and both Haxell (the general secretary) and Foulkes were removed.

John Freeman began his broadcasting career – as he did his journalism for the *New Statesman* – when he was still a Member of Parliament. He was an infrequent contributor from 1951 to the long-running *Week in Westminster* and *At Home and Abroad*, both discussion programmes on the BBC Radio Home Service. He also broadcast on the BBC World Service – his first paid contribution being an 'unscripted discussion' with Wilfred Pickles for *London Calling Europe*, answering the question 'What is socialism?' The date was 5 October 1952.

Following a six-week tour of eastern Europe in the summer of 1956 (see Chapter 7), Freeman became something of an expert on communism and delivered his 'Impressions of Warsaw' and 'The Iron Curtain' on *At Home and Abroad*.

A more adventurous programme was *Radio Link*, which connected speakers 'live' in studios around Europe. He took part in the opening programme on 5 July 1956, when the subject was Khrushchev's speech denouncing Stalin at the 20th Party Congress, held the previous February in Moscow. The other speakers were Raymond Aron in Paris and Thomas Barman in Warsaw; Robert McKenzie was the chairman. Afterwards Freeman wrote to the producer: 'Next time I shall be very much less scared of this hellish technique of headphones' – a curious admission for one with apparently steely nerves.

Freeman enjoyed radio and was keen for more work. If he had been asked why he worked hard to establish a broadcasting reputation, he would have retorted, no doubt, that he needed the money. But there was more to it than that. Freeman was never interested in financial enrichment for its own sake, nor was he interested in social status or being an intellectual snob. Provided the subject interested him, he was keen to find out more about it and shape it into the report, interview or discussion form that the broadcast media required, whether for *Panorama* or schools radio. His interests were wide. Themes emerged: foreign affairs, particularly the United States, eastern Europe and South Africa; anything to do with crime and punishment and the law; the human mind, from brainwashing to beliefs; the stage and cinema. To BBC staff, he was always polite – even to his paymasters, as the many notes in his files indicate. Perhaps this was no more than was to be expected, but Freeman had been a senior soldier and government minister and was considerably older than most of the staff he dealt with.

From 1956, Freeman combined radio broadcasts with television appearances. His most regular programme before *Panorama* was *Press Conference* – a format taken from American television, in which three or four journalists questioned a public figure in the news. After his first two appearances, the producer Felicia Elwell spread the word:

> He has taken part in a couple of *Press Conferences* and he seems to me to be an exceptionally able broadcaster who is very interested in popular exposition and any possible broadcasting for children. He has a good and sympathetic delivery and would be a very good person to add to the current affairs team.[12]

Freeman soon graduated to 'leading panel member' (his fee went up from 17 to 20 guineas) and it is easy to see why. His striking looks, authoritative manner and complete command of language made him the centre of attention whenever the camera allowed.

Watching *Press Conference* today, over half a century later, it is notable how cerebral and reasoned the arguments were. A good example was the appearance of Sir John Wolfenden on 6 September 1957, answering to his Report on Homosexual Offences and Prostitution. Apart from recommending that homosexual acts between consenting adults should no longer be illegal, the report recommended a crackdown on prostitutes soliciting in public and on pimps living off immoral earnings, but not a ban on prostitution itself. Freeman opened the 25-minute discussion by questioning Wolfenden about prostitution:

> FREEMAN: The criticism in a good many quarters is that you [the committee] tuck prostitution itself out of sight, sweep away scandals, so that you have been humbugs about it. Is that fair?
>
> WOLFENDEN [PUFFING ON HIS PIPE AND IN PARAPHRASE]: Not trying to abolish prostitution ... Our concern is with crime, with offences against the law, not with sin.
>
> FREEMAN: You are begging the question. It's your recommendations that determine what is crime. Now, how do you distinguish between crime and sin?
>
> WOLFENDEN [IN PARAPHRASE]: We are concerned with public order and decency and protection and the safeguarding of those who need it. We're not concerned with private and personal responsibility. Is that a fair distinction?
>
> FREEMAN: Yes, I think so.[13]

Between 1955 and 1960, Freeman's portfolio widened to include: schools programmes (television and radio); religious programmes like *Meeting Point* (television); *Woman's Hour* (radio); *Frankly Speaking*, *Commentary*, *Call from London* and *This is Britain* (all World Service); *Home and Abroad* (Home Service); and, of course, his first forays in the television talks department, like *Panorama*, *Press Conference* and *Face to Face* (see Chapter 6).

Even television light entertainment pursued him, with offers to appear on *What's My Line?* and *Ask Me Another*. These he declined, although he did accept the role of host on the *Chan Canasta* show. The truth was, unlike other Goldie boys, Freeman was keen to get away from politics. 'Find something you like doing and get someone to pay you for it,' he told his stepdaughter Lizi. He obviously succeeded.

The *Chan Canasta* show – in which Chan (his stage name) carried out feats of 'mental magic', displaying phenomenal memory and some telepathy – was of personal interest to Freeman, but it came to a bad end. Perceptive viewers told Freeman they could tell that the BBC production team was collaborating with Chan behind Freeman's back. Obviously, his credibility was at issue, and, as Freeman was a man of firm principle in his public life, he refused to host any further shows until a contract of trust was agreed; then he ended his association as soon as he could.

Occasionally, Freeman worked for the opposition. In its early years, ITV ran a popular discussion programme on Sunday afternoons called *Free Speech*. The regular panellists were the historian A. J. P. Taylor, independently minded politicians like Bob Boothby and Michael Foot, and the trade unionist W. J. Brown, who was known as 'the rustic philosopher'.

The chairman, Edgar Lustgarten, and the producer, John Irwin, were both freelancers, which is significant because the whole team had originally been employed by BBC TV, making exactly the same programme but calling it *In the News*. In 1952, it had been hugely popular, with an audience of about 50 per cent of all TV owners.

Nevertheless, early in 1955, the BBC gave in to the politicians who wanted more orthodox spokesmen and women to argue party politics. An early suggestion from the Conservatives was Margaret Roberts (later Thatcher), who the BBC rejected because no one had heard of her. So, led by Taylor and Lustgarten, the iconoclastic team of *In the News* resigned before they were pushed, and took their programme to the Associated Broadcasting Company, later ATV. Tom Driberg had been a contributor, and now he introduced Freeman as an occasional contributor to *Free Speech*.

In *The Best of Both Worlds*, Driberg describes the pleasures and perils of this form of live broadcasting in those pioneering days. No wonder even Freeman said that in the last moments before transmission he would be 'shaking with nerves'. After an expensive meal in a private room at A l'Ecu de France on Jermyn Street, Piccadilly, the *In the News* team was driven by Rolls-Royce to the studio in Shepherd's Bush for the rehearsal:

> In one corner of the huge warehouse-like studio, a table has been set in front of a bookcase full of incongruous books. Our names are inscribed on cards round a table. We are told to sit on chairs and rehearse our opening lines. When the cameras are focused, workmen fix the chairs to the floor; we mustn't move them. Penned in his chair, strong lights glaring in his face, it is difficult to marshal a case philosophically.

That still left lots of time before transmission. Time to wander the streets near the studio or sip a nervous half-pint at the British Prince pub at the top of Lime Grove, imagining the public in their scores of thousands settling down to watch the television. Then back to the studio:

Now and then one of those anonymous technicians who are always moving about in that huge place will give a friendly nod or a wink, or even a whisper, 'Give it to 'em tonight, Tom!' At last the summons to the table comes: a moment of relief and pounding tension. The lights are on, the fearsome-looking cameras trained all about us. Silence. A hand signal. We're off…

The time passes in a flash. The arguments tumble out pell-mell. It is a hot free-for-all between four garrulous, provocative, experienced politicians. There are other than verbal tricks to this trade; the old hands, such as Bill Brown, are adept in the art of camera stealing by fiddling interestingly with cigarettes or pencil or by raising the eyes to heaven in mock agony.

When it is over you lean back with a 'Whew!' and mop your brow. The make-up ladies give you little boxes of grease to take away, and you hurry off in the waiting Rolls to John Irwin's house.[14]

At the end of December 1957, Freeman wrote to radio producer Leslie Smith, with whom he made several Home Service programmes on crime and criminals: 'The affectionate letters I've had from a great many friends really have been a comfort at a time of utter misery.' Mima had died of cancer on 17 December. Although they had led very separate lives, her slow death caused him much grief. 'I have not really left the hospital since I last saw you,' he wrote to TV producer Christopher Burstall on 12 December. 'I am not easy to reach because I am sitting with my wife.' Lizi recalls 'a lovely last holiday John planned for us':

He took me on the Orient Express to Athens and my mother flew. When we changed countries we got a new restaurant car, which was exciting. We would sit separately either end of the restaurant car because we had breakfast at different times.

She got skin cancer skiing in the Swiss mountains and this developed into a brain tumour. In Athens a nurse used to come and give her injections, but no one said anything. Then in November she went into hospital because she had lumps on her arms and by this time she was virtually unconscious. My father took me out for coffee and told me she wasn't going to come home. This was just three weeks before she died. I really wished I'd had more time, just to talk.

A month later, Freeman recorded a discussion for religious broadcasting entitled 'The Intrusion of the Press into Private Grief'. That Easter he took Lizi to Paris:

My lasting memories – he took me to the Rodin Museum and to see the Toulouse Lautrec posters. We did nice things and had nice meals. We went halfway up the Eiffel Tower but he would not go further because he said he suffered from vertigo.

He always said, 'I don't think I'm much of a family man,' but he always made everything fun. On Saturday afternoons he would take me to his favourite record shop on the Finchley Road and listen to records, everything from 'Guys and Dolls' to opera.[15]

Lizi was sixteen when Mima died, after which Freeman formally adopted her.

Freeman's first *Panorama* had been broadcast on 8 July 1957 and his second on 7 November, the subject of the latter being 'brainwashing' – a topic of contemporary controversy because of the allegation (and refutation) that US and British prisoners of war had been brainwashed in the Korean War. In both programmes, Freeman's role was as discussion chairman. Suddenly he was in demand and *Panorama* was paying him 40 guineas per programme, plus another 10 guineas to cover interviews and commentary dubbing. A review of his TV schedule for the first half of 1958 shows how busy he was, bearing in mind he was also deputy editor of the *New Statesman* magazine.

At the time of Mima's death, Freeman and Christopher Burstall had been trying to set up an item on freemasonry, using Freeman's father's former clerk in Lincoln's Inn as the contact. 'The approach', wrote Christopher Burstall to Michael Peacock, 'is one of hard curiosity, a refusal to take things on trust. John Freeman is very interested and I'm sure he will fit the bill.' This was one *Panorama* project that did not come off, because the Grand Lodge would not cooperate. That same spring, 1958, Freeman was in Cyprus and France sending back film reports on civil wars for *Panorama*, while also filming in Dr Barnardo's village for an item on adoption.

In the midst of this he presented a hard-hitting programme on 'family tensions' for *Meeting Point*, 'cutting across the sentimentality of the day'. The producer, the Reverend Oliver Hunkin of the religious affairs department, had written persuasively to Freeman to book him:

> The star is a woman doctor, Dr J. E. Mackworth. She is 6 ft tall, uses psychoanalytic methods [on dysfunctional families] and states in her prospectus that her clinic is a meeting point for priest, doctor and psychologist. I hope you will do the programme because I feel you will go a certain way with her, and therefore scrutinise her closely.

This was a shrewd invitation that may have reminded Freeman of his time living in the Hubback household ten years before. That *Meeting Point* episode was broadcast on 16 March 1958, and Hunkin was delighted: 'My dear John, to have someone so practised and perceptive in the chair certainly eases a producer's tensions!'[16]

The same month Freeman agreed to script and present a schools TV film on Algeria for its *Spotlight* series. He was working overtime, recycling material for different audiences and finding new storylines. The producers were delighted until even Freeman's meticulous planning went wrong. He wrote to Ivan Gilman of the schools TV unit on 25 April: 'I owe you an apology. I mistook a film viewing on Monday afternoon for *Panorama* when it should have been with you. I am very sorry.'

By mid-summer, Grace Wyndham Goldie was fending off producers wanting to use Freeman.

As overworked freelance reporters are bound to do with the BBC, Freeman fell out with the television bookings department over expenses. Sometimes he could not produce all his receipts – 'Dear Miss Knight, you must be beginning to think I'm mad as well as incompetent: I'm sure I had 11.5 francs on 19 May!' – and on one occasion he claimed for hardship outside the line of duty:

From: Jeremy Murray-Brown, television talks
To: Miss D. E. Knight, television bookings

2 June 1958

In view of the fact that John Freeman has, in fact, put in rather more work on the French story than was originally intended (and also met with temporary imprisonment in Paris) I should be grateful if he could be paid an additional fee of 15 guineas.

———

To: Jeremy Murray-Brown, television talks
From: Miss D. E. Knight, television bookings

> We feel he has already received a very adequate fee. The temporary
> imprisonment is one of the risks of the job for which he would surely
> not expect monetary compensation.[17]

Had Miss D. E. Knight been aware of the circumstances she might
have been more sympathetic. That last weekend in May, with the
French people expecting an army coup in Algeria and a consequent
civil war in France, Charles de Gaulle was invested as President. In
Paris there was pandemonium:

> Gaullists, communists, plotters and police clashed all over the city.
> There was a vast eruption of motorcars, jamming the Champs-Élysées
> and spilling into side streets, their horns tapping out in extraordinary
> unison the beats of 'De Gaulle au pouvoir' and 'Algérie française'.[18]

Presumably it was while filming this 'pandemonium' that Freeman and his crew were arrested and imprisoned for between four
and five hours that Sunday (1 June). They knew that if they did
not get the film back to London the same evening, they could not
have it developed, the negative would not get cut and the positive
would not get printed in time for *Panorama* the following evening. Technical limitations in those days added to the stresses of the
TV reporter's job.

And so it went on for the next two years. In February 1960, with
ITV also after his services, the BBC programme contracts department
took Freeman out for a smart lunch at A l'Ecu de France and offered
him an exclusive contract of £3,750 per year, to which TV talks, light
entertainment, schools, the Home Service etc. all offered to contribute.

Catherine Dove had joined the film department after attracting
BBC attention to her acting at Oxford University in the early 1950s.

She soon met Grace Wyndham Goldie, who was on the prowl among the dingy Victorian terraced houses of Lime Grove (where the TV talks department was based), looking for new talent.

Grace recruited Catherine to work on the general election programme of 1955 and then appointed her *Panorama*'s first producer-director. She was responsible for some remarkable programmes – two in particular found their way into *Panorama* history.

One, on natural childbirth, aimed to be the first film on television to show a baby being born, although by the time BBC managers had taken fright and heavily edited the film, all the viewer saw was the baby's head – then it was in its mother's arms.

The other was a live interview with the Irish playwright Brendan Behan, who, Catherine remembers, stumbled into the studio 'virtually comatose'. 'Millions see drunk man on TV show' splashed the *Daily Sketch* the next morning.

Catherine also managed to lure the poet T. S. Eliot into the Lime Grove studio, and was very proud to have done so. Her *Panorama* colleagues were less enthusiastic because, as she admitted, his performance was disappointingly wooden.

On the *Panorama* team was Charles Wheeler, an ex-marine who had become a newspaper reporter in Germany after the war. Initially colleagues, they became lovers and lived together at his mews flat in Primrose Hill, north London, travelling to work in his MG and motoring around Europe on holiday. He was keen on the idea of getting married, but Catherine didn't think it would work: 'I felt that he was too nice and too young to be good for me and that probably I needed an older man. I was a bit of a handful in those days.'

At work, Catherine was beginning to press the department for a magazine programme dedicated to the arts. And so, eventually, *Monitor* was born. Grace appointed Catherine as its editor, but proposed Huw Wheldon, a senior producer, as a back-up: 'You're very young, Katie, and Huw will be able to help you.' Catherine takes up the story:

> Wheldon was a macho ex-soldier who had had a very good war, having been awarded the MC in Normandy – very much a man's man. He was keen to take on a major magazine programme like *Panorama* and, at that time at least, did not seem very interested in the arts. At our first meeting he said, 'Listen, Katie, our audience isn't going to care about what the artist wrote or painted. What they want to know about is their sex lives – were they queer or straight?' I was terribly shocked, being young and priggish, and also worried because his approach boded ill for our collaboration. I was also aware that he didn't like me very much.[19]

After this little demonstration of powerplay by Wheldon, and in the absence of Catherine (who, with terrible timing, was nursing a broken knee in hospital), *Monitor* went on air in February 1958. Wheldon became editor and presenter and moulded the show in his own image for over 100 editions, until he had 'interviewed everybody I wanted to interview'. He handed over to Jonathan Miller in 1965.

Wheeler, meanwhile, had transferred to the news department. His departure from *Panorama* had displeased Grace; she called him 'a traitor' for leaving. He visited Catherine in hospital and once again tried to persuade her into marriage:

> You'll never get *Monitor* back from Huw. You're twenty-six and you won't meet the man you think you are going to meet. We get on really well together so why not give it a try? But make up your mind now, because I'm off to India for the BBC in three weeks and there's not much time to arrange things.

At a low ebb in hospital, depressed about losing *Monitor* and considering leaving the BBC, Catherine gave in, against her better judgement. They were married in the Church of our Lady of the Assumption (she was a Catholic) on Warwick Street in May that year. Wheeler left immediately for India as the BBC correspondent there and Catherine intended to join him in Delhi in October when the weather was cooler. Left on her own, she recognised that the marriage had indeed been a mistake. She spent a wretched summer feeling guilty, ashamed and confused because, as a Catholic, she didn't want to consider divorce. Finally, she resolved to go out to India, explain to Wheeler how she felt, and arrange a separation. She booked her passage on the P&O liner *Chusan*.

That September, Freeman was the 'leading panel member' in three editions of *Press Conference*, produced by Catherine. This was the first time they had worked together and, as far as Freeman was concerned, it was love at first sight. He told her later that he decided to marry her as soon as he set eyes on her in the studio. At the time she lived near Kensington Church Street in west London, where a neighbour – the journalist Peregrine Worsthorne – knew them both: 'She was, of course, very beautiful, extremely attractive and mischievous. I was an admirer of John, though he was a mystery figure who was very hard to know. It was the sight of him that was really splendid. He was formidable; his appearance, his charm, his high principles.'[20]

The last programme of the three was a *Press Conference* with Bertrand Russell. After the production meeting, which in those days was always held in the Gay Hussar restaurant in Soho, Freeman told Catherine how sorry he was that she was leaving: 'I've never enjoyed working with anybody so much.' She told him how miserable she felt about her marriage and that she was going to end it. That evening her phone rang: 'John asked, "Are you too busy packing or would you come over for a drink?" I did, and that was that. I realised with amazement that this was the man I'd been waiting to meet. It was not difficult to promise to come back as soon as possible.'

When she went on board the *Chusan*, she found her cabin filled with red roses.

Wheeler met her off the boat in Bombay. He was appalled when she immediately confessed – 'I thought Freeman was a gentleman' – but he asked her to stay with him in Delhi over Christmas, partly to save face and partly because he thought it possible that she would change her mind. But at New Year, when Wheeler discovered letters Freeman had sent to Catherine, he was generous enough to accept the situation. In May he saw her off at the airport and Freeman met her the other end.

Freeman immediately asked her to give up her career. 'I have no right to ask you this, but it would be wonderful to find you here in Heath Mansions when I come home.' And so she ended her pioneering work at the BBC.

Was she disappointed?

> Not at all! I enjoyed the BBC for five years. They were good to me
> and I'd done quite well. But I was in love and all I wanted was to
> settle down with John and have a family. He said that I needed him
> to look after me. The age gap between us was sixteen years and he
> could be positively paternal, which I liked.

Soon Freeman became an actual father. Matthew was born in June 1961 – John was present at the birth, which was rare in those days – and they married as soon as Catherine's divorce from Wheeler came through the following year, despite her Catholic scruples. Charles Wheeler married again soon after, to an Indian lady named Dip Singh, with whom he had two daughters. He went on to become the longest-serving foreign correspondent in the history of the BBC and received a knighthood for his work. After his memorial service in Westminster Abbey in 2008, the bells were rung.

Freeman never did sign the exclusive contract the BBC had offered him. In the summer of 1960, he knew he would soon be editor of the *New Statesman* (not that he revealed this to the BBC) and, in any event, he wanted to cut back on his broadcasting commitments. It was probably no coincidence, therefore, that he then wrote two articles highly critical of the BBC. This was not exactly biting the hand that fed him, though it could well have felt like that at the BBC for he was still under contract for the last series of *Face to Face*.

In May 1960, Freeman was in hospital for a few weeks and therefore a 'Captive Viewer'. This was his title for his *Listener* article:

> I cannot help feeling depressed and alarmed by the utter triviality of nine-tenths of the flood of pictures that are so earnestly and expensively hurled at us. What ought we to expect of this medium, which now dominates the leisure life of most of the people most of the time? Ideas? Instruction? Entertainment? Or just the gentle, ceaseless, scarcely perceptible erosion of the angularities of free will and personal responsibility?

Then he focused his attack on Lime Grove, criticising in the *New Statesman* the BBC's all-embracing rules of 'impartiality' and 'balance' for factual programmes:

> The BBC is antithetical to both good art and good politics, because it excludes not only malice, sex and evil, but the possibility of intellectual offence and above all the decisive conclusions that are the proper end of civilised dialogue.

It is an appalling reproach to our civilisation that having developed the most pervasive means of communication in history, we
have taken the necessary steps to see that nothing more potent than
the carefully measured platitudes of *Panorama* can be communicated through it.

The archetypal BBC liberal is, in his own habitat, such an ambiv-
alent and emasculated creature.[21]

Freeman was finding it difficult to reconcile his role as deputy editor
of an opinionated left-wing political magazine with being a prominent
public service broadcaster. He had already been criticised by the new
director-general, Hugh Carlton Greene, for his *Panorama* description
of France's war in Algeria as 'colonial': 'He is slipping into his bad
habit of speaking as a deputy editor of the *New Statesman*.'

Freeman was then rebuked by the director of television broadcasting for writing in the *Daily Telegraph* that he strongly deplored the
amount of lying that went on during a *This Is Your Life* programme.

Grace Wyndham Goldie's policy of employing guest stars with
minds of their own was showing signs of wear and tear.

When Freeman was appointed editor of the *New Statesman* in
January 1961, the time had come for him to end his primary career
as a broadcaster. He continued to appear on both BBC TV and
radio (as well as ITV), and made one more series of *Face to Face*,
but another door was closing in his life as a new one opened.

Chapter 6

Television interviewer –
Face to Face

T HE FIRST INTERVIEW in *Face to Face* was broadcast
live from the BBC TV studios in Shepherd's Bush in
February 1959. The subject was Lord Birkett, the famous
cross-examiner in murder trials of the 1920s and '30s.

The screen opens to reveal a sketch of Birkett, drawn earlier by the
Polish artist Feliks Topolski, and the camera then moves to a very simple
title sequence of cut-out cardboard ('*Face to Face*, John Freeman interviews') before continuing to pan over more Topolski sketches.

Underneath runs the title music – the overture from an unfinished
opera by Berlioz – *Les Francs-Juges*. (After the programme, Birkett
wrote to the producer, Hugh Burnett, informing him that the opera

actually concerned the sinister tribunals of the Middle Ages in West-phalia, which saw condemned men disappear for ever. 'What do you think the damages would be,' he asked, tongue in cheek, 'if a powerful broadcasting corporation were to play this music to a television programme consisting of an interview with a celebrated judge?!') The music rises to a crescendo then fades, and the camera moves into a profile of Lord Birkett against a black background.

His voice is heard saying, 'It's the strain of waiting that's so hard' – evidence that the programme is live and he does not know his microphone is on! – and then another camera takes an over-the-shoulder shot from behind John Freeman, before moving in on Birkett. Freeman begins: 'Lord Birkett, you are known to the world, I suppose, as one of the greatest three or four criminal lawyers of this century…'

After a few minutes, the unique style of *Face to Face* was apparent. The studio setting was simply an armchair and a side table mounted on a plinth, with black drapes to isolate the interviewee. The camera remained focused on a close-up shot of the subject's face, showing, in Freeman's words, 'every bead of sweat, every flicker of the eyelid, a dimension that had not existed in television before'. The camera, in fact, was a second interrogator, or, as Freeman put it, 'the interviewer and the camera and the lights and the studio environment are all integrated into a single concentration on the individual'.

Freeman's face was rarely seen: 'That would be a total distraction,' said Freeman, 'and I strongly applauded the style.' The idea was one of Hugh Burnett's. He was a producer in talks television who had spent two years trying to persuade Grace Wyndham Goldie to accept the series, but far less time persuading John Freeman to present it:

> I wanted him because he was highly skilled at probing closely without causing offence. Walking round the block at Lime Grove we discussed

the series and the second time round the block he agreed. He also accepted the idea of sitting with his back to the camera, a tiny but important detail that gave rise to a brand new programme format.[1]

So the interview unfolded. Freeman's speech was unhesitatingly firm and precise, his pace unrelenting, his manner persistent. Unlike TV interviews before that time, there was nothing deferential or reverential about his manner. Unlike TV interviews of today, there was nothing hectoring or impolite. Freeman told Anthony Clare in 1988 that his intention most of the time had been simply to ask 'the sort of questions I thought an intelligent person, given the chance, might want to ask'. In the case of Birkett, that must have been true:

FREEMAN: Did you always believe in the innocence of your clients when you defended them?
BIRKETT: To be quite, quite frank, no – I just ought to add that whatever your belief is, you're not allowed to state it in the court. You're allowed to speak as an advocate, but you mustn't give your opinion.
FREEMAN: Did you ever personally have any qualms about defending someone on a murder charge whom you thought was guilty?
BIRKETT: None. You see, the view I took of the advocate's duty is this: he's there to present one side only, and he must do it to the best of his ability, and what he thinks really is irrelevant.
FREEMAN: Would you think it your duty as counsel to use every possible trick within the law to get your man acquitted?
BIRKETT: I would be against tricks of all kinds, but if you would alter the question to saying, 'Do you regard it as your duty to do everything within your *power* to get him acquitted?' then I would say yes.
FREEMAN: Yes. And that would include bamboozling a jury?
BIRKETT: Well, shall I say, *persuading* a jury.

FREEMAN: Have you ever got a man or a woman acquitted on a murder charge whom you believe in your heart to be guilty?

BIRKETT: Yes.

FREEMAN: Any regrets about that?

BIRKETT: None.

FREEMAN: Have you ever defended a person on a murder charge whom you *knew* to be guilty?

BIRKETT: No. Indeed, you're not allowed to. You may think he is guilty, and of course it's really quite impossible for any man of sense to defend a man and read all the facts without coming to some conclusion in his mind, but that's quite irrelevant. He's not the judge.[2]

Over four million viewers watched that first *Face to Face*, and they loved it. Its reaction index (a BBC viewer panel evaluation) was 83 per cent – the highest of all the interviews that were shown over the next three years. *Face to Face* became history. It was the most famous interview series on British television, and the Topolski sketches and Berlioz signature tune became its brand label.

Face to Face sold throughout the English-speaking world and, on its fiftieth anniversary in 2009, the BBC released a DVD box set of all thirty-five interviews. The series became a benchmark for later generations of TV interviewers, like Michael Parkinson: 'People of our generation revered John Freeman as one of the foundation stones of early television. I watched him with a mixture of awe and admiration. He was a great man and the present generation who know not of him don't know what they are missing.'[3]

Despite the world fame of many of the contributors to *Face to Face* – Carl Jung, Bertrand Russell, Martin Luther King etc. – it is known as 'that interview series with John Freeman'. It is the work he is best known for, yet he disliked the celebrity status the series conferred. In his *Who's Who* entry, he didn't even mention the BAFTA for Outstanding Television Personality he won for the series in 1960.

Kingsley Martin, the editor of the *New Statesman*, growled sourly: 'John is the only man who has made himself celebrated by turning his arse on the public.' Undoubtedly, his anonymity contributed to his celebrity. He was a man of mystery and the public loves trying to uncover mysteries. Exposing the real person behind the celebrity was, of course, exactly what he was doing with his guests on *Face to Face*, but he gave absolutely nothing away about himself.

He carried this anonymity to extreme levels when other programmes or press articles tried to turn the tables on him. In 1961, the other famous interviewer of those days, Malcolm Muggeridge, did his best on Granada's *Appointment.* The *Guardian* TV reviewer Mary Crozier wrote: 'The most curious thing was that John Freeman remained virtually the faceless man. Nothing came out that could not have been known without this interview. We were left with the impression that Mr Freeman was an almost alarmingly impersonal person.'[4]

Perhaps Lord Birkett would have been more successful than Malcolm Muggeridge, but when Birkett suggested a reverse *Face to Face* to end the first series, he was given short shrift. Many journalists made attempts to try a *Face to Face* on Freeman, but none got further than Anthony Clare in 1988.

Freeman was prepared to talk about the programme, but not about himself. He had the gift of thinking up an interesting reply that did not answer the question. He never said what *sort* of man he was.

The interviewer for an article in *Tatler*, 'The Grillers Grilled', got closer than most:

INTERVIEWER: In the broadest terms, a psychiatrist would classify you as an introvert rather than extrovert, wouldn't he?

FREEMAN: Probably, yes.

INTERVIEWER: Dr Carl Jung says that introverts tend to be governed at the unconscious level by their emotions. Could that come across to your audience?

FREEMAN: One can't know for oneself. Someone else must answer that.

Interviewers got more out of Freeman when he was talking about his cats, who roamed around Heath Mansions when the press came to call. Indeed, the press probably turned to the cats in desperation, as 'television's most penetrating interviewer' was full of insight about them: 'Pushkin has all the male characteristics in that he's bossy, sometimes bad tempered, with a logical brain and an engineer's approach to life; Dulcie is flighty, silly on occasions, but very affectionate.'[5]

The myth about *Face to Face* is that it was 'trial by television' with Freeman as the 'grand inquisitor'. The interviews with comedian Tony Hancock and TV entertainment celebrity Gilbert Harding were undoubtedly forensic in a highly personal way, and perhaps that is why they are among the best known, but they were the exception. Most of the others were unremarkable 'the real person behind the public façade' interviews, and, in fact, only fourteen of them were 'live' broadcasts.

Yet there *was* something inquisitorial about the interviews. Freeman often let the subject know what was coming with a semi-jocular opening question: 'Are you going to come clean?' Then 'his matchless voice, ultra-polite, devastatingly persistent', dominated the studio in the absence of any glimpse of its owner. He admitted that, for him, interviewing was 'a psychological exercise':

I am, I think, a purely intuitive interviewer. I read a lot about the person I am going to interview, and I think up questions, but most of my work is taken up with making up my mind about what *sort* of person I am dealing with. After the opening question, I tend to play the whole thing by ear, though usually I have an idea with which question I shall end the interview.[6]

The ambience, then, was inquisitorial but the substance only rarely justified the press term 'trial by television'.

Freeman's second guest, in March 1959, was the renowned philosopher and mathematician Bertrand Russell. He was eighty-seven and campaigning vigorously for nuclear disarmament. Before the recording, which took place at Russell's home, Hugh Burnett found an obituary that Russell had written about himself. Beaming widely, Russell read it out at the start of the interview:

> His life, for all its waywardness, had a certain anachronistic consistency, reminiscent of that of the aristocratic rebels of the early nineteenth century. His principles were curious; but such as they were, they governed his actions. In private life he showed none of the acerbity that marred his writing, but was a genial conversationalist, not devoid of human sympathy. He had many friends but had survived almost all of them and politically, during his last years, he was as isolated as Milton after the Restoration. He was the last survivor of a dead epoch.

Freeman took Russell through his life with probing but courteous questions and the old genius replied succinctly, sometimes with an air of mischief. He was well capable of avoiding Freeman's traps:

FREEMAN: Do you think, on the whole, the fanatics in the world are more useful or more dangerous than the sceptics?

RUSSELL: I think fanaticism is the gravest danger there is. I might almost say that I was fanatical against fanaticism.

FREEMAN: But then are you not fanatical also? In your current campaign in favour of nuclear disarmament you encourage your supporters to undertake extreme demonstrations. Isn't that fanaticism?

RUSSELL: I don't think that's fanaticism, no. I support them because everything sane and sensible and quiet that we do is absolutely ignored by the press and the only way we can get into the press is to do something that looks fanatical.

Two years after the recording, Russell was sent to prison for taking part in an anti-nuclear sit-down in London.

In May, the guest was the poet and critic Dame Edith Sitwell, the 71-year-old *grande dame* of English letters. This was an extraordinary encounter, partly because of her eccentric attire. With a headdress she called her 'bird-king's hat', an ermine jacket, and huge, exotic rings on her fingers, she looked like what she said she was – 'a throwback to ancient ancestors of mine' (an impression the Topolski caricatures did nothing to dispel). Her deathly white, sharp features stood out against the black background. Some of her answers made her sound less like a medieval 'throwback' than a witch in a fairy story:

> There was a peacock, you see, and he and I loved each other very much. I was four years old. He would fly up to the leads outside my mother's bedroom, when I went to say good morning to her, and would give a harsh shriek. Then he would give another scream and fly down to the garden to wait for me. We would walk round the garden arm-in-arm, excepting he hadn't any arms; I would have my arm around his neck; and I was asked why I loved him so and I said, 'Because he is proud and has a crown, and is beautiful.' And then my father got

him a wife, with his usual tactlessness, after which he never looked at me again, and my heart was broken.

Freeman's questions on this occasion were gentle, almost flirtatious. He tried to coax her into frank answers, though not always successfully:

> FREEMAN: Have you ever – I hope I may ask this – seriously contemplated marriage?
> SITWELL: That I think I can't answer.
> FREEMAN: No reason why you should at all. Do you consider, looking at young people today, that the standard of taste and behaviour is lower than it used to be?
> SITWELL: Well, you see, I think you said that I was a forbidding old lady – well, I'm very forbidding. No young person would dare misbehave in my presence, and I can think of one very great poet who died some time ago – I never saw him behave in a way that a great man shouldn't behave.
> FREEMAN: Would you tell us who he was? I can guess and it would be nice for you to…
> SITWELL: …Dylan Thomas. He always behaved impeccably in my presence.

The interview was another success. The *Daily Herald* declared: 'Here was a living legend captured on the popular screen.'

Grace Wyndham Goldie was delighted:

8 May 1959, from assistant head of talks television

My dear John,

I have already told Hugh Burnett how superb I thought the Sitwell programme was, and how beautifully he had handled it visually. I thought I must write to say that it seemed to me also the best thing I have ever seen you do on television.

I don't know how you made her so obviously at ease and happy that she could reveal herself, in ways that were fascinating and resounded to her credit as a person, in front of the television cameras. Thank you very much. I enjoyed it enormously.

Yours ever, Grace

—————————

12 May, 8 Heath Mansions

Dear Grace,

Thank you so much for writing. I value your praise more than anybody else's – without exception.

Yours ever, John[7]

He must have been relieved to get it, for she did not dispense praise lightly. Indeed, a few weeks before, at the morning-after meeting of the *Panorama* team, she had reprimanded him: 'Mr Freeman, I can't tell you how bad you were last night.'

Considering the popularity of *Face to Face,* it is remarkable how many of those 'approached' (not quite the same as 'invited') for interview between April and December 1959 turned the offer down. Of seventy-two 'approaches', only ten were successful. There was a 'no' from Danny Kaye, Laurence Olivier ('not interested'), Eamon De

Valera ('constitutional reasons'), Igor Stravinsky ('definitely no'), Pablo Casals, T. S. Eliot ('not inclined to appear on TV'), Lord Beaverbrook ('dislikes personal publicity'), Noël Coward ('not coming to England') and Charlie Chaplin ('working on memoirs'). There were no replies from Groucho Marx, the Shah of Persia, Alec Guinness, Maria Callas, Ernest Hemingway, Ed Murrow and Frank Sinatra. There was a 'perhaps' from Evelyn Waugh ('for a larger fee' – the standard fee was 100 guineas) and Stanley Spencer ('scarcely worth the while'), but a 'yes' from Cecil Beaton, Harry Belafonte, Augustus John, Gilbert Harding and Stirling Moss. Later Evelyn Waugh relented and gave Freeman a prickly interview.

There was also a category of 'not approved', meaning that the choice of Burnett and Freeman was rejected by Grace Wyndham Goldie or Cecil McGivern (the controller of television programmes). This category included Oswald Mosley, the Dean of Canterbury, Jomo Kenyatta and Albert Schweitzer. The odd one out was Schweitzer, as his 'English was no good'; the others, presumably, all had political black marks. Mosley was the former fascist leader; the 'Red' Dean of Canterbury was an unyielding supporter of the Soviet Union; and Jomo Kenyatta was allegedly the leader of the Mau Mau revolutionaries in Kenya, who had just been released from prison. However, this does not mean, necessarily, that the interviews were censored for political reasons. Grace Wyndham Goldie may well have thought that these three subjects would be so unpopular with a British audience that she would lose her precious viewing figures, plus there were more straightforward talks programmes, like *Panorama*, which could take them on.

The *Face to Face* with Carl Jung, recorded at the professor's home in Zurich in June 1959, was an historic coup. It was the only TV interview ever given by the world's greatest living psychologist and founder of the concept of the collective unconscious. He was eighty-four and would be dead within two years. For this reason, the tape, script and then DVD of the interview were, and still are, in demand all over the world.

Curiously, wrote Hugh Burnett, Jung was the only one of thirty-five guests to refuse to have his portrait sketched for the opening credits:

> Instead, we filmed paper captions floating on the lake by his house. He stood nearby, leaning on his stick and smiling as he watched us trying to drift the paper past the camera lens. I said to him, with a straight face, 'Professor Jung, perhaps we could start this film with a shot of you coming out of the water from your morning swim?'
>
> 'Ah yes,' he replied, 'emerging from the unconscious.'[8]

At one stage during the interview, Freeman's usual presence of mind seemed to desert him:

> FREEMAN: Do you now believe in God?
> JUNG: Now? Difficult to answer. I know. I don't need to believe. I know.
> FREEMAN: Well, now what made you decide to become a doctor?

Millions of viewers must have been beside themselves with frustration not knowing why the world's greatest psychologist *knew* that God existed. Several of them wrote to Jung, who replied:

> Mr Freeman in his characteristic manner fired the question you allude to at me in a somewhat surprising way, so that I was perplexed and had to say the next thing that came into my mind. As soon as the answer had left 'the edge of my teeth' I knew I had said something controversial, puzzling, even ambiguous. I was therefore waiting for letters like yours.[9]

Freeman himself wrote to Jung for the answer to the question he should have asked, and received this in return:

> I did not say in the programme, 'There is a God.' I said, 'I do not need to believe in God: I know.' Which does not mean, 'I do know a certain God' (Zeus, Jahwe, Allah, the Trinitarian God etc.), but rather 'I do know that I am obviously confronted with a factor unknown in itself, which I call God.' I remember him, I evoke him, whenever I use his name overcome by anger or fear, whenever I involuntarily say, 'Oh God!' It is an apt name given to all overpowering emotions in my own psychical system, subduing my conscious will and usurping control over myself. In accordance with tradition, I call the power of fate in this positive as well as negative aspect and, in as much as its origin is outside my control, 'god', a 'personal god'; since my fate means very much itself, particularly when it approaches me in the form of conscience or *vox dei*, with which I can converse and argue.[10]

In the cutting room back home, Burnett was finding Jung hard going:

> Dear John,
>
> I enclose a copy of the Jung script. Unless you press me very hard, I shall cut this programme on viewer appeal rather than psychiatrist's significance. I realise I might be hacking a very significant statement. However, from page fourteen onwards, some of Jung's statements are very difficult to follow. Up to thirteen, the material is excellent in terms of *Face to Face* technique, change of subject and vivid autobiography.[11]

Freeman, on the other hand, was most intrigued and keen to know Jung further. The opportunity came in a scarcely believable way. The *Face to Face* interview had been watched by the publisher Wolfgang Foges. He thought Jung should write a book for educated readers who understood Freud's basic theories of psychoanalysis, but were unfamiliar with Jung's. Sensing Freeman's interest, Foges asked him to persuade Jung.

'I jumped at the idea,' wrote Freeman, 'and set off once more to Zurich. Jung listened to me in his garden for two hours almost without interruption – and then said no.' That might have been the end of what would become *Man and His Symbols* had fate, or Jung's subconscious, not intervened. Jung had a dream in which 'a multitude of people were listening to him in rapt attention and *appearing to understand what he said*' (Freeman's italics). Crucial to Jungianism is the belief that man should be guided by his 'unconscious', as revealed in dreams. So Jung changed his mind – on two conditions: Freeman had to be a co-editor and he had to include essays from disciples chosen by Jung.

Freeman accepted, but the second condition tried his patience beyond the limit. Urbane and charming he was, but Freeman was also used to getting his way, and neurotic European psychoanalysts were not his company of choice. He wrote in the margin of the essay by Jolande Jacobi, 'I puke on this' and – scarcely restraining himself from throwing it in the bin – handed over the entire manuscript to his friend Norman MacKenzie.[12]

Man and His Symbols was completed in the month of Jung's death, June 1961, and published with an introduction by Freeman.

Freeman wrote that Jung had initially laid down the subject matter and outline of the book, but then 'the last year of his life was devoted almost entirely to [finishing] it'. Jung had asked him to be co-editor (with his closest professional friend Dr Marie-Louise von Franz of Zurich) because he, Freeman, was the 'average reader' and therefore what he could understand 'would be intelligible to all'.

Freeman (and Norman MacKenzie) took their job seriously: 'I have scrupulously insisted on having every paragraph written, and, if necessary, rewritten, to a degree of clarity and directness that enables me to say that in its entirety this book is designed for the general reader.' Freeman prided himself in his writing more than in his interviewing, and later said he wished he had spent more time as a teacher. Here he introduces the subject of the book:

> Jung's thinking has coloured the world of modern psychology more than many of those with casual knowledge realise. Such familiar terms, for instance, as 'extravert', 'introvert', and 'archetype' are all Jungian concepts – borrowed and sometimes misused by others. But his overwhelming contribution to psychological understanding is his concept of the unconscious – not (like the unconscious of Freud) merely a sort of glory-hole of repressed desires, but a world that is as much a vital and real part of the life of an individual as the conscious, 'cogitating' world of the ego, and infinitely wider and richer. The language and the 'people' of the unconscious are symbols, and the means of communication are dreams.
>
> Thus an examination of *Man and His Symbols* is, in effect, an examination of man's relations with his unconscious. And since in Jung's view the unconscious is the great friend, guide and advisor to the conscious, the book is related in the most direct terms to the study of human beings and their spiritual problems.[13]

The comedian Tony Hancock was Freeman's twelfth guest, the interview pre-recorded in January 1960. For Hancock, it was a huge honour to be invited. He was the first popular entertainer on a roll call of world-famous philosophers, lawyers and writers. He was an autodidact whose shelves at home in Sussex contained the works of

Russell and Jung – and now he was going to occupy the same chair as them! Hancock did not want to be regarded as a professional buffoon, but rather as an introspective thinker who spent much of his leisure time working on self-improvement, and he therefore took the interview very seriously. According to his brother, this was literally fatal, as it set him on a course of unhealthy introspection and self-destruction: 'It was the biggest mistake he ever made. I think it all started from that really. He should never have done it. Tony was an intelligent man, but he was not an intellectual. He was carried away by John's intellect. Self-analysis – that was his killer.'[14]

Before the interview, he compiled and answered his own questions, despite the advice of his foil in *Hancock's Half Hour*, Sid James: 'For God's sake, don't answer everything truthfully – you'll be right in it!' But Hancock ignored the well-known warning among comedians to not take themselves too seriously. He was determined to tell the truth.

Freeman's aim was to push this to the limit, although he did not quite put it that way. He said he set out to explore 'the old *Pagliacci* theme, the sorrow behind the mask of laughter, of which he was a prime example. I thought the public would be interested in seeing a little of the torment that goes into the making of a great comic.'[15]

On *Face to Face*, Hancock was obviously nervous – pursing his lips, puffing on a cigarette butt and grimacing. He answered questions about his childhood, about why he was childless, about his ill health, about whether he was happy and about why he was anxious, but it was only in the last few minutes that Freeman became persistent and intrusive.

FREEMAN: There appears to be something that is troubling you and I would like to know what it is?

HANCOCK: I would not expect happiness. I don't think that's possible. I'm very fortunate with my work.

FREEMAN: You would not change your life at all? I wonder if you really get very much out of your triumphs. You've got cars you don't drive; you've got health you tell me is ropey. You find it difficult to learn your lines; you've got money you don't spend; you are worried about your weight.

HANCOCK: I spend the money. I do. I enjoy it.

FREEMAN: I want to put to you one last question. You could stop all this tomorrow if you wanted to. Tell me, why do you go on?

HANCOCK: Because it [my work] absolutely fascinates me, because I love it and because it is my entire life.

The audience research report on *Face to Face* with Tony Hancock was mixed. The reaction index was well below average, at 64 per cent, and some found the interview 'painful'.

'John Freeman hit below the belt and at times was impertinent,' reported one of the panel. 'His questions seemed barbed with antagonism,' said another. There was even some sympathy for Hancock: 'He was like a fish out of water.'

Others, however, thought the interview was 'painfully effective' and 'most accomplished'.

Freeman wrote to the *Daily Telegraph* in self-defence: 'I judged that more of Hancock's complex and fascinating personality would appear on the screen if he was kept at full stretch. I hope viewers did not equate that with hostility. I am sure Hancock didn't.'

Hancock certainly did not. He went round to Heath Mansions to watch the programme being broadcast and afterwards he stressed that he had felt no embarrassment: 'After all, we know that if you go on a programme like that, some of the questions are going to be tough.

They were tough, but good, and I'm sorry that Freeman got the worst of the criticism.'

The two became friends, and the self-improvement continued. Catherine remembers spending the weekend with the Hancocks at Lingfield in Sussex and falling asleep (she was heavily pregnant), much to John's displeasure, while he and Hancock discussed a chart on the wall linking quotations from Kant, Hegel and Descartes. 'This man has a fine mind,' Hancock said of Freeman, 'and he was very good for me because he used to listen and then he would say, "Some of your points are very good, but you are talking like a student." I'm very fond of him.'[16]

After the Hancocks' marriage fell apart, Tony took refuge in Freeman's flat at Heath Mansions. When the Freemans were in India, Tony stayed with them in New Delhi on his way to Australia to do a new show. Soon after arriving in Sydney he committed suicide.

On 11 April, some months after the Hancock *Face to Face*, John Freeman was Roy Plomley's guest on *Desert Island Discs*. His choice of music was eclectic but familiar. In fact, Kathleen Ferrier singing 'What Is Life?' ('the voice that has moved me most in my lifetime'), Dylan Thomas ('whom I have met') reading his own 'And Death Shall Have No Dominion', Billie Holiday singing 'Strange Fruit', and Toscanini conducting Verdi's 'Agnus Dei' are among the most popular records chosen in the long history of the programme. However, Freeman must be one of the few guests to have welcomed the desert island – 'I have often thought that an enforced spell in prison or hospital would be a good way of collecting my senses' – but did he really mean that, or was it an example of an interesting but untruthful answer? He admitted, surprisingly, that before *Face to Face* he was 'absolutely shaking with nerves'.

Roy Plomley was most interested in Freeman's interviewing technique:

PLOMLEY: Some rather rough words have been used about your interviewing technique in *Face to Face*. Brutal is one; aggressive is another; third degree is a third. Fair comment?

FREEMAN: Not really. I think occasionally I have been aggressive when I thought it necessary, but I hope never brutal and never third degree.

PLOMLEY: I watched your programme with Tony Hancock. One of the questions you asked concerned his degree of affection for his mother. Now, surely that is more suited to psychoanalysis than a TV interview?

FREEMAN: It depends entirely what you're trying to get out of a person and whether he's willing to answer. After all, no one has to appear with me on TV unless they want to. I was anxious to find out some of the things that worked on Hancock in his childhood, and this appeared to be relevant. He answered, as far as I remember, quite happily.

PLOMLEY: Well, the camera was showing, to put it mildly, that your questions were disconcerting Tony Hancock. In fact, once or twice he was squirming, but you still pressed home the attack.

FREEMAN: It wasn't an attack at all. It was an attempt to keep him at full stretch, because I thought in this way people would understand more about him. He's a very shy man – inarticulate when separated from his script-writers – and there was a danger that if I let him relax too much he would just talk in comfortable platitudes, as showbiz people sometimes do.

From Freeman's perspective, the high point and low point of *Face to Face* occurred, respectively, with the racing driver Stirling Moss and the painter Augustus John.

He told Anthony Clare that his interview with Moss (with Albert Finney, the only *Face to Face* subject alive in 2015), broadcast in June

1960, 'was almost the only one I can ever recall doing on *Face to Face*, or anywhere else, for that matter, from which I came away reasonably satisfied'. He had expected a playboy with a talent for driving fast cars, but he instead found an 'intensely serious professional'. Moss dismissed the concept of fear and replaced it with a matter of calculation: if you got the calculation right, there was nothing to be afraid of. Freeman observed: 'This was a man of cold, precise, clinical engineering judgement, and that surprised me very much indeed.'

Freeman revealed that the notion of a man who could live so closely to the edge of death and danger, but trust entirely his own judgement to keep on the right side of the line, appealed to him very much. The analogy could be applied to Freeman's live broadcasting of *Face to Face*. In front of an audience of several million and with no escape, Freeman had to trust his own judgement to keep on the right side of the line and deliver a winning interview. John Freeman and Stirling Moss had much in common, and perhaps this was why he found the interview so satisfying.

The *Face to Face* with Augustus John, pre-recorded but eventually broadcast after retakes in May 1960, was a near disaster. The old painter appeared semi-drunk and slightly senile. For once, Freeman appeared to have no empathy and little courtesy; in fact, he could barely contain his irritation. Afterwards he let rip to Burnett:

> It was a fiasco. I feel sure that nothing can be salvaged that could be worthily used in *Face to Face*. You may be able to sling something together but I shall take the strongest exception to this being put out as one of a series that has very high standards. Throughout a long afternoon he said little that was coherent and absolutely nothing that was interesting.
>
> The important lesson is that we should never undertake a *Face to*

Face without thoroughly reconnoitring the subject. On the whole, we should fight shy of octogenarians for all sorts of reasons, but please let us never try this one again.[17]

John Freeman and Hugh Burnett did not always have an easy relationship, and it was going to get worse.

In December 1960, the *Face to Face* guest was pop star Adam Faith. Lizi Freeman says he was her choice, after she dissuaded her stepfather from inviting Tommy Steele. She and some friends watched the live programme from the gallery. The interview was, said Adam Faith afterwards, 'a pleasant talk with a pleasant man', and that is how it seemed to viewers. Proof again that Freeman was not always the grand inquisitor. Perhaps the subject and style were chosen deliberately as a reaction to the notorious *Face to Face* with Gilbert Harding three months previously.

Although a minor figure compared with most of the other guests, Harding was one of the best-known faces on BBC television and, in an age of deference and politeness, he was known for his irascibility. 'The rudest man in Britain,' the tabloids called him, partly for his performance as a panellist on the quiz show *What's My Line?*, where he bullied or insulted the participants. Harding was a fellow TV professional and he had actually approached *Face to Face* for the interview himself, so Freeman and Burnett considered him fair game. Their plan was for Freeman to question Harding about his reputation for rudeness. Did it make him happy? Freeman intended to suggest that a professional life as a panellist and disc jockey after a Cambridge University education meant Harding was working 'below his capacity' and that this disappointment had made him the rude man the public saw.

So the interview began. But then, in a more psychoanalytical approach, Freeman asked Harding if he had 'obsessive thoughts about punishment and discipline?' Then: 'Are you good at enduring pain? Then: 'Do you fear pain?' Then: 'Can you stay with other people who are suffering pain? Then: 'Do you fantasise about punishment for your enemies?' Then: 'In your dreams are you a dominant figure?' Then: 'Have you ever been with a person dying?' Then: 'Is that the only time you have seen a person dead?' Quite where the interview was leading no one could tell, because at this stage Harding was close to tears, with beads of sweat running down his temples under the studio lights. It turned out that Harding's mother had died recently and he had been at her bedside. Freeman did not know this and he was distressed when he was told afterwards – more so by the suggestion (typical of the myth of *Face to Face* in the tabloid press) that he had consulted Harding's psychiatrist before the show to discover his most vulnerable point. Mary Crozier, reviewing in *The Guardian*, was unimpressed: 'Mr Freeman kept on in a really tedious way about pain, disappointment, punishment, discipline, dreams and childhood. I begin to think he attached far too much importance to this amateur psychoanalysis. I fancy Mr Harding's answers showed considerable control.'[18]

The interview revealed that under Harding's grumpy persona was a sad and lonely man. Burnett wrote that letters of sympathy flooded in. During the interview, Harding said: 'I'm afraid of dying. I should be very glad to be dead, but I don't look forward to the process of dying.' Eight weeks after the transmission, he suffered a fatal heart attack as he was leaving Broadcasting House. He was fifty-three.

In January 1961, John Freeman took up his new post as editor of the *New Statesman*. He was shortly to turn his back on *Face to Face*, literally. That month, anticipating Freeman's departure, Burnett wrote to Ed Murrow and asked if he would like to present a *Face to Face* series in America, featuring, it was hoped, Marilyn Monroe, Mae West,

Professor Oppenheimer (of A-bomb fame) and Mort Sahl. Murrow was 'very interested', but the series came to nothing.

In due course, Freeman resigned, but he told Burnett he might return after he had settled into the editor's chair, provided he was billed as 'John Freeman, editor of the *New Statesman*' and paid more money than the 100 guineas a performance. In the meantime, Burnett piloted a programme with *Panorama*'s Robert Kee.

In July 1961, Freeman wrote to Burnett denying that he was being 'uncooperative or superior' and agreed to present one more series in the autumn, if the money was right. Showing a cool nerve that Stirling Moss would have admired, Freeman did not sign a contract until within days of the series starting in October. He was polite but insistent: more money, and first-class air travel. Burnett complained about Freeman's 'militant attitude'. 'Katie [Catherine Freeman] is doing her best to persuade him,' said someone in the talks contracts department, and Leonard Miall dined Freeman at L'Escargot in Soho. In the end, the BBC caved in and the series went ahead, but it was doomed from the start.

The series opened with the trade union leader Frank Cousins. It was a straw in the wind when Burnett wrote to Leonard Miall: 'I would like to place on record that to put the first of a new series of *Face to Face* between an appeal for the National Old People's Welfare Council and the Venerable F. W. Cox doing an *Epilogue* is death and destruction to this programme.'[19] The series continued with a very popular interview in London with the American civil rights leader Martin Luther King.

Shortly after, in November, Freeman agreed to squeeze in a few American recordings of *Face to Face* when he was over in New York for the *New Statesman*. It says something about the self-importance of the BBC that it expected its New York office to book, at short notice, Marilyn Monroe, Tennessee Williams, Ella Fitzgerald and General Douglas MacArthur. All said no and the American venture was abandoned.

In January 1962, the series continued in Britain. There were two weak interviews, with the actor Albert Finney and the playwright John Osborne. Freeman seemed unprepared and, for the first time, lacked drive and persistence: as a result the interviews fell flat. The Osborne *Face to Face* scored the lowest reaction index of all: 54 per cent. On 6 February, Leonard Miall wrote a terse memo to Burnett:

> Freeman is not interviewing as well as he used to.
>
> He and you are not pulling in harness.
>
> The look of *Face to Face* is nearly stale. The opening is slow and laboured.
>
> The real trouble is two [that Freeman and Burnett were no longer working as a team]. Sort that out and all will be well.[20]

This was the sort of memo Burnett could not ignore. He had a frank talk with his interviewer and reported back to the head of talks:

> John has come clean. He thinks that as editor of the *New Statesman* he can no longer afford to be regarded as a star of gladiatorial combat, which is what the viewer expects from *Face to Face*. He says he has deliberately abandoned the tough form of questioning because his TV personality has threatened to overshadow his *NS* personality. He regrets embarking on the present series and says he is too busy to do more. He will not undertake any more series of *Face to Face*. You will remember that when I suggested to you my position was like a man with a rope around his neck with you pulling one end and Freeman the other, you said that is what a producer is for (!!!). Further, I have

watched John repeatedly turn down names of subjects approved by the BBC. It is the harness that is at fault, not the relations between the horses.[21]

The director-general had also noticed Freeman's weak interviewing. He said he did not rule out a future *Face to Face* with Oswald Mosley, but not for the present, given Freeman's interviewing had lost its 'toughness'.

Burnett suggested to Freeman one last *Face to Face* – this one with the artist whose sketches had introduced nearly all the programmes, Feliks Topolski. 'He turned it down flat,' Burnett told Miall.

Burnett then invited Robert Kee to take over from Freeman as interviewer and the schedulers placed another series (the seventh) for the summer 1962, with Lady Astor as the first guest. Nothing came of it.

This was the unhappy ending to the BBC's most famous series of interviews. It had made John Freeman a household name and TV Personality of the Year in 1960. He said genuinely that he disliked the celebrity status, and gave this as his reason for turning his back on *Face to Face*. But the truth was more complicated.

The fame of *Face to Face* invited parody. *The Stanley Baxter Show* produced a sketch called 'Nose to Nose'. More significantly, on 7 December 1962, BBC drama broadcast a play specially written for television by Terrence Rattigan called *Heart to Heart* (the *Daily Mirror* billed it as 'the largest theatre in the world', as the two-hour play was expected to reach an audience of eighty million having been produced for television in thirteen versions in thirteen countries over one week). The lead was the inquisitor (played by Kenneth More), a cynical, womanising journalist with a drink problem, who had rocketed to fame 'taking people apart' on television. Not surprisingly, Freeman had a case for a libel action, although the scenario was unrealistic. The *Daily Sketch* said: 'As a serious attack on the *Face to Face* type show, it probably made John Freeman giggle into his mug of BBC canteen tea.' Nevertheless, Freeman protested in the *New Statesman* office, 'The allegation of alcoholism I just about accept; that of amorousness I reject absolutely', to which Catherine would later comment, 'That should have been the other way round.' Freeman consulted a lawyer and settled with the BBC after 'an amicable exchange of letters'.

As a postscript, a few months before *Face to Face* ended, the BBC audience research panel reported its poll on possible future guests. Over 400 names were suggested, of whom the most popular was the conductor Sir Malcom Sargent (fifty-two votes), followed by two TV personalities – Richard Dimbleby (twenty-nine) and Eamonn Andrews (twenty-four). Radio quizmaster Wilfred Pickles and pop singer Cliff Richard were also popular choices.

Sir Winston Churchill polled fourteen votes. As Leonard Miall wrote on the bottom of the list: '*Sic transit, gloria mundi.*'[22]

Chapter 7

Political journalist –
Freeman and the Cold War

F OR FOURTEEN YEARS, John Freeman wrote for the *New Statesman* (1951–65). For the last ten of those years, he was either deputy editor or editor, thereby exercising editorial control at the height of the Cold War over a socialist magazine that had a reputation for pro-communist beliefs. As such he seemed to invite rumours. He was a public figure on the left who guarded his privacy, and that in itself was suspicious. He was also well known for his dubious friendships, as with Tom Driberg, who was suspected of being a spy. One rumour at the time was that Freeman worked for the intelligence services; another, preposterous now, was that he was the 'fourth' or 'fifth' man in the spy scandals surrounding the defection of the three spies Burgess, Maclean and Philby.

These rumours were not true but undoubtedly two of his co-writers and close friends on the magazine were 'spies' for one side or the other, or both. Less emotively and more accurately, they worked part-time as informants, couriers and photographers, answerable to the secret services of the state. There was, after all, a Cold War on at the time and those who travelled to the other side of the Iron Curtain considered it their patriotic duty to prevent it becoming 'hot'. Freeman, as we know, was a socialist on the left of the Labour Party. Was he a Soviet sympathiser? How far did his political views shape his editorial policy? And in what direction? First, I need to place Freeman in the *New Statesman* offices and account for his promotion to editor.

When John Freeman took over from Kingsley Martin as editor of the *New Statesman and Nation* in January 1961, the circulation was 75,000 – but falling – and the advertising revenue was almost £100,000 per year. When Martin had become editor in 1931, the circulation had been 12,000, the advertising revenue £7,000 per year, and the magazine losing money. In other words, Freeman succeeded a thirty-year editorship that had turned the *New Statesman* into the most successful political weekly magazine in Britain, although arguably it was past its best.

It was a political magazine based firmly on Martin's socialist principles – and everything that Freeman did was bound to be in his shadow. Freeman described his predecessor as 'an angular, argumentative, exuberant Nonconformist, who never acquired the good taste and discretion to keep quiet in the face of injustice and folly. In his magazine he weekly wrestled with doubts and proclaimed the conviction of a whole generation.'[1]

Despite his patriarchal appearance and pedagogic manner, Kingsley

Martin was notoriously indecisive; 'wrestling with doubts' was a good description. The nickname of the *New Statesman and Nation* – 'Staggers and Naggers' – referred to Martin's fickle conscience and nagging morality. When he retired from the editorship, A. J. P. Taylor sent a message: 'The end of an era! It is most distressing to think that the *New Statesman* may now follow a consistent line two weeks running.'[2]

Kingsley Martin could not make his mind up between pacifism and preparations for war. In the late '30s he was one of the first appeasers of Hitler and then one of the first to turn against Chamberlain for appeasement. In the late '50s he could not decide whether to support the campaign for nuclear disarmament or not, alternating between enthusiasm and ambivalence. Freeman accused him of having 'a half-baked love affair' with unilateralism.

Kingsley's agonising over the right path was shared by his readership. When Norman MacKenzie, who was an assistant editor from 1943 to 1962, spoke at his memorial service in 1969 he said that Kingsley Martin 'was not so much the conscience of the left as the unconscious of the middle class, and that's why he had so much power. He had a very deep sense of his readership, their anxieties and hopes, and of himself in behaving justly.'[3]

Transparently honest, often angry at the state of the world but funny about the idiosyncrasies of the British character, Kingsley's journalism 'played a crucial role in shaping the thought of a generation'. That was Freeman's view writing in the 1960s.

The critics of the *NS* labelled it indecisive, irresponsible and pessimistic, but:

> It is difficult to deny that had Martin's *New Statesman* not existed, public opinion on such varied and momentous issues as anti-fascism in the '30s, war aims, the welfare state, and – perhaps above

all – the anti-imperial revolution of India and the British colonies, for the three decades of his editorship would have been very different from what it was.[4]

Such was the seminal influence of the magazine that Freeman inherited.

Norman MacKenzie lived just long enough to write in the April 2013 centenary edition about the literary and social traditions of the magazine, which was often referred to by the name of its location – an alley in a Dickensian corner of London leading off Lincoln's Inn Fields called Great Turnstile:

> If I have to fit Great Turnstile into the English tradition of radical writing, I would say it goes back directly to Richard Steele's early coffeehouse congeries of mid-eighteenth-century London that gave rise to the *Tatler* magazine. That's certainly how Kingsley saw it. The *New Statesman* interlocked the old Whig radicalism, centred round Whitehall, with the Fabian parliamentary radicals of the LSE and the art, crafts, music and theatre crowd from Bloomsbury. Great Turnstile Street was right in the middle, literally.
>
> When Kingsley Martin had become editor his first deal was to acquire *The Nation* with its Lib–Lab viewpoint. In the 1920s, *The Nation* had bought up that great Victorian literary weekly, *The Athenaeum*. When Martin added *The Week-end Review* the following year (1934), he found himself master of a vehicle he had largely designed himself, a literary omnibus carrying star writers from the left spectrum – H. G. Wells, J. B. Priestley, Malcolm Muggeridge, C. E. M. Joad, Harold Laski and a coach load of glitterati from political and artistic circles. It was all grist to Kingsley's mill. He was a very inclusive editor. That remained the strength of the *NS* for forty years.

We were a sort of club of intellectual gentlemen like the Savile or
Garrick: not so high class but similarly collegiate.[5]

John Freeman first wrote for the *New Statesman* in 1951. Kingsley, then
in his mid-fifties, was looking for a successor and already had Freeman in mind, partly for his chief of staff capabilities. As Freeman said:
'Kingsley hated work, all other forms of work except writing, which
he loved.' Freeman was in the process of resigning from the government, and his resignation principle of welfare before re-armament was
in tune with the Labour left on the staff, from the editor downwards.
So Martin took Freeman out to lunch and, on 23 May 1951, Freeman
accepted by letter the offer of a part-time staff job:

> I would ask you to have two things in mind. First, that you will really
> try – having regard to your judgement of my capacity – to find me
> a proper, reasonably secure and remunerative job in the *NS and N*;
> secondly that you will exercise some care and patience in teaching me
> the rudiments of the job, which is new to me, and not lose patience
> if I show initial clumsiness and ignorance. I'm sure I shan't regret tak-
> ing the decision even though, on the face of it, it's financial lunacy.[6]

Within months, Freeman was de facto editing the paper when Kingsley Martin was abroad. He was learning journalism too, although as a
former editor of *Cherwell* and a writer of political reports, it was hardly
from a standing start. What united all Freeman's careers was his talent
as a communicator. He told C. H. Rolf, another regular *New Statesman* writer and the editor of Kingsley Martin's *Letters and Diaries*:

> Kingsley was one of the formative influences in my life. And one of
> the things to remember about him is that, for all his 'good causes' and

so on, he was a very crafty and skilful old journalist; he knew all the tricks of the trade and could teach them. I find constantly, in writing or in making other people write, that I am embodying Kingsley's rules into my own work.[7]

For the next four years, Freeman combined being a backbencher in Parliament with writing for the *New Statesman*. His promotion to deputy editor became assured in 1955, in circumstances that would have embarrassed anyone with a less 'ice-cold temperament' than Freeman. Richard Crossman MP – considered one of the most brilliant political journalists in Britain, and chief leader-writer for the *NS* on foreign affairs since the war – had made clear to Kingsley Martin that his spiritual home was the *New Statesman*, not Parliament, and he wished to succeed Martin as editor. If he knew he was the heir apparent, he told Martin, he would resign his parliamentary seat. Martin had not responded. Then, in July, Crossman was offered a tempting job on the *Daily Mirror*. He tried to use this offer, clumsily 'holding a pistol to Martin's head', with the threat that, unless Martin named him formally as deputy editor, he would defect to the *Mirror*, which was offering him four times as much money.

Freeman's reaction to this was clever, and possibly duplicitous. Crossman claimed in his diary that Freeman wrote him a note to the effect of 'rather than lose me he would like to see Kingsley resign and me take his place, in which case he would serve under me'.[8] This is quite possible, bearing in mind that they had been Bevanite colleagues in Parliament until Freeman's resignation. The opinion in the *NS* office, however, was that Freeman outwitted Crossman by a lateral move. Realising that Kingsley Martin would find it easier to lose Crossman if there was another fluent, polemical leader-writer waiting behind his typewriter, he travelled to Paris and persuaded Paul Johnson, the very young *NS* correspondent in France, that there might be a job on the London staff. Johnson was delighted.

Kingsley Martin sacked Richard Crossman, by phone, at 8.30 a.m.: 'I've thought it over and it's quite definite that there is no room for the three of us [meaning himself, Freeman and Crossman] on the paper.' Later, C. H. Rolf discovered among Martin's papers this note about Crossman: 'I have never worked on the paper with anyone so brilliant but so impurely motivated. I think he lacks the qualities that will bind a staff in loyalty to him and the integrity, disinterestedness and judgement that will make him a good editor.'[9] The implication of this damning note must be that Crossman's attempted putsch was doomed before it even started. John Freeman wrote Crossman a chivalrous letter:

> I think the loss of you from the *Statesman* is a terrible blow; but the blow is to us rather than to you. I am sure you are right in saying that your chances of inheriting the editorial chair at Great Turnstile in the long run are made neither worse nor better by your going off now.
>
> I would just like to say that the last few days have been exceptionally unpleasant ones for me, since I cannot help being aware that, had I never arrived at Great Turnstile, it is almost certain that the present situation would not have arisen. Nevertheless, I think you do probably understand – and I would certainly wish you to – that I have tried my best to behave towards you as a good colleague; for many reasons, not the least is that I regard you as a very much better journalist than I am.[10]

The trouble with writing about John Freeman – so private; so 'hard of access', in Paul Johnson's own terms – is that it is sometimes impossible to find out what his motives really were. At my suggestion, Norman

MacKenzie asked Freeman why Kingsley Martin had preferred him to Richard Crossman. Freeman replied: 'You know, he was like a Tudor monarch with court favourites of the moment. I was preferred at that time.' Possibly true, but not a revealing answer.

That was not quite the end of the story. Two days after the breakfast phone call, Martin met Crossman face to face. He was less candid than he might have been, but forthright nevertheless:

> KINGSLEY MARTIN: There can be no question, I've thought about it and I would never trust you to put the *New Statesman* first in your politics.
> RICHARD CROSSMAN: I've told you – I'd give them up.
> KINGSLEY MARTIN: I don't believe it – you're a politician, and John Freeman isn't. He's really given up politics to live for the *New Statesman*.
> RICHARD CROSSMAN: I knew you brought him in for that purpose, Kingsley – to get rid of me.[11]

Watching this bloody battle for succession from the sidelines was the gossipy political philosopher Isaiah Berlin. Confined to bed at All Souls College, Oxford, he wrote to the American historian Arthur Schlesinger with a running commentary:

> The story is that John Freeman is going to become editor of the *New Statesman*. I don't know who he is except that he's a fanatical left-wing socialist – a Bevanite – with violent and stupid views on almost everything. His judgement is appalling and the reason for seeking to appoint him is that he's about to marry someone else's wife in such circumstances as to make his departure from politics advisable. I shall be sorry to see old Kingsley go. He was a kindly, old-fashioned, idiot journalist of an absurd, irresponsible, madly irritating, but, in some

sense, human sort, whereas Freeman, by all accounts, is a humourless monster, a dreary third-rate fanatic.[12]

This commentary, of course, was wrong in most respects. Martin did not leave until 1961, Freeman was not on this occasion 'about to marry someone's wife' (as far as I know) and he was hardly a third-rate fanatic either; but it shows Isaiah Berlin's dislike of socialism and, perhaps, Freeman's reputation with women.

Freeman was appointed deputy and, from then on, it was simply a matter of time before his succession, for Martin thought the editor had to be from within the paper. But when was the best time for Martin to retire?

Like many chief executives, Martin claimed he wanted to retire – his 'Sunday painting' and book-writing were tempting him – but he could not bring himself to do so. Initially, Freeman was content to edit the paper as deputy while leaving Martin to write the diary, 'into which', said Martin, 'I put my heart, and which I was determined always to keep fresh and gay, as well as writing other articles.' Freeman was loyal, comfortable with his de facto editorship and on the crest of a wave at the BBC. But by 1960 their roles had changed. Martin wrote that he was tired and had little new to say. Freeman added to that; he considered that Martin's writing had deteriorated because he could not make his mind up what he wanted to say. He told C. H. Rolf:

> I think there are basically two kinds of journalist: one that wants to expound a situation, and one that wants to *redress* a situation and doesn't care much about the facts – he wants to preach a sermon. Kingsley was a preacher. While he was absolutely certain about his tenets and what he wanted to say, he wrote like an angel.

> I think if there was a decline in his writing it was at least as much
> due to the decline in his certainty as to any decline in his powers
> to concentrate.

Further, said Freeman, Martin's incoherence was spreading. He was increasingly incapable of making decisions and, in this general confusion, the circulation was beginning to fall. For Freeman's part, he had received several other offers of work and, although he did not say so, it was clear that broadcasting was no longer offering the challenge he needed. He told Martin: 'I should find it difficult to stay unless you made way fairly soon.' He was more explicit to C. H. Rolf:

> The point was not that I wanted to edit the paper above everything
> else – though perhaps I did – but that his continued retention of the
> editorial chair had become seriously damaging to the paper. I saw
> no purpose in continuing what I could not longer support. It seems
> that he never quite got the point, and this is why he felt so resent-
> ful afterwards.[13]

The breakdown of friendship between the second and third editors of the *New Statesman* was to follow.

After the defection of Guy Burgess and Donald Maclean to Moscow in 1951 – and their subsequent unmasking as communist spies, followed by a similar defection and revelation about Kim Philby in 1963 – the British press was on the hunt for the 'fourth man' and indeed the 'fifth man'. There had to be another member of the ring who had tipped off the others. The 'fourth' turned out to be the art historian and Surveyor of the Queen's Pictures, Anthony Blunt, who was secretly granted immunity in 1964. Speculation about the 'fifth' still lingers. The wildest speculation extended as far as John Freeman. His three surviving colleagues on the *New Statesman* to whom I spoke (Norman MacKenzie, Paul Johnson and Anthony Howard) had all heard these rumours – indeed, it was Norman who alerted me to them – and all dismissed them as preposterous. Nevertheless, they must stem from the reputation of the *New Statesman* during the Cold War as a nest of 'fellow travellers' (communists who were not party members), MI6 informers, or both at once. 'Walking on both sides of the street' was the phrase used.

In fact, the *New Statesman* had form. The very first editor, Clifford Sharp, had worked secretly for the Foreign Office political information department in 1918–19 writing strongly anti-Bolshevik reports. When they later appeared in the *New Statesman* he changed the content to a condemnation of counter-revolutionary excesses, because he thought this is what his public wanted to read about.

George Orwell has a lot to answer for. After the war he wrote for *Tribune* magazine, which represented the socialists on the left of the Labour Party (later the Bevanites). He and Michael Foot would frequently lunch with Norman MacKenzie near Great Turnstile. That did not stop Orwell in 1949 from presenting to the government's Information Research Department a notorious blacklist of 'crypto-communists and fellow travellers … who should not be trusted as propagandists'. The *New Statesman* was strongly represented. The list included: the present and future editors, Kingsley Martin and Richard Crossman (though Orwell thought Crossman was 'too dishonest to be an outright FT [fellow traveller]'); the revered columnist J. B. Priestley ('a strong [communist] sympathiser'); another writer, Dorothy Woodman (Kingsley Martin's future partner); Tom Driberg; and assistant editor Norman MacKenzie. At the same time, according to a later *New Statesman* editor, Anthony Howard (1972–78), some staff were also reporting to MI6: 'The relationship between journalism and the secret intelligence services has always been a grey one.

It was probably most closely consummated in the offices of the left-wing *New Statesman*.'[14]

This apparent dual allegiance is not hard to unravel. All the staff at the *New Statesman* in the '40s and '50s were campaigning socialists, including Freeman, of course. Some had been communists, like, for example, Tom Driberg, and briefly Norman MacKenzie. There was a Cold War; the government was convinced that the Soviet Union might well invade or at least infiltrate western Europe. The *New Statesman* writers often travelled to eastern Europe, the Soviet Union or China for their work (MacKenzie was the expert on communism). What could be more reasonable than to use socialist credentials to access the other side of the Iron Curtain? What could be more professional for MI6 than to ask these journalists to act as couriers, photographers and contacts? What could be more patriotic than to accept? Norman MacKenzie, later a gentle, bookish professor of educational technology at Sussex University, was a dramatic example.

When MacKenzie left for academia in 1962, John Freeman wrote: 'He has long been our expert on communist affairs on both sides of the iron curtain. His interpretation of the Soviet CP since Stalin has proved far more accurate in his prognosis than many of his more publicised rivals in the field.'[15] Freeman was probably hinting at Mac-Kenzie's extraordinary scoop in 1955.

MacKenzie's Bulgarian contact, Tseko Etropolski, had summoned him to a meeting on a pedalo at a Bulgarian Black Sea resort. Khrushchev had just tipped off the Cominform at a secret meeting in Sofia about the extent of Stalin's purges, a full four months before he stunned the communist world by revealing everything at the notorious 20th Party Congress. MacKenzie's Bulgarian contact had memorised much of Stalin's highly secret disclosures and repeated them to MacKenzie at this out-of-eavesdropping meeting. His scoop fell on deaf ears. Neither

MI6 nor the Foreign Office nor, even, Kingsley Martin, wanted to take any action. When MacKenzie read reports of Khrushchev's speech the following February he recognised passages word for word.[16]

MacKenzie had been a member of the Marxist socialist Independent Labour Party (ILP) in the late 1930s. It is even possible that MI6 had asked him to join the Communist Party in 1940 for its own purposes. To add to his credibility with the Kremlin, he sometimes wrote for Telepress, a Soviet-backed news agency in Fleet Street that published atrocious communist propaganda. Leonard Woolf, a director of the *New Statesman,* must have been taken in by MacKenzie's pro-communist stance since he once described him as 'the most dangerous man in the *New Statesman*'. MacKenzie found this 'rather strange' because he was a patriot. In fact he had worked under the protection of MI6, part of the British security service, since the early 1940s. As the war ended and east Europe fell into the Soviet-occupied zone, so MacKenzie travelled increasingly into communist Europe on an MI6 ticket, though he received no other payment. His special areas were Romania and Bulgaria.

On one occasion MacKenzie was caught photographing the outside of a prison camp near Bucharest. He was briefly imprisoned before being moved to a hotel, but still under arrest. Drifting in through his window, he heard the mellifluous tones of a violin played by, he was soon to discover, David Oistrakh. Soon after he was handed two tickets by the Security – one was an air ticket to London, the other was for a seat at Oistrakh's performance. MacKenzie said the whole episode was like 'a fairy tale' but that can't be how it appeared at the time. Many years later he met an old friend at a school reunion who sounded embarrassed: 'I've been feeling guilty all these years. Didn't I see you in chains on Bucharest station?' (This story is independently verified). MacKenzie admitted it was true and added that he had got worried when the plane transporting him out of Romania appeared to be heading north towards the Soviet Union, before it circled back and landed him in Yugoslavia. 'I gather you're doing useful work in the Balkans,' said Kingsley Martin enigmatically when he returned to the office.[17]

Anthony Howard recalled that after one press trip to eastern Europe he noticed a *New Statesman* colleague reporting to MI6: 'When I raised the matter with him, he got quite shirty and inquired whether I regarded myself as a patriot or not?' The trouble with 'walking on both sides of the street' is that it's sometimes unclear in which direction you are walking.

With MacKenzie there can be no doubt. In the spring of 1956, for instance, at the request of Kingsley Martin, he travelled to Budapest to assist a former *New Statesman* writer and BBC broadcaster, Pál Ignotus, who had just been released from jail in the wake of the Khrushchev disclosures. This was months before the Hungarian Revolution but nonetheless a mission of some danger. Ignotus had spent the war years in London but had decided to risk a return visit to the land of his birth in 1949, just after Hungary became a communist state under the severely repressive Mátyás Rákosi. MacKenzie had warned him not to go back. He had been right to do so because, on his arrival, Ignotus was seized, thrown into prison, tortured and kept in solitary confinement. There is a coda to this story. On his release Ignotus married Florence, the woman from the neighbouring cell with whom he had exchanged months of increasingly romantic 'tapping' messages without once seeing her. They decided to remain in Hungary but fled in November 1956 after the Soviet puppet, János Kádár, betrayed the ideals of the October revolution.

The next year MacKenzie was one of the first journalists, with Woodrow Wyatt, to detect the vote-rigging scandal in the Electrical Trades Union (ETU). Freeman wrote: 'It was entirely due to his

Father Horace: 'He did not suffer fools.'

Mother Beatrice: 'My pretty, silly mother.'

Baby John at his christening.

JF in the second rowing VIII at Westminster School, 1930 (back row, second from left): 'He rows like the village blacksmith.'

Hunger marchers demonstrating in Trafalgar Square, October 1932: 'The school has heard the voice of England's forgotten people.'

Major Freeman home
on leave.

General Montgomery surveys the desert battlefield at 22nd Armoured
Brigade HQ, August 1942. Freeman's CO, Brigadier Roberts, is on
Monty's left.

Allied victory parade through Tunis, May 1943.

John Freeman MP, 1946: 'On every side is a
spirit of high adventure.'

The Minister of Supply tries to show interest while visiting an aircraft factory in 1948.

JF looking unwell on his election poster, Watford, 1951.

Groom and bride: Tom Driberg and Ena Binfield.

The best man with Lizi and Mima in the front pew. Nye Bevan is behind, in the centre.

The Goldie boys in a *Panorama* production meeting, 1958. On the left is Richard Dimbleby; four from left is Christopher Chataway; then JF and Woodrow Wyatt; then, two along, Robert Kee.

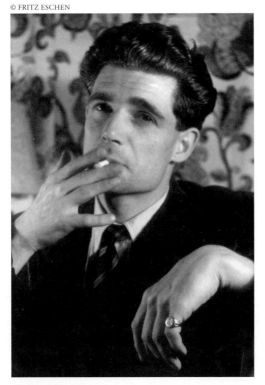

Charles Wheeler, 1955.

Catherine Dove, 1955.

Face to Face with Tony Hancock, 'pursing his lips and grimacing'.

Face to Face with Augustus John: 'It was a fiasco. He said little that was coherent and nothing that was interesting.'

The wedding: John and Catherine, with Lizi behind, in Hampstead, 1962.

The Freeman family at 2 KG, New Delhi, 1967. From left to right: Tom, Catherine, Lucy, Matthew, John.

Burns Night in
Washington, 1970.
JF submits to
'flummery'.

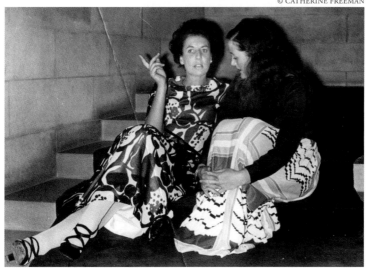

The ambassador's
wife and her social
secretary: Catherine
with Judith.

In the Oval Office:
President and Mrs
Nixon, Henry Kissinger,
the UK ambassador and
Mrs Freeman.

Professor Freeman
on his bicycle at UC
Davis, 1986.

Judith with Tors and Jessie
at the home of Jean and
Dan Snyder.

JF at Triggsy's
wedding in
Barnes, 1998.

foresight that the *NS* became committed to liberate ETU members from the communist caucus.' No one could deny then that MacKenzie had done his bit for Queen and country. MacKenzie told me in 2004: 'I'm sure John [Freeman] had some kind of intelligence connections.' He should know.

Aylmer Vallance was more mysterious. His story is worth telling because he became one of John Freeman's few real friends. In fact, Freeman nursed him on his deathbed in 1955 and in 1961 he named his first son after him, Matthew John Aylmer.

Vallance turned up at the 'Staggers' offices at the outbreak of war in 1939 wearing the uniform of a lieutenant colonel in the War Office. He worked part-time for military intelligence. At the same time he was about to marry a member of the Communist Party who was close to its leadership, including general secretary Harry Pollitt. This must have strained the marital relationship during the Nazi–Soviet Pact 1939 –1941 when they worked for opposing sides; but perhaps it didn't, no one knew with Vallance. At the end of the war Lieutenant Colonel Vallance slipped this unsigned editorial into the *New Statesman* when it was at the printers, thereby avoiding the red pencil:

> Its foundations [the new world order] must be based firmly on recognition of the essential unity of the working people of all nations. Their needs and desires – work and security and a 'dinner of herbs where love is' – are one and the same. The Captains and the Kings have made, between them, a century of greed, aggression, hatred and blood. They may now depart. (12 May 1945)

George VI and the Chief Captain (Churchill) had just received the ovation of the crowd at Buckingham Palace. Leonard Woolf, who was in the editor's chair that week, was furious: 'It [the editorial] is full of the slants, snides, sneers and smears that communists and fellow travellers habitually employ as means for building a perfect society.'[18]

During the war years the strongest patriots could be communists because the common enemy was fascism. A number of *New Statesman* staff worked secretly for the Political Warfare Executive (PWE) writing propaganda for dissemination into Nazi-occupied countries. Prominent among them was Richard Crossman, who was dubbed 'a master of psychological warfare', and Aylmer Vallance's job was to ensure they did not give away military secrets. But during the Cold War that followed, the enemy was the Soviet Union and its communist satellites in eastern Europe, so allegiances were severely tested. On which side of the street did Vallance walk between 1945 and 1955? The jury is still out. Evidence that it was on the west: he kept his military rank of lieutenant colonel in his passport until his death, which must have provided some sort of cover, and he travelled behind the Iron Curtain frequently using a travel agency in north London, Gateway Tours, that was rumoured to be money-laundered by MI6. Evidence that it was on the east: he was a huge admirer of Yugoslavia in particular, named his son 'Tito', and several of his articles had a pro-communist bias. C. H. Rolf, who shared a *New Statesman* office with him and happened also to work part-time for the police, offers this verdict:

> It seems likely enough that he was playing a fairly devious game, using the *New Statesman* with the knowledge of the Intelligence Department to plant useful items of pro-allied propaganda, but also planting, under cover of the two-way prestige this gave him, 'fellow travelling' material about war theatres like Yugoslavia. This was a source of constant friction; and the commonly-heard accusation that the *New Statesman* was a fellow-travelling paper was due not only to Kingsley's ambivalence about Russia, but also to Aylmer's stealthy insistence on putting

in, deliberately too late for censorship or amendment, extreme statements about eastern Europe.[19]

After Vallance's death in 1955, John Freeman wrote to his son 'Tito' (real name Philip): 'My own friendship with him [Aylmer] was close and very rewarding. And yet, looking back forty years and more, I realise that I never really knew who he was or what he believed in.' About this time, when Philip introduced himself in a London club the response was: 'Not Aylmer's son? He was a damned fine intelligence agent.'

Vallance's shady past life must have appealed to Freeman. It could have fitted into John Buchan's *Greenmantle* spy story. A neat, spry man with a goatee beard beneath a long face and glasses, he normally faded quietly into the background as those with something to hide normally do. Yet he had led an extraordinary life. He had joined the intelligence services in 1915 and played the 'great game' across the Himalayas. The 'game' included fighting a duel in the jungle and walking, disguised as a Sikh, from Karachi to Singapore.

In the 1930s he had become editor of the *News Chronicle* but had been sacked for a sex scandal that involved the female motoring correspondent, the editor's table and a surprise visit from the prudish chairman, Lord Cadbury. He had joined the staff of the *New Statesman* in 1937. A consummate journalist he turned out well-informed copy on finance, fisheries and food, filling any gap necessary at short notice where a few hundred words were required. He was a quick and calm editor, working at the printers with a hand poised over the copy ready for a last-minute change, or, for that matter, a last-minute addition.

Although a lifetime socialist, he spent many a weekend at a Scottish castle fly fishing, drinking heavily with his house party and then driving back to London for a Monday editorial. He looked like a Scottish laird and behaved more like a *bon vivant* than an earnest socialist. He loved European travel and had European wives: the first a White Russian émigré who deserted her family to be with him; the second, Helen Gosse, a member of the Communist Party and granddaughter of the distinguished literary polymath Sir Edmund Gosse; the third a destitute German refugee, Oertie Christina Fischinger. Vallance was more than a friend for Freeman: he was a mentor and even, perhaps subconsciously, a role model.

On his deathbed in 1955, Aylmer summoned his young daughter Margaret, asking her to open the drawer of his desk. Inside was a long-barrelled revolver. She left it where it was:

> I was taken off to live in John Freeman's house with John and Mima and Lizi. She was thirteen and I was fourteen. Mima was very tall and beautiful and really kind to me. John was aloof – quite strict too. It was quite a big flat they had near Hampstead Heath. One day Oertie arrived and I saw at once from her expression that my father was dead. So I was fourteen and an orphan.[20]

Three years later Mima died, also from cancer.

Was Freeman a communist sympathiser, even a fellow traveller? In his more extreme 'leftist' period from Oxford through the war he no doubt admired Lenin and the revolutionary ideals of Trotsky: he was not called 'Trotsky Freeman' for nothing. But he was never in the Communist Party and, according to Edward Hyams, who knew him well on the *New Statesman*, he was never taken in by 'Uncle Joe' Stalin. He always considered him a tyrant and villain: 'The villainy of which he held Stalin guilty was the perversion of socialism so as to make a lie of what Freeman believes to be essentially true.'

In the summer of 1956, Freeman travelled for six weeks through the so-called 'People's Democracies' of Poland, Hungary and Czechoslovakia. It was a formative experience. He wrote a long piece for the *New Statesman* on his return – 'A Profile of People's Democracy' – and spoke about his impressions several times on BBC radio. The timing of his visit was significant. It was after Khrushchev's revelations at the 20th Party Congress in February of that year but before the Russian invasion of Hungary in November, a brief period when Soviet communism appeared to be showing a human face. Yet his article was severely critical of the very basics of Soviet communism:

> To define the beginning of error as the Soviet decision to enforce collectivisation overlooks the fact that defects must have already existed in the Leninist system of democratic centralism, which amounted to betrayal of first principles. So that, even for the Russians, the claim that a return to Leninism is a sufficient blueprint for future legality is a hollow one.

Freeman wrote that the 'Peoples' Democracies' were fundamentally different from the Soviet Union because Poles, Czechs and Hungarians knew that they had until recently belonged within the mainstream of European social democracy. Yet their form of socialism was 'here to stay' and in 1956 that was a reasonable assumption. As a socialist he saw evidence for optimism: 'Despite the cruelties and the bungling that have characterised the People's Republics hitherto, social attitudes and the economic pattern are gradually evolving, which bear *some* relation to what *any* socialist must recognise as being his aim.'

Nevertheless, the over-centralisation, bureaucracy and interference from Russia was blighting individual initiative, and underneath that *suffocation* was something worse:

> When all the achievements have been listed and all the allowances
> made, the fact remains that the Peoples' Democracies do not yet offer
> the generality of their citizens the chance of a decent life, free of fear,
> free of want – or even free of graft. But the central failure is that a
> disregard for freedom has corrupted individuals.[21]

This is not the essay of a starry-eyed communist sympathiser, many
of whom were members of the Labour Party at this time; still less of
the hard-line, Russia-right-or-wrong ideologue, who were the fellow
travellers and party members of the 1950s. It is obviously a perceptive
analysis by an independently minded journalist within the democratic-
socialist context. That was Freeman. To gossip that he may have been
a spy is completely ridiculous.

Any doubts where Freeman stood on nuclear disarmament, a
subject on which pro-Soviet sympathies quickly showed themselves,
should have been dispelled the next year, 1957. Once again, as in
the '30s and '40s, the *New Statesman* set an agenda and moulded
public opinion. On 2 November, it published the most seminal
article in its 100-year history: 'Britain and the Nuclear Bomb' by
J. B. Priestley. Goaded by Aneurin Bevan's crushing of unilateralism at the recent Labour Party conference ('it is not statesmanship
– it is an emotional spasm') and using his father-of-the-nation style
that had served him so well in his BBC Home Service *Postscripts* of
1940, Priestley ended:

> The British of these times, so frequently hiding behind masks of sour,
> cheap cynicism, often seem to be waiting for something … great and
> noble that would make them feel good again. And this might well be
> a declaration to the world that after a certain date one power able to
> engage in nuclear warfare will reject the evil thing for ever.

After this, the birth of CND was just a matter of time. The editor that week was John Freeman. He agreed to sign off the article although, wrote C. H. Rolf, 'he was himself in sympathy with Bevan and the party's decision'.[22]

Later that month a meeting of opinion shapers was held in Kingsley Martin's flat. Bertrand Russell was there, J. B. Priestley and his wife Jacquetta Hawkes, the former American ambassador to the Soviet Union, George Kennan, whose recent Reith Lecture series 'Russia, the Atom and the West' had stoked up anxiety about nuclear warfare, and the Labour MP Denis Healey, a specialist in defence. The new *New Statesman* leader-writer Paul Johnson watched it get off to a bad start:

> Someone spoke advocating a unilateralist line and Denis Healey replied, 'Yes, yes, that's all very well, but what we've got to do is to be responsible about this.' Whereupon Priestley exploded, 'RESPONSI-BLE! RESPONSIBLE!! How many times have I heard that dreadful word?! It has led to two world wars and the prospect of a third.' I noticed that Bertie Russell was cackling. He thought that was very funny because if anybody knew how to be irresponsible then he did! I knew then that this was going to be a lot of trouble.[23]

That was the beginning of the Campaign for Nuclear Disarmament.

Over the next few months the *New Statesman* became a global forum where world leaders protested their commitment to world peace. Bertrand Russell began the exchange in November 1957 with 'An Open Letter to Eisenhower and Khrushchev'. It came down to the exhortation 'to agree to disagree' (this being the mantra first coined in the *New Statesman* by Richard Crossman): 'It is not necessary that either side should abandon belief in its own creed. It is only necessary that [East and West] should abandon the attempt to spread its creed by force of arms.'

Khrushchev himself replied a month later, in an article written in Russian and accompanied by a personal letter to the editor. When the package arrived from the Soviet embassy, Kingsley Martin suspected it to be a hoax. The Soviet premier endorsed Bertrand Russell's hopes for a sunlit future for mankind and condemned 'the criminal policy of militarism'. With that scoop the sales of the *New Statesman* went up by 2,000 to well over 70,000, then an all-time high.

The uplifting tone was soured by the eventual reply of the implicit villain of the piece, US Secretary of State John Foster Dulles. He pointed out (February 1958) that the Soviet Union had never renounced the use of force to solve international affairs, as its invasion of Hungary in 1956 had proved. It was left to Spike Milligan, appropriately, to poke fun at the Dr Strangelove concept of Mutually Assured Destruction (MAD). He was one of hundreds who joined in the *New Statesman* debate:

> Let me be the first to say it. Mr Krushchev's letter in reply to Bertrand Russell is all a fiendish plot. It is a deliberate attempt to rob us of the promised American bases on our soil. We must arm, arm, arm, arm, arm. For the Russians must be taught that the only way to end war is to have it.[24]

During this period Freeman was often in the editor's chair. J. B. Priestley said: 'John Freeman was against us, but editorially he behaved superbly.'[25] Freeman's view was that distinguished writers of the left were perfectly entitled to write polemical 'ban the bomb' articles, but the *New Statesman* should not identify formally with a pacifist pressure group, particularly one that would require Britain to leave NATO. So he reinforced Kingsley Martin's indecision, so to speak. Paul Johnson told me: 'Barbara [Castle], John and I would not let him [Kingsley Martin] take what we considered a pacifist line. Kingsley referred to us as the 'red-headed league' [they all had red hair] and thought we were ganging up on him.' Tony Howard amplified this:

> Freeman remained an unrepentant believer not only in adequate national defence but also in the eighteenth-century notion of the advantages of a 'balance of terror'. Week in, week out he battled, with the help of his colleagues, to prevent Kingsley Martin from committing the paper to the Aldermaston marchers.[26]

It is surely significant that Major John Freeman had been a soldier with four years of defending Britain by force of arms behind him.

The New Statesman *cartoonist Vicky shows Kingsley Martin*
handing over to John Freeman.

Chapter 8

New Statesman editor

WHEN FREEMAN BECAME editor of the *New States-man* in January 1961 he did not intend to stay long:

> The task I set myself, on becoming editor, was to tidy things up, modernise the paper a bit, and then hand over to some-one else who should preferably be of a younger generation. I did think that what had been a marvellous operation until the mid-'50s had sadly deteriorated, and that what was needed was a short incumbency by a non-genius to see if a certain amount of order could be put back into it.[1]

There speaks Freeman as chief of staff. But there was a more fundamental issue beneath the surface, which Edward Hyams identified in his *History of the First Fifty Years* (of the *New Statesman*) – an issue endorsed by Freeman in his introduction to the book.

For the first twenty years or so of Kingsley Martin's editorship, the paper and most of its readers believed in the implementation of socialism. Martin was a preacher who believed in socialism just as his Nonconformist minister father had believed in Christianity. To deny socialism was almost wicked and during the '30s and '40s its advent could be preached with revolutionary zeal. After that time, however, the identification of socialism with Soviet communism and the iniquities thereof, together with an aggressive American capitalism, meant that democratic socialist parties in the West were on the defensive. In Britain the socialist hopes of the 1945 generation, fully endorsed by John Freeman, had turned into the Butskellism of the 1950s. Freeman wrote in his introduction:

> The political and social course of the '30s and '40s had been mapped out in advance with astonishing accuracy by the socialist thinkers of the inter-war years and the prophets of that generation were confident that they knew the answers.
>
> In the face of the problems of the '50s and '60s there is no certainty. British socialist practice and precept has, so to speak, come to the end of the homework done by the early new statesmen and a period of intense disputation and inquiry is now needed to relate socialist morality to the modern world.[2]

Edward Hyams put it more graphically: 'The *New Statesman's* cry of dissent will be sustained, but it will not cry, "You are wicked!" but, rather, "You are mistaken!" John Freeman's *New Statesman* is more likely to be more "grown-up", more rational, penetrating and enquiring.'[3]

Tony Howard said much the same thing: 'Soft-heartedness went out and hard-headedness came in, with adjectives like "well-balanced" and "judicious" replacing familiar epithets such as "outrageous" or "unforgivable".'[4]

Anthony Howard was one of Freeman's first appointments. He came from *The Guardian* and was the first professional parliamentary correspondent the *New Statesman* employed. He had no preconceived view and had access to information from all sides. The second was Karl Meyer as Washington correspondent. John Kennedy was now President and Freeman was determined that the *New Statesman*'s anti-American bias of the Cold War should be replaced by a recognition that the centre of power in the western world must lie in Washington. The third appointment was Karl Miller as literary editor. Having poached him from *The Spectator*, Freeman let him get on with the job of professionalising the literary criticism in the back half of the paper. At editorial meetings he occasionally offered suggestions for the music coverage, music being his first artistic love (his favourite composers were Ravel, Mahler and Shostakovitch), but otherwise he left well alone. 'Culturally I am a complete conservative,' he said.[5]

A good example of the *New Statesman*'s 'more rational and penetrating' articles to point up the inequalities of the 1960s and the need for social justice, were the essays by Peter Townsend on 'The Meaning of Poverty' and Richard Titmuss on 'Income Distribution and Social Change', both published in 1962. The four essays of Richard Titmuss are hard going. Norman MacKenzie introduced them with an article on 'The Double Standard' that resonates today: 'Professor Titmuss has reminded us that all through public life there runs a double standard – one criterion for the "fiscal welfare" of the prosperous payer of income tax and another for the "benefit welfare" of the retirement pensioner, the chronic sick and the claimant of national assistance.'

On 9 January 1962 the *New Statesman* published an obituary of the economic historian, socialist and educational, R. H. Tawney. It has Freeman's imprint:

> Tawney never believed in the inevitable triumph of socialism. Both *The Acquisitive Society* and *Inequality* are passionate assertions that man cannot be whole or dignified until he lives in a community where his private motives lead him to seek the public good. For him, humanism was an act of will, not history. He believed in the rule of decency and reason.

After six months of Freeman's editorship, Anthony Howard reported that:

> The paper has felt the new editor's impact. It has shifted from the wild frontier of the far left to a position more in line with today's socialist thought. In place of the drain of readers it suffered in the latter half of 1960, has come almost a flood of new ones.

In July 1961, the circulation rose to a record 85,000.

These changes were taking place while Kingsley Martin was editorial director, an appointment Freeman had given him for twelve months after his retirement. It was a mistake. 'The paper had to be given a new look,' said Freeman, and this was difficult while Kingsley occupied 'half the editor's chair'. For his part, Martin could not stop interfering, demanding an office and attending the Monday meeting. As a friend of his said, 'Kingsley had a genius for stepping back into the limelight.' Freeman's method of coping with this was to encourage Martin to take long trips abroad, to South America, to Cuba, to the United States, and then to cut his copy very short – without explanation – when it was sent in. On one occasion the price of this cutting down to size was heavy. Kingsley correctly predicted the 'Bay of Pigs' invasion of Cuba by Florida exiles in April 1961, and wrote a despatch to that effect from Washington, but Freeman did not use it. Kingsley expressed 'grave concern about your [Freeman's] attitude to me in the future'; Freeman rang him in Washington and told him to write 'very short or not at all'. After Kingsley ceased to be 'editorial director' relations improved but were never resolved until both had left the *New Statesman* behind them. Freeman told C. H. Rolf after that happened: 'We had conversations of apparent friendliness. It may be that on some days he felt genuinely affectionate and on other days remembered past bitterness.'[6] Martin continued to write for the *New Statesman* until he suffered a stroke in 1963.

What sort of editor was John Freeman? According to Norman MacKenzie:

> The paper was meticulously planned. We knew what was going into it, who was being commissioned to write what. John ran the paper as a totality. He was a proper executive editor. The price was that he was not very imaginative. He didn't respond to sudden change and the Monday meetings were nothing like as unpredictable, as exciting as when Kingsley had come and announced that over the weekend he had had a new idea.

Freeman, said MacKenzie, was a chief-of-staff type of editor – with a radical streak: 'He could have been a kind of radical soldier in Cromwell's army. I could well imagine him taking part in the Putney debates. He liked the army very much, its structure and its sense of a well-oiled machine. He brought some of that to the *New Statesman*.'[7]

One or two of Kingsley's old guard thought the magazine had become 'professional' and this was not said as a compliment. They preferred the wild enthusiasm of the old days to Freeman's insistence on 'getting it right' and selling more copies. Tony Howard agreed with MacKenzie; Freeman's editorship was one of administrative and editorial efficiency: 'It was a tight ship, with John Freeman every inch the captain. He set himself high standards and expected, and exacted, them from his staff.'[8]

MacKenzie and Howard agreed that Freeman gave little away about himself, that he hated intrusions into his privacy. Howard recalled when a professional photographer took photo after photo of the editor at his desk. He was trying, he said, to 'catch you in an unguarded moment'. 'Alas,' Freeman told him, 'there are not many of those.' Howard noticed Freeman's 'thin-lipped smile with just a suggestion of self-mockery in it'.

MacKenzie and Freeman would visit a pub on Thursdays near the *New Statesman* printers in High Wycombe. On one occasion MacKenzie remembered 'a man at the bar put his finger up at John and said, "You can't get away without me recognising you. I know who you are. Yes, you're the chap on the *Chan Canasta* show." John was absolutely livid and stalked out. He hated any kind of personal publicity.'

He was very self-aware and on guard. Someone said: 'John Freeman gives a brilliant impression of being John Freeman – and he will never turn in other than a good performance.'

MacKenzie found Freeman's manner 'intimidating':

He walked as stiff as a ramrod. I think he actually did wear a corset at times because of a bad back, but he always walked as if he wore a steel corset. He kept his temper under stiff control too. He was always charming, but in a sort of opportunist, febrile manner; 'My dear fellow, how good to see you' kind of thing. But he was frequently contemptuous of people and did not suffer fools. He was a man of principle in his public life and contemptuous of people who did not do what they said they would do. I remember once when Harold [Wilson, Prime Minister] had been slippery he said, 'I'll put some backbone into that little runt.'

He was reserved, impersonal, but under that he could be very kind and frequently funny.[9]

Francis Hope experienced the contrasting sides of Freeman's office manner. He joined the staff as Karl Miller's literary assistant and in his first week he had the temerity to tell the editor, who had just given him advice on a minor typographical point, that he would just check it out with the literary editor: 'I was confronted by steady, if not steely, blue eyes. "My dear Francis. Let me make one thing quite clear. What I have just said was not a suggestion. It was a decision."'[10] Later, Freeman took him out to the Garrick Club, perhaps before making him diplomatic correspondent: 'I suppose I feel more at home here than anywhere,' said Freeman to Hope. Then he qualified this as a 'shaming confession'. And so he might because, although the Garrick was and is most popular among writers and actors, it is still one of the bastions of clubland, and Freeman was a professed 'non-joiner' with strong egalitarian views. He wriggled out of this by claiming that he preferred the conversation of the Garrick Club's servants to that of its members.

The editor's prerogative was the 'London Diary', although other writers contributed to it. Freeman, writing as Flavus, did not enjoy the weekly duty. He would shut himself in his office on Tuesday afternoons and 'slog it out', as Howard put it. MacKenzie remembered that he wrote carefully and competently but he was not a diarist:

When you work in an office you soon pick out the way people write. Kingsley would take his coat off – he always wore a short-sleeved shirt

– get a pen out and write, just like that. He was a show off and readers
knew Kingsley's personality from what he put in his diary; there were
many light pieces about his gardener and his weekends in the country.
John was not willing to show anything of his personality so there was a
stiffness about his writing. It lacked the fun, the vivacity of Kingsley's.[11]

Howard went further and said Flavus was 'boring and flat' because
Freeman 'would not give anything of himself'. Considering that Freeman was writing scripts for broadcast during this time, which had
to be direct and precise, Flavus could be infuriatingly passive, devoid
of the letter 'I':

> The numbed silence in which the audience is left at the end of 'The
> Representative' gave way to a stir of excitement last Monday as the
> lights went up at the Aldwych Theatre and onto the platform filed
> four speakers to launch an open discussion. (15 November 1963)

Or:

> This journal has played in recent years an important, and honourable,
> role in championing the cause of the homeless and very poor. Par-
> ticularly in trying to protect them from the indignities, which even
> a well-meaning bureaucracy is quick to put upon them unless the
> bureaucrats themselves are made to feel someone is watching them.
> (4 September 1962)

A welcome exception was a mellow Flavus bringing in the New Year of
1962 from the village of Chilham in north Kent. Freeman had bought
a cottage here from Edward Hyams, the 'countryside correspondent'
of the *New Statesman*.

Five minutes to midnight on New Year's Eve in the church belfry;
with the new snow deep on the ground and the thermometer at
16 degrees. The bells bobbed their way through a cheerful peal, which
splendidly proclaimed the New Year to a deserted countryside. Round
the walls of the belfry sat the revellers, glowing with wine and love,
momentarily hushed by wonder. Afterwards, whisky in the White
Horse and a snow fight. The appeal of the year's turn seems to be
deep, archetypal magic.

John and Catherine were spending their Christmas holidays at Chilham
with their baby son. He told her that 1961 had been an 'annus mirabilis'
because of his editorship of the *New Statesman* and Matthew's birth: 'I
never knew it was possible to be so happy.'

Freeman admitted that 'he was not primarily a writing editor'. He
said afterwards: 'The greatest satisfaction I found was discovering
new talent who would take over from me.'[12] Reading Flavus over the
years of Freeman's editorship, I am struck by the prominence of two
themes. The first is the *New Statesman*'s traditional support of colonial
revolution, from Indian independence onwards. He wrote many para-
graphs about the iniquities of apartheid and the emerging nations of
Africa. The second is more Freeman's own: a fascination with crime,
vice, law and order. Many weeks Flavus is in a magistrate's court, a
reception centre, a prison; exposing legal anomalies, the working of
the Street Offences Act and the wrongness of capital punishment.
He even notices the new fashion in soft porn magazines of displaying girls from the Iron Curtain countries: 'Nothing I have read of the
relaxation of communism is as totally convincing as the bare bosom
of Manya Gaspararovna, "a jazz-digging dental technician from Len-
ingrad"': hardly the style of Kingsley Martin.

In October 1962 the world came as close as it ever has done to nuclear war. Once again the *New Statesman* was an important forum for national debate; once again it showed the confused thinking of the late Kingsley Martin era. The occasion, of course, was the Cuban Missile Crisis.[13]

American spy planes obtained photographs of Soviet nuclear missiles recently moved to Cuba in retaliation for similar American missiles placed in Turkey and Italy. The United States considered attacking Cuba by sea and air but decided instead to blockade the island, a military and legal 'quarantine', to prevent the delivery of more offensive weapons and as a way of demanding the removal of those already in place. When the *New Statesman* went to press on 25 October these facts were not clear and the Soviet response to the blockade was unknown. It was a fearful time. The day before Khrushchev had written a public letter to Kennedy accusing him of 'an act of aggression propelling human kind into the abyss of a world nuclear-missile war'. Russian ships attempted to run the blockade and two days later a Soviet missile crew shot down an American spy plane.

That week, editor John and Catherine Freeman were in Paris and the leader was written by Paul Johnson. Contrary to expectations, particularly to those who remembered his anti-American leaders of the late '50s, he placed the *New Statesman* dogmatically behind the United States:

> The Russians stand accused of an act of provocation unprecedented since the outset of the Cold War, carried out in haste, in secrecy and behind a curtain of falsehood... Kennedy has chosen the least of three evils [the other two being diplomacy and invasion]. Russian response suggests that Khrushchev will not allow the operation to degenerate into conflict. He will accept humiliation over Cuba.[14]

This prediction proved correct. On 28 October the Russians withdrew from Cuba taking their missiles with them. The *New Statesman* leader had been courageous. Even the *Daily Telegraph* had hedged its bets by calling for the United States to act through the United Nations.

Behind the scenes, however, there was dismay in Great Turnstile. Anti-American feelings on the nuclear issue could not be eradicated overnight. It so happened that Kingsley Martin had been booked to write the 'London Diary' for 25 October. He began, jauntily, 'I presume Kennedy's military blockade of Cuba has not yet triggered off a nuclear war?' Even more contradictory was the introduction above a doomsday essay by Bertrand Russell 'Can Nuclear War Be Prevented?': 'This article was written before the Cuban missile crisis became acute. Kennedy's recent irresponsible warmongering illustrates the truth of all that follows.' The early nickname of the *New Statesman* as 'the naggers and staggers' was proving all too accurate – as in, staggering from one view to another. Presumably it was Freeman's absence in Paris that accounted for this lack of 'editorial efficiency' as Howard called it.

Norman MacKenzie had retired from the *New Statesman* the previous week to return to academia. Now he wrote a long and anguished letter to John Freeman. He blamed Paul Johnson's leaders for taking away 'the conscience of the paper':

> Paul cannot bear those aspects of English radicalism for which the paper has traditionally stood – scepticism, uncertainty, the small battalions, even emotional responses if you like. The paper's job is not to be bedevilled by taking sides, but to have the courage to stand alone, to rise above the sterilities of Cold War polemics and to offer a view that may not be 'practicable' but is desirable as an alternative to cynicism and stupidity.[15]

What was the editor's view? Freeman had delegated the editorial to Paul Johnson, as he often did, so he stood by him. It so happened, however, that he took part in a BBC Overseas Service discussion a day or so after the *New Statesman*'s publication. In it he argued (against Peregrine Worsthorne) that President Kennedy had over-reacted by blockading Cuba. If the Russians tolerated having American missiles so near their borders in Turkey, why should not the Americans tolerate having Russian missiles so near their borders in Cuba? Was this Freeman's dispassionate view or did he simply want a robust argument? In either event, he was at variance with his own paper.

The fiftieth anniversary of the *New Statesman* was celebrated in the edition of 19 April 1963. It was the 2,605th edition in the magazine's history, as Freeman pointed out in his leader, 'The 50-Year Itch'. The magazine's most established writers wrote on their favourite themes: J. B. Priestley on 'Fifty Years of the English'; Kingsley Martin on 'The Way of Dissent'; Richard Crossman on the 'Newstatesmen'; and Malcolm Muggeridge on 'Life with the Staggers'. Robert Graves contributed 'Four Poems' and Graham Greene a short story 'Mortmain'. To this galaxy of home writers, every bit as distinguished as those in the 1930s and '40s, were added eight once, present or future heads of state who sent greetings: President Kennedy; prime ministers Macmillan, Nehru and Nyerere; Earl Attlee; Harold Wilson and others. In his leader Freeman asserted the 'fundamental purpose' of the *New Statesman*:

> It is to show our readers by scientific analysis and reason how they may apply to public affairs and great issues the standards of personal morality, good order and common sense, which civilised men take for granted in their private dealings. That individual men and women should take personal responsibility for asserting that principle at the

level of national and international affairs is the fundamental proposition on which democratic socialism must be based.

When Freeman was supposed to be at the *New Statesman* printers on
a Thursday afternoon he was sometimes somewhere else, so he left
phone numbers with the office where he could be contacted. One of
these was for the home of the Irish novelist Edna O'Brien. In 1968
she published a collection of short stories called *The Love Object* – the
title of the first story. It is about a young woman's obsession with an
older man and her breakdown, almost suicidal, when he leaves. It is
sexually explicit:

> 'Hey,' he said, jocularly, just like that. 'This can't go on, you know.'
> Then I raised my head from its sunken position between his legs and
> I looked at him through my hair, which had fallen over my face. I
> saw that he was serious. 'It just occurred to me that possibly you love
> me,' he said.

Edna O'Brien disguises the identity of 'the love object'. He is a famous
lawyer, not a broadcaster or journalist, but in many small and intimate
ways, such as the descriptions of his face and body and his obsessive
habits like folding his trousers along their creases before getting into
bed, he is clearly John Freeman. There is a scene Catherine remembers when 'Martha' (Edna) identifies 'Helen' (Catherine) at a party:

> I noticed a dress I quite admired, a mauve dress with very wide,
> crocheted sleeves. Looking up the length of the sleeves I saw its
> owner's eyes directed at me. Perhaps she was admiring my outfit.
> People with the same tastes often do. I have no idea what her face
> looked like, but later when I asked a girlfriend which was his wife

she pointed to this woman with the crocheted sleeves. The second time I saw her in profile. Those eyes into which I looked did not speak to my memory with anything special, except, perhaps, slight covetousness.[16]

'The Love Object' ends with the man saying, 'I adore you but I'm not in love with you. With my commitments I don't think I could be in love with anyone.' In real life, the commitments were that Freeman and his family were about to leave for India, news that he conveyed to Edna on a postcard. Gossip spread soon after publication among Washington high society that this very autobiographical story was about the British ambassador but no one ever said that to Catherine. As often, the wife was the last to know. Much later, she reproached him for not warning her about the book. 'I suppose,' he said, 'I thought it was too trivial to mention.'

In her memoir, *Country Girl,* Edna O'Brien adds a small postscript. She remembers an unexpected ring of her doorbell one Monday evening. Standing on the doorstep was the actor Richard Burton. He had read 'The Love Object', which she describes as a story 'in which the spiritual and carnal ramifications of a love affair were laid bare', and 'maybe because of this, he took me to be more libertine than I was'. I invited Edna O'Brien to contribute to Freeman's biography. She replied: 'I know it would be more generous, were I to say yes, but I am not the person I was then and therefore I am declining your invitation to contribute.'

In April 1963, Freeman was profiled in the *News of the World* by the popular columnist Nancy Spain in her article 'Dish of the Week':

Physically John Freeman is dishy. He has aggressively red hair, a fair skin burned brick red by the wild tropical suns of Hampstead Heath, his voice has the caressing, undeviating power of all male stars, whether of the theatre or screen, and his hands are beautiful – well-kept, and somehow ruthless.

Voice and hands, as all the girls will tell you, are very important in a Dish. The public knows very little about his private life. This is not a bad thing either. Women like a bit of mystery.

He is also gentle, very big both mentally and physically, and his probing kindliness, applied with such strength and power, is the quality that most of the public remember him for in *Face to Face*.

'I believe in trying to find out the truth,' he said, 'and then in handing it on to the public analysed in such a way that it is easily understood by them.'

Charm, charm, charm … this is the thing that counts in a Dish. And when you get allied with it a passion for the truth that almost amounts to obsession, then, indeed, you have a Dish of the Day.

Freeman wrote the page ten column in the *News of the World* at this time, alternating with Randolph Churchill, so Nancy Spain's gushing piece may partly be excused as a plug for the paper. He made two comments in the interview that are worth remembering: 'I don't see myself as a political figure; I am a journalist, pure and simple' and 'I would rather like to forget my time as a TV journalist. I found out everything I could about that medium, and now I'm much more interested in the old-fashioned, written word.' Freeman, as always, had moved on, 'closing each door firmly behind him'.

Explaining why he wrote for the mass-circulation, scandal-sheet *News of the World,* Freeman said, 'it enabled my role at the *New Statesman* to be rather more episcopal than it might otherwise have been'. The delicious use of the word 'episcopal' shows his precision with words, his pomposity, but also a self-mockery. As usual, he added that he wrote for the money. He was paid a guaranteed minimum of £2,500 per year by the *News of the World*. Added to his *New Statesman* salary and his continuing broadcasting work as a freelance, he would have been earning £12,000–15,000 a year in the mid-'60s, a good income. His page ten column consisted of 1,000 words or so of comment on the week's news. At best it was an opinion piece, popularly expressed. 'Damaging Questions the Premier Must Answer' referred to the Profumo scandal. In the article Freeman wrote that he had known, and liked, Jack Profumo since their first days at Oxford. 'Empty Seats? Don't Blame Your MP' was an argument for more pay for MPs. 'Why the Premier Won't Hand Over' referred to a failed putsch by the Tories to remove Macmillan. 'This We Risk To Guard Freedom: the press must sometimes be ready to cause offence – and damn the consequences' was an argument for press freedom in the light of the Vassall Report.[17] Freeman's reporting of the Vassall case landed him in trouble.

John Vassall was an admiralty clerk caught spying for the Russians and sentenced to eighteen years in prison in 1962. He was a known homosexual rumoured to be having an affair with his boss, Tam Galbraith, Civil Lord of the Admiralty. This gave rise to rumours that despite going through the normal security procedures, Vassall had been protected by someone in the admiralty with the result that he had got away with his treachery for many years. In November 1962 Freeman wrote an unsigned article for the *News of the World* to this effect: 'Is it possible, MPs are asking, that somewhere among senior officials lurks a Mr Big who is able to protect homosexuals from the stringent enquiry to which others are subject when they take over secret jobs?' The Radcliffe Tribunal, conducted by three judges, was set up to investigate the supposed lapses in security. Freeman was summoned to appear. Anthony Howard remembers him slipping out of the *New Statesman* office 'looking a bit sheepish'. Freeman agreed that a 'legitimate inference' of his article was that there was a person in the admiralty or security services protecting homosexuals, but his language had been, perhaps, 'over-colourful'. In any event, he said, he was only expressing the concern of MPs. The tribunal concluded that Vassall had not been helped, shielded or favoured by anybody in government. Freeman had got it wrong.

In May 1963, after Parliament had debated the Radcliffe Report, Freeman wrote 'This We Risk to Guard Freedom'. It was a provocative piece that has resonance today. He hoped that 'we've now heard the last of this squalid little traitor [Vassall]' and he admitted that the press 'didn't emerge from the trial with much credit'. Nevertheless, he argued, 'There are times when the press must cause both scandal and offence – and damn the consequences.' The alternative was a 'press condemned to have its face washed by a government nanny' – in other words, some form of state control. He implied that this had happened to the BBC already, despite *Panorama* being 'good and responsible': 'The TV channels are run by men who are virtually civil servants. Their first concern is not to cause offence, not to create scandal.' He recommended an independent chairman – perhaps Lord Radcliffe himself – for the press council. History has shown that this innovation has not worked either.[18]

At the general election in October 1964, the first Labour government for thirteen years was voted into power. Freeman, who had been sounded out for office in it (see Chapter 4), placed the *New Statesman* firmly behind new Prime Minister Harold Wilson in his efforts to modernise the party and turn it into 'the natural governing party of Britain'. In December, Wilson visited the White House for talks with President Johnson and Freeman was in the press corps. He wrote a long *New Statesman* article 'Wilson at the White House' on

11 December. It was very complimentary: 'Wilson certainly won the respect of his host – and probably his liking. The acceptance of Wilson as a responsible statesman is the first achievement of this week's talks.' Anthony Howard thought that Freeman was 'trailing his coat' for a diplomatic appointment and therefore directing his well-known charm at Wilson, although it was common knowledge in the *New Statesman* offices that the editor had little time for the Prime Minister. He once said, to approval from his fellow writers, 'If there were a word "aprincipled" as there is a word "amoral" it would describe Wilson perfectly.' It was nothing new for him to praise in public and criticise in private, but probably Howard was wrong on this occasion.

A few months later Wilson did invite Freeman to be the High Commissioner in India (the title equivalent in Commonwealth countries to ambassador elsewhere). Freeman said he had gone along to 10 Downing Street with his notebook expecting that he had been summoned for interview. Then the Prime Minister 'took the wind out of my sails completely by asking me whether I would go and lead our diplomatic mission in India. I was absolutely flabbergasted and said that with his permission I would like a little time to take it over.'[19] This has the ring of truth about it.

Why did Freeman leave the *New Statesman* after only four years as editor for a completely different assignment? – advertiser, soldier, politician, broadcaster and now diplomat? Richard Crossman said that, having 'seen through' politics and journalism, Freeman said to himself: 'Let me find a career so chilly and austere that I can never see through it or be bored by success.'[20] How wrong he was! MacKenzie agreed that Freeman was bored by the *New Statesman* and no longer enjoyed it. Driberg saw Freeman more as a good citizen answering the Prime Minister's call to undertake a task for his country. Freeman himself might well have said that although the invitation to become a diplomat came out of the blue, he had made it perfectly clear in 1961 that he saw his editorship as a consolidation of Kingsley Martin's rule and had always intended to put a younger editor in place after a few years. Paul Johnson was the man he had in mind.

In fact Johnson's appointment stalled at the last moment. Kingsley Martin, exhibiting his customary indecision, was worried at the prospect of a Roman Catholic editing a traditionally agnostic paper. It was left to Freeman to find a choice of words that augured well for his next role as diplomat: 'The board has unanimously decided to appoint Mr Paul Johnson acting editor, with full editorial responsibility.' Johnson accepted this and said he had no doubt that the position would soon be 'regularised'. It was and he remained editor until 1970.[21]

Freeman's move from Great Turnstile to Whitehall caught the attention of the press. Particularly perceptive was this profile in the *Daily Mail* by Marshall Pugh:

> Mr Freeman was in High Wycombe yesterday, bringing out his last edition of the *New Statesman* with his usual gun-drill efficiency.
>
> I don't know who his close friends are and I don't know anyone who does. But the mention of his name is guaranteed to start a debate among people who know him *slightly*.
>
> Some say he is cold, yet he has a very warm manner, and I know of his kindness. It was Freeman who visited a dying colleague in hospital when the jollier lads couldn't face it. He is a courteous man who can be suddenly cruel. He is a shy man who can stand around in chilling silence or suddenly expand on any subject, except John Freeman. He is a highly disciplined man who can suddenly explode. He is diffident, with enormous reserves of self-confidence.
>
> I have drunk with him for many an hour and I am not certain I know the man at all.[22]

Chapter 9

Diplomat – High Commissioner to India

THE FREEMANS SPENT the eight days over Christmas and the New Year deciding whether to accept the India posting. Civil servants in the Commonwealth Relations Office (CRO), probably regarding him as a typical journalist in their eyes – that is, superficial and untrustworthy – sent Freeman a few files. Then he asked for more. Then he asked for a full background briefing to extend over Christmas. Perhaps it was the army that had drummed into him the necessity of 'prior preparation' and he followed that order ever after. Freeman was not a career diplomat, of course, but his previous careers had all trained him for the job in hand. He was well organised, could assimilate a brief quickly and speak to it, was a good listener and judge of character and, above all, he was a precise and fluent communicator. Over the next seven years it was to be the writing of despatches that would give him most pleasure. 'I don't think I would have been too ashamed', he said later in his self-deprecating way, 'to send a newspaper some of my despatches from India.'[1]

The round of press interviews he gave in January 1965 showed that Freeman the role player was perfectly capable of turning from journalist to diplomat overnight. He drew the curtain on one interview with the courteous put down: 'Any such opinions that I do form are then the property of Her Majesty's government [HMG].'[2] Wilson wanted an independent High Commissioner who would work to him more directly than a career diplomat who had progressed through the Foreign Office. He knew since his school days that Freeman had been a believer in Indian independence and his previous job as editor of the *New Statesman* would serve him well in India because of the reputation of Kingsley Martin as an ardent anti-imperialist. All in all, Freeman was one of Wilson's astute appointments.

The press approved of Freeman: 'Tall, red-haired, powerfully built, he radiates from behind a manner of winning charm an aura of drive and effortless executive ability'[3] was one press description. Another was more physically descriptive: 'Freeman's face has the ruddiness of a yeoman farmer. His close-cut hair is pale ginger. He stands 6 ft 2 – taller than you imagine.'[4] It was his connection with India's nationalist politicians that Freeman was most keen to talk about. On 11 January he was interviewed on the BBC Home Service *Ten O'Clock News*:

When I was at university in the middle of the '30s I became acquainted with Krishna Menon who was a rather prickly political agitator for Indian independence living in London. I absorbed all his thinking.

I am clear in my own mind that one of the tasks I must now address
is to make certain that we in Britain understand the mood and aspi-
rations of the younger generation of Indian politicians and also the
writers and artists.[5]

This would become the theme of the High Commissioner's parties
at the residence.

On 31 January Freeman gave a speech at India House on the sev-
enteenth anniversary of the assassination of Mahatma Gandhi. He
recalled their meeting in 1932 at Westminster School: 'How many
converts to the cause of Indian independence the Mahatma made
that evening I'll never know. But I remember the sense of surprise,
awe and – perhaps "melting" is the word – which his visit evoked.' He
concluded: 'I talked to him [Gandhi] for a few minutes in private as
he left and from that day on the cause of Indian independence concerned me.'[6] What a pompous assertion! Freeman may have been a
precocious schoolboy but he was no more than seventeen at the time!

Soon after, the High Commissioner designate took the sea route for
India on the P & O liner *Chusan*, arriving in Bombay on 26 March.
It so happened that another new member of the High Commission
arrived the same way and nearly at the same time. He was John Rimington, newly appointed First Secretary of Economic Affairs, travelling
with his young wife Stella, who would eventually become the first
female director-general of MI5. In fact she was recruited into the spy
world while in Delhi. In *Open Secret* she describes arriving at the very
end of the Raj. The British Empire in India had formally ended in
1947 but the Raj, as it became known after Indian independence, had
enjoyed an 'Indian summer' through the 1950s, extending though
diminishing until the death of Prime Minister Nehru in 1964. An
'Indian summer' stands for the unexpected warmth after the season

has ended. Applied to the British Raj, it means the continuing privileged, un-'Indianised' lifestyle of the remaining 18,000 or so UK
citizens resident in India in 1965. This became one of Freeman's main
concerns as High Commissioner. Stella Rimington observed them
on her ship the RMS *Caledonia*:

> Underneath an awning at the stern a cast of traditional characters
> assembled at noon each day to drink their chota pegs [measures of
> whisky or gin]. There were planters in knee-length khaki shorts, going
> back from leave to their lonely lives in the hills round Darjeeling or
> Assam, businessmen and engineers bound for Bombay, Calcutta, Delhi
> and upcountry too. There were missionaries, lots of them, travelling on
> the bottom decks of the boat but joining us in the evenings to watch
> films under the stars or make up bridge fours, playing interminably in
> a smoky lounge. At Port Said the magic man, the goolie-goolie man,
> boarded the ship and travelled with us through the Suez Canal, with
> white chickens up his sleeves, making them and various watches or
> rings disappear and reappear, just as he had done for forty years. But
> in 1969, when we returned from India, the Suez Canal was closed,
> the British businessmen and tea planters were leaving forever and
> India had shifted the whole direction of her diplomacy and indus-
> trial development.[7]

This was on Freeman's watch: it would be a traumatic four years.

After the *Chusan* docked at the Gateway of India on the Bombay
waterfront, Freeman flew to Delhi. The Rimingtons, fresh off the
Caledonia, travelled by train:

> We were met by a superior-seeming person from the Deputy High
> Commissioner's office, whose job was to put us safely on the train

for the 24-hour journey to Delhi. I was taken aback by what seemed to me the immense luxury of his style of life – servants in cockaded hats and long sashes offering tea and whiskies in cut tumblers, in surroundings of opulent furnishings and oriental rugs. We were further amazed on being presented with a hamper of provisions for the train journey. There was everything in there, whole chickens, pudding in a tin, and the inevitable bottle of whisky. We were told on no account to touch a morsel of food or drink offered us on the train; that way lay certain death.[8]

The new High Commissioner arrived in his Rolls-Royce at his official residence, known as '2 KG' standing for 2 King George Avenue. It is impressive: a two-storey whitewashed mansion, designed by an Indian architect after the style of Lutyens, with a pillared veranda giving onto three and a half acres of lawns and shrubs – prime diplomatic real estate. The Union flag announces the High Commissioner's presence. Obsessively tidy since his army days, Freeman found the High Commission itself, a '50s Indian design in Chanakyapuri, to be run down and shabby. He sent for a 'competent shit' to sort things out so the Commonwealth Office gave him Counsellor John Waterfield. At the residence, Freeman waited for Catherine and the two boys, Matthew aged three and Tom aged eighteen months, to arrive by air. They did so in the company of former BBC boss Leonard Miall, who was on his way to advise the Indian government on setting up a television service.

Soon after Freeman arrived, the Minister for Overseas Development asked the High Commissioner for the transfer to her department of a member of his staff. Legend has it that, as she was Barbara Castle and he was John Freeman, the exchange went something like: 'John, dear, could you possibly spare young Snooks, love Babs'; to which the reply was along the lines of, 'The High Commissioner is considering your request and you will be notified as soon as a decision has been reached.' No doubt this story was not strictly true but the fact that the rumour circulated round the High Commission shows that the staff were getting to know their boss. Another door had closed.

Stella Rimington found herself surrounded by the last vestiges of the Raj:

> In New Delhi, statues of British governor-generals still stood on their plinths at the intersection of the major roads, which were still called by British names. The largest and grandest colonial-style bungalows were lived in by British and American diplomats and most of the bathrooms contained lavatories and wash basins by Shanks and Thomas Crapper, their brass pipes polished to a brilliant shine. The dignified bearers in their splendid turbans and smartly pressed uniforms knew how to make a pink gin and how to cook jam roly-poly and bread and butter pudding. Any attempt to modernise the menus was met with firm resistance.

Once again, however, she notes that the echoes of empire really were dying to a whisper:

> But India was changing fast and by the time we left in 1969, that era with its recall of the Raj had ended. The British were out of favour. The statues were being pulled down and replaced by local heroes and the roads were being renamed [2 KG is now 2 Rajaji Marg]. Mingled with a certain sadness at seeing the statue of King George V being pulled from beneath his canopy on Rajpath, there was a certain understanding among the British community of the justice of these proceedings. The British had simply stayed too long.[9]

Two specific events hastened the exodus. On 6 June 1966, a date referred to by the British in India in apocalyptic terms, the rupee was devalued against the pound by one third, thus slashing the income British businessmen could send back to the UK. The devaluation, coupled with heavy taxation and the need to obtain Indian government approval for high salaries, meant that it became virtually impossible for an 'expat' to earn more than £2,750 per year in India. The second event was the looming 1969 India Companies Act that would abolish the system of management agencies. These mostly British conglomerates ran portfolios of Indian companies in Calcutta, the business centre of British India, and enabled young men out from public schools to earn a good income. By the time Freeman left, only a rump of 1,400 expats remained. Thus, wrote Geoffrey Moorhouse in *Calcutta*, 'The British are reduced to roughly the same number of people as were in Calcutta a few years before the Black Hole happened.'[10]

This lugubrious comparison would not have been wasted on the High Commissioner, nor that it happened during the regime of Indira Gandhi. Freeman's difficult relationship with the Indian Prime Minister would dominate diplomatic relations for the second half of his posting. Already, however, soon after his arrival, he was reminded that the legacy of the British Raj could be an embarrassment; that a nostalgia for the past had to be replaced by a hard-headed view towards a commercial future. Lord Mountbatten came to stay. In May 1965, Mountbatten was Britain's chief of the defence staff, but he had been the last viceroy of British India and the first governor general of the newly independent India. Mountbatten had supported Freeman's appointment as High Commissioner, but now he embarrassed him with his Raj attitude, culminating in an incident at the residency when he suggested showing guests round his 'old house up the road'. He was referring to the Viceregal Lodge, now the state home of the Indian President, the *Rasthrapati Bhavan.* This patronising insensitivity, Freeman noticed, played on the 'neurosis' of the Indian government and press, ever ready to feel slighted when none was intended. Catherine Freeman noticed this too: 'He was an embarrassment. He wanted his old troops lined up outside his old house. I thought our Indian hosts were very decent.'[11] Mountbatten himself noticed a change in atmosphere. At a meeting with Indian military commanders, 'He sensed a feeling of restraint on the Indian side and it was clear to him that relations were very different from the last time he had visited India.'[12] Always keen to receive honours of one kind or another, he was dismayed that plans to offer him the honorary colonelcy of an Indian Army regiment were vetoed.

A year later Freeman was more explicit about the legacy of the Raj. The CRO asked him to advise on a possible visit from Jennie Lee, a left-wing government minister and widow of Aneurin Bevan; also an old friend of Mrs Gandhi. Harold Wilson's proposal was that she would 'establish a cordial atmosphere for his own visit' later in the year. Freeman replied:

> A most friendly welcome awaits those who had sympathised with India during the final stages of the struggle for independence. At the same time we must be under no illusion that these slightly nostalgic associations with the past play no real part in shaping present-day Indian attitudes towards contemporary events. In a rather different context we have experienced something of this in the diminishing returns yielded by Lord Mountbatten's recent visits.
>
> My own feeling is that the Prime Minister would be well advised to relate his visit to the future pattern of Indo–British relations. Events of the last eight months [the British attitude to the Indo–Pakistan War,

see later] have made a clean break with the sort of associations that India wistfully held for the Labour Party of the '30s and '40s. We can no longer depend on warm feelings from the past and we must look forward to a pragmatic relationship of mutual benefit in the future.[13]

Indians felt they were entering a new era too. With the death of 'Panditji' Nehru after seventeen years of shaping Indian independence, the sophisticated Indians of New Delhi were hoping for the end of the *maa-baap sarkar,* that is the paternalistic 'mother and father state' of the Congress Party that had smothered India politically and socially since 1947. There was a growing sense of liberation. This was reflected in the parties the Freemans gave at the residency. The writer Prem Shankar Jha told me that they were like going into 'a room full of fresh air'[14] and the novelist Khushwant Singh agreed. Both gave the credit to Catherine. 'I found Freeman cold and distant,' Khushwant Singh wrote, 'despite his socialist pretensions he behaved like a pukka sahib',[15] meaning in this context an aloof administrator of the Raj.

One of their visitors was Tom Driberg. He agreed that John Freeman was spoken of with respect rather than affection, since 'he retained his cool, withdrawn (though courteous) manner'. Catherine, on the other hand, was the subject of affection because she was most definitely not a patronising, affected, memsahib:

Catherine Freeman is the most un-memmish of women. With her dark hair, lovely oval face, creamy-pale skin, and lustrous eyes, she might almost be Indian herself: though her looks are, in fact, Irish. She has in conversation an Irish, slightly fey, highly humorous *abandon*. Some Indians paid her the highest compliment they could: they compared her with Edwina Mountbatten, wife of the last viceroy, who had the same gift for warm, unforced, un-self-conscious friendship; and, of course, real equality in companionship included the right to contradict – even to tease, which she does enchantingly – without causing offence.[16]

So the Freemans' entertaining had none of the stiffness of the Raj. They attracted a diverse assortment of cultivated guests without the Raj protocol and strict hierarchy. Catherine's own production skills came into play when she was planning a party for top civil servants out from London:

> We organised a moonlit, midnight picnic among the ancient graves
> of Old Delhi. I got a flute player to sit on top of one of the marble
> tombs and he tootled away. We took silver candelabra, which lit up
> the ruins. It was such a beautiful evening, never to be forgotten.[17]

Catherine loved the Indian experience and sought it out. John stayed more in the High Commission, hearing about it from her. 'He sends me out into the market place and tells me to report back to him,'[18] she said at the time. During the Bihar drought of 1967, he allowed Catherine to travel by Jeep through the stricken villages in order to write a report for the Foreign Office. Afterwards she raised funds to build wells in remote parts of the country to she staged the premier of the film *Shakespeare Wallah* as a glamorous fund-raising event. The writer Ruth Prawer Jhabvala was there with the director James Ivory and the producer Ismail Merchant. All became good friends. The actors Madhur Jaffrey and Marlon Brando came too.

'Camelot in Delhi' Driberg called the socialising at the residency, referencing Kennedy's Washington – but it was often Camelot without the King. 'Of course, John was there,' Catherine says:

He always did his duty, but he was very proud of his ability to shake hands and then disappear. If we were in a large reception tent, a *shama-yana*, he would greet his host and then slip out discreetly through the flap at the back. He had the whole routine down to three minutes.

When he did stay he would seek out the company of young journalists. The First Secretary at the High Commission was Robin, now Lord, Renwick:

> John was not the glad-handing type of ambassador. He was a reserved intellectual who enjoyed a quiet discussion over dinner with people he respected. He didn't especially enjoy 150 people swarming around his garden. He would give a reception if he had to – I don't think he really enjoyed it – but in terms of intellectual understanding of all the issues going on in the country he was absolutely first class.[19]

The young Rimingtons found themselves stuck in the High Commission compound where they were welcomed by the last British chief justice of the Punjab and the British chief administrator of Madras, both of whom had moved to the Indian civil service after independence and were still in post. It was 'the Anglo-Indian community, some still clinging to their topis',[20] she said metaphorically. On one occasion the Rimingtons had the Freemans to dinner and Stella, lectured in advance about the protocol of such visits, became anxious when a fat Indian woman sat on the right-hand end of the settee, the place formally reserved for the High Commissioner.

When Stella Rimington observed that the British were 'out of favour', a point picked up by Lord Mountbatten, she was not referring to the last fluttering of the Raj, embarrassing though that might be to hard-headed realists. The cause was the Indo–Pakistan War (the 'three-week war', as Freeman called it), which broke out in August 1965. This major conflict, leading to one of the biggest tank battles since the Second World War and, Freeman reported, 'causing in India more excitement than any other news since 1947',[21] quickly escalated to draw in the super powers. On the diplomatic front Freeman was heavily involved. On behalf of the UK, he found himself incurring the fury of the Indian government and at the same time he was 'driven to despair' by the attitude of the British government, in particular by Prime Minister Harold Wilson. It was a baptism of fire no diplomat would relish, least of all one so new to diplomacy.

Since 1949 a jittery ceasefire had existed between the two powers on the Indian subcontinent partitioned in 1947, India and Pakistan. The bone of contention was the beautiful Vale of Kashmir, which both countries claimed as their own – the Pakistanis because most Kashmiris were Muslim and the Indians because the ruler, the Hindu Maharaja of Kashmir, Hari Singh, had acceded his state to India. Since then Indian and Pakistan armies had been camped either side of a cease-fire line monitored by the United Nations. The Indian government refused to hold the agreed plebiscite until the Pakistan Army, which had originally begun hostilities in 1947, withdrew.

In order to test Indian resolve for border conflict, in April 1965 the 6th Brigade of the Pakistan Army launched Operation Desert Hawk several hundred miles to the south in the Rann of Kutch. This desolate region of salt marshes is partly in the Indian state of Gujarat with the Arabian Sea to the west, and partly in the Pakistani province of Sind to the north. One visitor described it as 'a reeking reach of black tidal mudflats bounded with sand dunes and etched by dead streams of salt and scum'; uninhabited save by a few camel herdsmen. 'It seemed ridiculous', wrote Freeman to the CRO, 'that two countries should quarrel so fiercely over a barren tract of land.'[22] The

Pakistan intention, however, was not ridiculous. It was to conquer a tract of land, bloody the nose of the Indian Army, wait for the UK to arbitrate between two Commonwealth countries and then agree to peace terms that would not include surrendering the land taken. This is what eventually happened at the end of June, but not before the two states threatened a general war against each other that could have led, wrote Freeman, 'to the double shock of widespread military conflict and communal massacre on a vast scale'.[23] Freeman and his opposite number in Karachi, Morrice James, acquitted themselves well in the successful negotiations, much to the pleasure of Harold Wilson, who received a note of congratulation from Lyndon Johnson, President of the United States, and the thanks of Lal Bahadur Shastri, the new Prime Minister of India. The British arbitration proved that 'credit was still good in the subcontinent', wrote Freeman but he added, ominously: 'We have remedied a symptom but the basic *malaise* still exists.'[24]

On the night of 5–6 August, Pakistan launched Operation Gibraltar. Over 1,000 Pakistani insurgents in civilian clothes crossed the 500-mile-long ceasefire line that had separated Indian and Pakistani forces in the Kashmir since the end of the first war in July 1949. This was the start of the second Indo–Pakistan War. Pakistan was clearly the aggressor and the paper trail shows that Freeman pointed this out to the CRO from the beginning. Yet in a most unfortunate statement that he later tried to excuse, Prime Minister Wilson blamed India, thus causing lasting resentment between the two countries. Wilson's gaffe, which he made worse with subsequent attempts to wriggle out of responsibility, cannot have improved Freeman's opinion of him, to say the least.

This is the story: the aim of the Pakistani insurgents in disguise was first to foment disorder leading to a popular uprising against Indian rule. Then regular Pakistani forces would enter the Kashmir on the pretext of restoring law and order. This would lead, President Ayub Khan hoped, to the external powers, led by Britain and the United States, stepping in and brokering a Kashmir settlement – to Pakistan's advantage. On 8 August, the Indian Minister of External Affairs, C. S. Jha, briefed the British High Commissioner about the Pakistan insurgency. Lest there be any doubt, the Pakistan newspaper *Dawn* carried the headline the next day: 'Revolutionary Council Held in Kashmir: Liberation War to be Waged'. Freeman reported all this to the CRO in his fortnightly summary of 17–30 August: 'The Indians are satisfied that they have ample evidence that Pakistan planned and organised a massive infiltration into Kashmir under the guise of a liberation movement.' He further reported on 25 August that the UN military observer, General Nimmo, was 'amazed and aghast' at the Pakistan infiltration and had warned General Chaudhuri, the Indian commander-in-chief, that there was more of it coming: 'suspicions of reserves, activity etc. behind the ceasefire line'.[25] On 28 August the Indian Army went on the offensive, crossed the ceasefire line in Kashmir and engaged enemy forces.

The attempt to raise a revolution in the Kashmir having failed, on 1 September Pakistan significantly escalated the conflict with Operation Grand Slam, an armoured thrust across not only the ceasefire line but also the international border dividing the two states in the Chamb area to the south of Kashmir. This endangered the Indian town of Jammu, sandwiched between the Vale of Kashmir and the Daman Koh Plains to the south. Jammu was of huge strategic importance to India because through it ran the only road linking India with Kashmir and beyond that to Ladakh, to the north of which Indian troops were facing the Chinese, who had successfully wrested land from India in 1962. The Pakistan Foreign Minister

Bhutto declared: 'We have taken a solemn pledge to [end India's] barbaric policy of eliminating the Muslim majority in Kashmir by Hitlerite extermination.'[26] On 2 September an Indian air strike on Chamb failed to dislodge Pakistani forces and the ensuing tank battle, considered the largest since the Second World War, was similarly unsuccessful. On 3 September the UN and the British government called for a ceasefire.

Three days later the Indian I and XI corps retaliated by a surprise lateral move. The army crossed the Indo–Pakistan border in the Punjab and headed for Lahore, Pakistan's cultural capital. This was greeted in Delhi by wild scenes of enthusiasm, reminding someone at the High Commission of the public reaction in Europe to the outbreak of war in 1914. Vigilantes roamed the capital rounding up suspected Pakistani agents, causing another High Commission official to warn 'to be a Muslim is now to be in some degree of danger'.[27] In the UK, Wilson told journalists that: 'The war between India and Pakistan is one of the gravest international developments since the end of the war against Japan.'[28] He responded by another call for a ceasefire 'in the most urgent terms'.

It was then, on 6 September, that the British Prime Minister deeply offended India, with enduring consequences. No. 10 Downing Street issued a public statement expressing Wilson's deep concern at 'the increasingly serious fighting, especially at the news that Indian forces have today attacked Pakistan territory across the international frontier in the Punjab'. The Indian offensive, the press statement went on, was 'a distressing response to the resolution adopted by the security council calling for a ceasefire'.[29] Wilson then asked Shastri to ensure that British weapons sent to India for use against the Chinese were not used against Pakistan.

Wilson's accusation caused a furious, self-righteous response. Shastri wrote to Wilson that the culprit was Pakistan, whose regular forces 'had launched a massive attack across the international boundary between the Indian state of Jammu and Kashmir and the West Punjab in Pakistan'.[30] The Indian High Commissioner in London said that Wilson's press statement would be received with anger not only in the Indian Parliament but throughout the world. 'Why was India pilloried without a mention of Pakistan's similar violations?'[31]

Wilson was chastened. He called off any further attempts to broker a ceasefire, leaving it to the United Nations.

Where did this leave High Commissioner Freeman? He was frustrated and embarrassed. He had reported the true sequence of events punctually. He had warned Wilson on 6 September against calling for a ceasefire: 'I feel obliged to express my view that any appeal to India to cease fire, which is made by our Prime Minister would be at this stage useless and might even serve to weaken any influence we might be able to start later.'[32] He now wrote that Wilson's call for military equipment to be withheld had caused 'particular resentment'. 'Britain's popularity in India,' he wrote to the CRO on 13 September, 'has taken a severe knock as a result of our open criticism of India's escalation of the conflict.' Wilson had jumped in 'with indecent haste' and scotched the Indian view that a Labour government was much less likely than its Conservative predecessor to display a pro-Pakistan bias. At the same time he thought that India was 'largely to blame' for the reaction in Britain because its publicity machine was inert and Pakistan's much superior. He gave as an example of this Wilson's criticism made to the Indian High Commissioner on 7 September of 'India's bombing of "open cities" including Karachi and Rawalpindi'. This was false information that had certainly not come from Freeman, but nor had it been refuted by the Indian government.[33]

He would soon find that Wilson laying the blame on India in

September 1965 'hung round my neck like an albatross'.[34] The following December the Labour MP Francis Noel-Baker returned from Delhi and reported to Wilson that he had received 'constant reproaches' about Britain's 'pro-Pakistan' attitude over the war. Wilson replied, partly repeating Freeman in fact, that it was attributable to the ineptness of India's public relations machinery and that the Indians had 'undoubtedly' exaggerated his statement, 'reading more into it than was intended'.[35]

The British press published this exchange and the Indian press was further outraged. 'Mr Wilson opens old wounds in Delhi controversy' began the Delhi correspondent of *The Times.* Freeman despaired. He wrote to the CRO: 'I must emphasise extreme embarrassment. This is by far the most serious embarrassment of the several we have had recently in the final stage of this tiresome controversy. It has gravely damaged our Prime Minister's prestige in India and undone careful work.'[36]

More would follow. In 1971 the *Sunday Times* serialised Wilson's memoir about his years in office, *The Labour Government 1964–1970: A Personal Record.* In it he admitted his mistake for the 6 September press statement but blamed Whitehall officials: 'I had been taken for a ride by a pro Pakistani faction in the CRO.'[37] This was refuted by the permanent under-secretary at the CRO, Joe Garner, the recipient of many memos from Freeman, who wrote to Wilson demanding that the record should be put straight:

> It is clear that the initiative for an early statement [on 6 September] came from No. 10 and that the CRO was under pressure from your office. A statement was drafted in the CRO and submitted to you with the specific warning that, if issued in this form, it would be likely to have serious repercussions on our relations with India.[38]

Significantly, the Cabinet Secretary, Sir Burke Trend, supported Garner: 'You were absolutely right to say what you did.'[39] The Wilson fib
was an unedifying tailpiece to the story. It probably came as no surprise to Freeman who had invented the word 'aprincipled' to describe
his old colleague.

Back to the war…

September 1965: both the United States and the United Kingdom
suspended arms supplies, leaving Pakistan in particular very short of
weapons power. China trumpeted its support of Pakistan and gave
India an ultimatum to withdraw its outposts on the Chinese border.
The Soviet Union, keeping the Great Power balance, spoke out against
Chinese bellicosity and supported the USA and UN in trying to bring
about a ceasefire. With Indian troops having the better of battlefield
exchanges and having frustrated Pakistan's invasion of Kashmir, Prime
Minister Shastri agreed to a UN ceasefire on 22 September. Ayub
Khan had no option but to agree. The Chinese, having made 'maximum noise with minimum risk' confirmed that their border dispute
with India was at an end. In January 1966 the Soviet Union brokered
a peace deal in Tashkent. Both India and Pakistan agreed to withdraw
their armed forces to positions held before the start of the war. This
was a diplomatic triumph for Russia and Britain was nowhere. John
Freeman gloomily made the best of a bad job. He told his opposite
number in Karachi, Morrice James, that the UK had little option but
to 'lie low for the time being and leave it to the Russians to make the
running, in the hope of gradually recovering our influence and making a comeback later'.[40]

Later, Freeman put the furore in context. In his valedictory despatch in 1968 (that is the final despatch by an ambassador in which
he is encouraged to air his views), he wrote that British–Indian relations were in a state of 'post-colonial tension'.[41] If the British displayed

outdated 'nostalgia' then the Indians showed 'neurosis' in being hyper-sensitive and 'suspicious'. He had told Indira Gandhi in May 1967 that the Indian press and politicians were constantly on the watch for any slighting remark by Britain and then 'replied in immoderate and occasionally abusive language'.[42] Indian political dialectic was more polemical than in Britain but the British public did not understand this.

While lying low, Freeman wrote a thirteen-page essay for the CRO entitled 'The Three-Week War'. It was of seminal importance. He challenged the traditional role that Britain played, as former colonial power and convenor of the Commonwealth, first to intervene in dis-putes and second to try to keep a balance between both sides. This role, said Freeman, was now outmoded. A much more pragmatic role was necessary:

> We are obliged to admit that India will not in any circumstances consent to a settlement in Kashmir that does not leave her in overall control of the Vale as well as Jammu and Ladakh. Moreover, Paki-stan cannot mount sufficient military force to make India change her view. There is nothing we or anybody else can do about it. Essen-tially we have reached the stage where India and Pakistan must settle their own problems. And, since Pakistan has opted for a military solution and demonstrably failed, the settlement is bound to be an Indian one, reflecting the natural realities of military power, popula-tion and resources in the sub-continent. If we continue to resist we shall only fail and our breach with India will become final; and then Soviet influence will become the dominant factor in Indian politics.[43]

This was a most significant statement and approved of by the profes-sionals in his diplomatic team. Sir Peter Hall was Second Secretary in New Delhi at the time:

The remarkable thing about John Freeman was that he recognised a basic truth, and got HMG to understand it, which was that although we had colossal ties with India it was literally a foreign country. This may seem blindingly obvious now but then it was not long after independence.

Whenever London, with a sort of hankering for the great role, put itself in the middle between Pakistan and India it was extremely uncomfortable and ineffective. I think Freeman made London understand that it was no good viewing India even in post-colonial terms. One had to view India with completely different eyes, which he did.[44]

Lord Renwick told me much the same:

The CRO still felt historical urges of responsibility to try to solve the Kashmir dispute. As John Freeman pointed out, that just got us into trouble with both sides. His message to London was, stop trying to solve the Kashmir dispute; they will either solve it one day, or they won't. He was fundamentally right that we needed to recalibrate our efforts and concentrate on what we could do properly.[45]

Fifty years later India and Pakistan are still in dispute over Kashmir. India administers 43 per cent of the whole area of Jammu and Kashmir with a strong military presence; Pakistan controls 37 per cent and in between are Kashmiri insurgent groups who either want accession to Pakistan or complete independence.

In July 1966, Lucy Catherine Mekhala Freeman was born in London and taken to Delhi six months later. She and her two brothers were now looked after at the residency by Cynthia Gomes, an Anglo-Indian nursery nurse whom the Freemans recruited when Lucy was on the way:

I was never treated as a nanny, no. Everywhere they went I would eat at the same table. Except when they had head government people, business people and then they had evening dinners set and I would be up with the children in the nursery. Mr Freeman was a very good father, in my opinion. He made the time. He used to come from his work in the evenings and say, 'Cynthia, shall I take over?' He would bath them, play with them, put on the boys' pyjamas and Lucy's nightie. Then he would read them a story and say goodnight. Then he would go and dress for the evening. Wherever his children were concerned, they came first, I would say.

Cynthia was familiar with the large domestic staff, nineteen in all:

There was the head butler (the *khitmatgar*) called Gopal; then we had four other bearers who did duties downstairs and upstairs, tidying up the rooms, making up the beds, this and that. Then I had a nursery bearer called Kachero who made up the children's beds and mine, and maids (*ayahs*) to help with the children. That's the life I had. In the kitchen were two cooks (*khansalah*) and a kitchen staff. Outside there were gardeners (*mali*) watchmen (*chowkidar*) drivers and so on.[46]

It was not a life of Catherine's choosing, but she adapted to it cheerfully enough:

Actually, you get used to it after about twenty-four hours because there is a hierarchy among the staff and an established routine, which works very well, and you would be foolish to interfere with it. It's not the kind of life one would have chosen for the children either. There's the danger they could have got spoilt. When Matthew was given a go-kart for his fifth birthday, which could not fit into my car, he said,

'Can't the Rolls-Royce bring it behind us?' I drew a deep breath and said, 'Now, look here...'[47]

Hours after signing the Tashkent Declaration, on 11 January 1966 Lal Bahadur Shastri suddenly died. He was sixty-two and had been in office only eighteen months. His successor was Jawaharlal Nehru's 48-year-old daughter Indira Gandhi. She was already a widow with two sons, one of whom would eventually succeed her as Prime Minister. From then on and for the rest of his period as High Commissioner, Freeman's diplomatic work was dominated by his relationship with Mrs Gandhi. He found this relationship difficult. It led him to write a memorable despatch in May the following year. It was not diplomatic but it showed a frustrated man venting his feelings with an almost surgical skill with words:

> Mrs Gandhi does not seek to be disobliging to, e.g. western ambassadors, but she knows she cannot have with such officials the sort of hair-down [uninhibited] and often recklessly self-indulgent exchanges she needs and can enjoy with sympathetic non-official visitors. This is perhaps another way of saying that it is the element of decision and responsibility in politics which she finds so crippling. When this is introduced she freezes up in an iceberg of suspicion, insecurity and indecision. Her relationship with official representatives – at least from the western countries – shows reticence and gaucheness.
>
> The point can be summed up like this: it is not too difficult for the private citizen to get through to her on an 'irresponsible' network. It is not too difficult for intimate colleagues with leftist views to steer her prejudices into attitudes or statements damaging to western interests. Her femininity does, of course, play a considerable role in all this – both in her approach to subjects and in other people's

approach to her. But simple sex is not all. Before one really can get through to her, one has not only, as it were, to squeeze her hand, but to dress up in her political clothes. Since her most deep-seated and darkling neuroses concern Britain, this is not always a course which can be commended to HM High Commissioner.[48]

As it happens, Catherine Freeman recalls that particular May confrontation, but her experience of Mrs Gandhi was somewhat different:

> I always found her very friendly and human. She lived at the end of our road and I remember John going off to see her on a rather serious and difficult political matter. He came back very frustrated: 'God, that bloody woman! She absolutely stonewalled me, completely, on everything I had to say. I was there for at least an hour with no result, and then, as I was taking my leave, she changed her tone completely and asked me most solicitously how you were finding the heat with the new baby. That made him very cross, but I rather appreciated her woman-to-woman concern.[49]

The May 1967 meeting did find the Prime Minister and the High Commissioner in agreement on one point. Freeman wrote:

> Mrs Gandhi said: 'You [the British government] seem to us to be always trying to achieve some sort of balance of power in Asia and this leads you to interfere in matters we think don't concern you.' She was referring to Pakistan and felt that we were trying to manipulate Pakistan against India.[50]

Freeman did not say that he had recently written a despatch making much the same point. He did, however, make this one of his main conclusions in his valedictory despatch written a year later. Speaking of 'Indo–Pakistan frictions' he wrote: 'We have the capacity to do calamitous damage to our interests in India by ineffectual intervention or conspicuous involvement.' Nothing could be plainer than that.[51]

The High Commissioner's Second Secretary, Sir Peter Hall, thinks that Freeman's despatches were one reason why the former journalist was chosen for the post. There was, he said, an art form in Foreign Office telegrams; lengthy, self-serving and downplaying difficulties. Freeman's despatches were the reverse. He remembered one that followed an unproductive meeting with Indira Gandhi when, on instructions, he argued against nuclear development. 'He wrote afterwards: "I saw Mrs Gandhi this afternoon and spoke in accordance with instructions. Her manner was frosty and unhelpful throughout and I am convinced my representations will have no effect on Indian policy. Freeman." Perfect, but how many people do it?'[52]

Freeman returned to London for his annual review shortly afterwards. On the previous occasion, in 1966, Wilson had displayed his political antennae, as Freeman remembered: 'As I went into No. 10 Wilson shook me dramatically by the hand and put an arm around my shoulders, murmuring as he did so "This will be good for forty seconds on TV tonight. Ted Heath is speaking in Gravesend and I don't have an engagement."'[53] On this occasion, Wilson had a substantial offer to make. He asked Freeman if he was interested in another posting. Freeman had obviously seen this coming because he said he would be interested in only two: the Soviet Union or the United States. They agreed that he would end his term as High Commissioner a year later. Wilson then offered Freeman the customary knighthood and Freeman declined, as ever impervious to flattery or status. He did, however, accept the title of Privy Counsellor with a 'Rt Hon.' before his name and 'PC' afterwards. Presumably he did so because the Privy Council does have an advisory role to the sovereign that is a little more than just honorary.

Back in New Delhi he became embroiled in an incident that, like many involving MI5, had its farcical element. The British complained to the Indian government about the Soviet influence on Indira Gandhi, exercised through the Indian Foreign Ministry, so the High Commission must have been just a little smug when in December a Russian defector, Aziz Oulougzade, sought asylum in the American embassy and applied for admission to the United Kingdom. Freeman allowed it, despite the objections of the Indian Foreign Ministry. The Soviet ambassador demanded a protest interview. Freeman asked Robin Renwick to sit in: 'The Russian ambassador was full of bluster: "This man is misguided. He is ruining his life. All is forgiven". That sort of thing. Freeman was impassive. He did not give one inch. He just sat there in silence. He was a very tough guy.'[54]

With the defector still camped in the American embassy after four days and all the potential publicity of a Cold War incident in the offing, proceedings needed to be communicated to the UK in secret, that is by cypher telegram. Stella Rimington was now working 'behind the baize door' in the High Commission where MI5 had its office, but she had not been taught how to use the cypher machine. The girl whose job it was could not be contacted because she was in bed with her Sikh boyfriend. 'I was aware of earnest and angry consultations in huddled groups outside on the lawn during a High Commission cocktail party,'[55] Rimington wrote.

In May 1968, Wilson's government passed the Commonwealth Immigration Act. It limited the right of entry to the UK to citizens of the United Kingdom and Colonies currently holding a British passport who were born in the UK or had at least one parent or grandparent born in the UK. This was damage limitation to the 'Africanisation' policy of

Kenya, which could have led to the flight of 200,000 African Asians, many of them Indians with British passports, who did not wish to become Kenyan citizens. Indian politicians were outraged. This was 'a breach of faith'. Britain had 'a legal, moral and political responsibility' to absorb the Kenyan Asians. Mr Om Mechta, deputy Chief Whip of the Congress Parliamentary Party, called for the nationalisation of British assets in India and for India to leave the Commonwealth. Mrs Gandhi 'made her strong views known' to the High Commissioner but said that India should 'not act in a huff'. Freeman probably regarded this as another example of Indian 'neurosis'. Once again, his advice to HMG was to 'talk little. It is a waste of time, and probably counter-productive, to attempt a hard sell on the Commonwealth in India. Eventually, it will be a combination of inertia and marginal self-interest that will hold India inside the Commonwealth.'[56] And so it came to pass.

The High Commissioner's own views on the controversial Immigration Act he kept to himself. Had he still been editor of the *New Statesman* he may well have written a strong article opposing it but now he was a correctly behaved diplomat. One of his team was the economist Robert Cassen, an advisor to the British Aid Programme in India. He had a regular Wednesday morning meeting with Freeman:

> I remember one at which John talked about the new Immigration Bill in these words: 'It has come to my attention that some of my colleagues have been critical of the new Immigration Act. I don't know what you think about this, but I must remind you of your duty as members of the High Commission to defend Her Majesty's policies and if you are unable to defend this one, keep your mouth shut.'[57]

In July, Freeman's time was up and the family returned to London by air after a formal farewell with the residence staff lined up outside, they and Catherine with tears in their eyes. The Freemans rented a home at Hamilton Terrace, in London's St John's Wood, and Freeman took stock of his diplomatic career, so far. He said he was impressed by the diplomatic service: 'extremely hard-working, highly efficient and not overpaid'. He admitted that he had found diplomacy difficult, particularly dealing with economic and financial matters, but he felt he had come into his own in the writing of despatches. A case in point was the customary valedictory despatch he had written just before leaving New Delhi.

Much of it concerned the end of the Raj and the change in Indo–British relations. He wrote that 'a little over twenty years ago we were involved in controlling almost the entire perimeter of the Indian Ocean. Now [because of the east of Suez withdrawal] we control none of it.' He noted that in the 1960s India's imports from Britain had declined by a half and Indian exports to Britain had declined by a third. Since 1965, the 18,000 UK citizens resident in India had fallen to fewer than 14,000. His conclusion was clear:

> Our position in the world and our relations with India are now such that we must attach primary weight to the promotion of our own interests. We must eschew nostalgic recollections of a special relationship that over most of the field no longer exists and we must brace ourselves to stand up to criticism when it arises.

He ended his valedictory despatch with an oratorical flourish in a style reminiscent of an eighteenth-century tombstone:

> Perhaps a regenerate sinner, plucked by a somewhat whimsical government from the stews of Fleet Street and the limelight of Shepherd's Bush, may be allowed to pay a disinterested and most affectionate

tribute to the kindness, the devotion to duty, the professional skill
and sheer quality of mind and imagination, which he has encountered
during his three and a half years as the guest of HMG.[58]

Isn't that the voice of an actor, tongue in cheek, who has written himself some good lines? Applause was not long in coming. In the margin
an FO mandarin has written: 'Very nicely put indeed. The tone of it
goes a long way to explain how popular he has become in the service.'

On 31 July Freeman called in to 10 Downing Street for an end of
term report. Wilson had been given notes in preparation, conveni-
ently written in the first person:

> I have followed with interest the evolution of our relations with India
> and much admired the patience and skill with which you have rebuilt
> our position. I think the results have entirely justified your adoption,
> after the hostilities of 1965, of the 'heads down' policy.
>
> What interests me in particular is that what we are now working
> towards is a relationship, which, in various, important, but perhaps
> not very marked ways, is different from that of the past. I'm sure this
> is healthy.
>
> Your valedictory despatch sums all this up very well.[59]

On the way out, Freeman bumped into his old adversary Richard
Crossman. Crossman wrote in his diary:

> John used to be a rather willowy, elegant young man with wonderful
> wavy hair but he's thickened out and his complexion has roughened
> so that he looks like an extremely tough colonel of a polo-playing regi-
> ment just back from India – big and bluff. Beside him was little Harold,
> relaxed and gay, having undoubtedly been drinking with John.[60]

No doubt the two had been celebrating Freeman's appointment as ambassador to the United States, a posting first announced the previous February.

Chapter 10

Diplomat – ambassador to the United States

'A MAN OF no principle whatsoever except a willingness to sacrifice everything in the cause of Dick Nixon. His defeat is a victory for decency in public life.' This is how John Freeman described Richard Nixon in the *New Statesman* on 9 November 1962, just after Nixon had failed in his bid to become Governor of California. In 1969 these dismissive two sentences almost cost Freeman his plum post as ambassador to the United States – before he even moved to Washington. The veteran American correspondent Stewart Alsop, writing in *Newsweek* in December 1968, remembered the article and launched a broadside. Freeman, he wrote, 'on the record and in print has savagely attacked the future President of the United States to whom he will shortly present his credentials'. This meant the death of the Anglo-American special relationship! Former President Eisenhower, no less, read the article and went further: the appointment of Freeman was an insult to the presidency itself.

The British government was to blame. When Freeman was appointed, Harold Wilson and his Foreign Secretary George Brown expected the Democrat Hubert Humphrey to win the presidential election in November 1968 and therefore their ambassador-designate would be working with an administration of similar political outlook. Instead the Republican candidate won and Richard Nixon was in the White House. According to his National Security Advisor, Henry Kissinger, Nixon 'swore that he would have nothing to do with Freeman'.[1] George Brown admitted that appointing Freeman 'was a mistake, but there was no reason to consider it a mistake at the time it was made'.[2] Twenty-two Tory MPs called for Freeman's dismissal and the appointment of a new ambassador 'on the same wavelength as the United States President'. 'US Call To Drop Freeman' was the headline in the *Sunday Telegraph.*

In the circumstances, Freeman was obviously miscast. He contacted his old friend Henry Brandon, the Washington correspondent for the British *Sunday Times,* and asked his advice about resigning. Brandon advised him to hang on but 'expect a difficult time' when he arrived.[3] So Freeman apologised instead: 'The qualities I admire most in public life are courage and guts, and I cannot recall any case in public life where a man has shown more by his fighting spirit that he is worthy to hold high office. I hope Mr Nixon will be prepared to wipe the slate clean and start on a new basis.'[4] Wilson doggedly stuck with his choice. He felt that Anglo-American relations could 'stand the strain'.[5]

Freeman did have a few influential supporters and one was the former United States ambassador in London, David Bruce. He said that the demands for Freeman to give up his post were 'foolish' and wrote in his diary: 'He [Freeman] is undoubtedly attractive, and reputed to be intellectually brilliant. Those who dislike him charge him with being arrogant and supercilious, but as a table companion today there was no trace of such defects.'[6] Henry Brandon was a supporter too. He reported that Richard Crossman had told him: 'He will do well because he is like an officer who stands erect under enemy fire'[7] – a double-edged compliment.

Despite the support of 10 Downing Street, Freeman's appointment, or at least its timing, was not universally welcomed in the Foreign Office. The outgoing ambassador, Sir Patrick Dean, was a career diplomat who felt he was relegated to 'lame-duck' status when Freeman was appointed fully nine months before he was due to retire; more hurtful than that was the rumour that Freeman had been appointed to restore British influence with the presidency. This rumour turned out to be true. The Foreign Office asked Sir Patrick's advice about a trip by Freeman to Washington around the end of the year to meet Nixon and mend bridges. He advised against it; he thought the trip would be counter-productive. Instead, Freeman asked Catherine to visit the ambassador's residence informally to see how suitable it was for family life. The Deans were polite but decidedly cool. When the White House announced that Nixon would visit Britain in February 1969 as part of the new President's European tour, both sides realised that this would force the issue. Freeman's controversial appointment would be resolved one way or the other.

Kissinger had warned the Foreign Office that the President 'might make Freeman's ambassadorial tenure as difficult and awkward as possible'.[8] That was borne out when Nixon and his entourage arrived in London. One of his White House aides, probably on his own initiative, sent a message that the President would boycott the Prime Minister's dinner to be held in his honour unless Freeman was removed from the guest list. The attempts of David Bruce to intervene, either by changing Nixon's mind or by requesting Wilson to remove Freeman from the guest list, were unsuccessful. At the last minute Nixon was persuaded to attend by his Secretary of State, William Rogers, but the stage of No. 10 Downing Street seemed set for a chilly encounter.

Nixon loved to surprise and here was an ideal opportunity. In his toast after the dinner on 25 February he charmed Freeman, saying that American journalists had written far worse things about him than had the *New Statesman*. Then his speech reached a memorable climax, carefully honed as it was by his brilliant speech-writer William Safire. Henry Kissinger was there:

> Looking squarely at Freeman, who sat on the opposite side of the table, Nixon said: 'Some say there's a new Nixon. And they wonder if there's a new Freeman. I would like to think that that's all behind us. After all, he's the new diplomat and I'm the new statesman, try-ing to do our best for peace in the world.'[9]

The impact was electric. Wilson wrote to Nixon on his menu: 'That was one of the kindest and most generous acts I have known in a quarter of a century of politics. Just proves my point. You can't guar-antee being born a Lord. It is possible – you've shown it – to be born a gentleman.' The usually imperturbable Freeman was close to tears.[10]

David Bruce adds his eyewitness account: 'A profound satisfaction was apparent throughout the room. I've never known anything more courteously or magnanimously done. The PM fairly glowed with pleas-ure.'[11] What a pity I could not persuade Freeman to recall the incident in old age. It ranks with his Humble Address to Parliament on 16 August 1945 as the summit of set piece speechmaking by him or about him.

During the dinner Michael Stewart, George Brown's successor as Foreign Secretary, commended the ambassador-designate to Secretary of State Rogers; Freeman was 'highly professional and intellectually gifted, with broad experience'.[12] Rogers needed no convincing. He replied that after their antagonism Nixon and Freeman would 'lean over backwards to be friendly' to one another. And so it proved. When Freeman arrived in mid-March at the White House to present his credentials, Nixon used the occasion to move the ceremony from the Oval Office into his residential quarters, a clear signal that the United Kingdom was still a special partner. He welcomed Freeman generously, implying again that the past was forgiven: 'Let me assure you that you are most welcome in Washington. Your impressively versatile career is well known to us. I was delighted to meet and talk with you in London and anticipate seeing you often in the future.'[13]

Meanwhile the *New Statesman* journalist Francis Hope was assuring Americans that the term 'radical socialist' did not have the revolutionary connotation in England that they gave it. In a long article for the *New York Times* – 'Meet the New Man from London' – he began, tongue in cheek:

> One must understand the English upper-middle-class radical. A little leftishness is not at all a dangerous thing in England: some of our best friends are socialists. The *New Statesman* is found in the nicest of households. The old Fabian tradition that the elite should be infiltrated rather than destroyed, dies hard. Ambassador Freeman is one of its finest blooms.[14]

He continued with a perception about the 'Class of '45', the parliamentary intake of soldier-socialist MPs that applied to Freeman as much as it did to more radical socialists, like George Orwell: 'The

Class of '45 has a complex attitude towards social change. They have lived through the war, which both caused and called for a greater equality, but also reinforced an affection for the British way of life.'

'How will he find Washington?' Francis Hope asked. Here I wonder whether he was briefed by his old *New Statesman* boss, so apposite were his answers:

> The suggestion that he would have been happier with Humphrey than with Nixon is as complete a misunderstanding of the man as one could hope to find. He has always disliked political parties. The Communist Party of the Soviet Union, he once said, is his idea of the nastiest institution ever devised by man. He is here to do a job.
>
> The idea that Freeman ran an anti-American paper is another that won't stand up. The insularity of the 'Class of '45' never touched him. During the war when he encountered American troops he was struck by two facts, the extraordinary speed of their learning from mistakes and their widespread sense of having something to fight for. He is a great clearer away of cobwebs. Sentimentality about the special relationship or nostalgia for the Kennedy era will not influence him at all.[15]

The Deans insisted on staying put until Sir Patrick's seventieth birthday, leaving the Freemans kicking their heels in Hamilton Terrace. Freeman was frustrated but for the rest of the family it was a happy time, as Cynthia Gomes remembers:

> Mrs Freeman said, 'Cynthia, I've got a surprise for you. John's been offered the post of ambassador in Washington: would you like to come with us?' So I said yes please. And so everything was arranged, I had no problem with passport and visa. We stayed at Hamilton

Terrace because Mr and Mrs Freeman were interviewing staff, butler
and footmen and all that was going on, while the children went to
school and I was doing other things. The nice thing about that was
when we were together in the evening Mr Freeman used to say to me
and Mrs Freeman, 'go and sit down and watch *Z Cars*, and I'll prepare dinner. And I used to stand and say, 'Oh no, I will do…' And
he would say, 'It's alright, go on, sit down, sit down, Cynthia.'
And so Mrs F. and I would sit down. And he used to make simple things, sardines on toast, but very nicely done! No really nicely
done! Table all laid out, everything done very nicely. Glasses put
out, everything. And we would come and sit down and at the end
he would rinse plates, put them in the dishwasher, do all of that.
To me, that's how I saw him, in Hamilton Terrace, before he went
to Washington DC.[16]

One of the vacancies in the embassy household was for a social
secretary, whose duties were to help the ambassador's wife with all
that she had to do. A major part of this was the secretarial work
involved in the endless entertaining, which is such a feature of the
diplomatic life. The social secretary lived in the residence, almost as
a member of the family, so the salary was modest and the relationship close. Catherine made enquiries for a possible candidate and
these reached as far as The Owl and Pussycat toy shop in Hampstead,
much frequented by the Freeman children. Its owner, Betty Mitchell,
happened to be the ex-wife of the famous documentary filmmaker
Denis Mitchell, whom the Freemans had known at the BBC, and
she recommended her 28-year-old stepdaughter Judith. Judith had
been brought up in South Africa, had worked as a playgroup leader
in London and an au pair in New York. She had also spent time at
Big Sur in California at the Esalen Institute, famous for its hippy

philosophy and lifestyle. She came for interview and both Freemans found her a breath of fresh air. They decided to employ her.

Catherine and the three children were due to fly out with the ambassador in mid-March but were delayed because they caught flu. 'It's all very annoying,' Freeman said, but went ahead anyway with Judith Mitchell in attendance. When Catherine, Cynthia and the children arrived in Washington three weeks later, he was waiting on the tarmac. She was taken aback to find him looking drawn and stressed. 'This is a loathsome place,' he said to her. 'We'll just have to make the best of it. I'm not sleeping at all well so I think we should have separate rooms.' She supposed that he was going through some kind of mid-life depression and would need a lot of support.

And so to the ambassador's residence at No. 3100, Massachusetts Avenue, the most impressive address on Embassy Row. It was so large, said Catherine, that she was not sure how many rooms there were. It is a vast red brick and stone palace, designed by Lutyens in the English country manner, with a dramatic columned portico and terrace overlooking the immaculate rose garden. The drawing room had seats for eighteen, the dining room for thirty-six and the ballroom held 'unnumbered multitudes'. It was perfect for entertaining, fortunately, for Catherine soon discovered that she was expected to give two lunches, two dinners and a reception each week, and attend on average four receptions or dinners every week as guest – much of it presented in a lavish style and in the glare of publicity. For this entertaining, the Foreign Office provided a budget of $100,000 per year to which the ambassador added his own contribution. There were constant demands for interviews from the press, demands that Ambassador Freeman shunned whenever possible and directed to his wife.

In January 1969, she had given an interview to the fashion queen of the *Sunday Times,* Ernestine Carter. It was revealing:

'John,' says Catherine Freeman, whose husband is the ambassador-designate in Washington, 'tells me that I expose too much of my surface.' She didn't mean skin. She meant herself. For candour is one of her outstanding traits. Those who think of diplomatic wives as carefully conventional, consciously gracious, hyper-discreet, will find that Mrs Freeman won't fit that mould. In fact, she fits no mould. She is careless of convention, and can afford to be, for she is equally at ease with chars and royalty and has the knack of making immediate contact.[17]

This candour had annoyed the High Commissioner and would annoy the ambassador. 'My husband is very critical of what I say,' she told another reporter. 'When I tell him I'm giving an interview, he says, "And just what is it you have to tell people? What are you trying to say?"'[18]

No. 3100 Massachusetts Avenue was by a long way the largest British overseas mission in the world. The total number of diplomatic staff in the United States in 1968 was 182, compared with 214 in the whole of eastern Europe. In Washington, working under John Freeman and his deputy, were twenty-three political staff, plus thirty-four working in commerce, consular and information services. The number of personnel working for the British defence staff was 198. Freeman's administrative work was limited but he also had to cope with the endless stream of UK ministers, MPs and VIPs who visited Washington. As in India, and despite his non-professional background, his staff thought highly of him. His First Secretary was Andrew Burns:

> He was a good man to work for. I asked him on one occasion how he found the job as ambassador, and he said, 'Really it's very much like being an editor except that you don't have to do so much writing. As an ambassador, you have to do more.' I thought he was quite good.[19]

Another junior diplomat, Andrew Wood, thought the same: 'I don't remember anyone feeling that John Freeman was not one of us. He settled in very quickly.'[20]

Freeman set about dispelling American fears that he was opposed to the Nixon regime. He did so successfully. In the words of Henry Brandon, who entertained the Freemans and the Kissingers at his summer home in Plymouth, Massachusetts:

> Although he arrived with his 'left-wing' coat tails still casting their shadow on the red carpet, he soon rose above prejudices, whether those of others or his own.
>
> I realised from our discussions how depoliticised Freeman's views had become, how scrupulously he adhered to the canons of the Foreign Office. In Washington, British professional diplomats tried hard to cultivate the manners of the amateur; in Freeman's case it was the amateur (as he was viewed in Washington) who cultivated the traditions of the professionals.[21]

Egalitarians in Washington should have taken heart from the fact that he was the first ambassador for over fifty years without a title except 'Mr'. He pronounced himself 'quite happy as I am', but did not say that this was of his own choosing.

Before Freeman had left the UK he had been given a 'Confidential and Guard' briefing from the Foreign Office. This was just before the victory of Nixon in the presidential election of November 1968, but the relevance to Freeman's work remained valid:

> The United States is our most important friend, ally and trading partner ... [Nevertheless] we no longer consider that our relations have a 'special' character. In fact there has been a recent tendency in the

United States regretfully to write Britain off because we seem to them to be failing to fulfil our part in maintaining world stability in the defence and monetary fields.

The Americans deplore our withdrawals east of Suez and, while HMG's attitude over Vietnam is understood, many Americans resent our unwillingness to support the war as, for example, Australia does.

The principal objectives of the ambassador's mission will be: to promote British trade; to maintain cordial relations against the background of our application to join the common market and our lukewarm support of Vietnam; to encourage an outward looking trend in Congress and American public opinion; to keep Her Majesty's government informed of United States internal and external policies and plans.[22]

Looked at from the American point of view, at least according to the influential Henry Brandon: 'Britain is still the most useful, most reliable ally and the easiest to communicate with. But economic and financial stringencies have left Britain very little elbow room in the big power game.'[23]

It was Freeman's great achievement during his two years as ambassador to provide a continuous flow of first-hand information from Washington to Whitehall, from the very highest level and on the most important subjects. In this respect, Britain punched above her weight. Freeman's personal 'elbow room' with the two most important men in the United States government, President Richard Nixon and his National Security Advisor Henry Kissinger, was unique. No British ambassador before or since can have been more confided in, more privy to presidential thinking on foreign affairs than he. As Kissinger put it:

I thought so highly of Freeman's judgement that I frequently consulted him on matters outside his official purview. On one or two occasions, I let him read early drafts of presidential speeches, tapping his talents as an editor. He had every right to report all his conversations to his Prime Minister; he almost certainly did so. But the intimacy and trust of the 'special relationship' were meant precisely for such cordial collaboration.

For his part Nixon came first to trust, then to like Freeman. Freeman was the only ambassador invited to the White House for a social occasion during his first term. He also became one of my closest friends; that friendship has survived both our terms of office. I consider it one of the greatest rewards of my public service.[24]

When Freeman wrote his annual review for 1969, he said it had been 'a pretty good year of Anglo-American relations':

> President Nixon has repeatedly made clear to me in terms I can no longer doubt that he regards his administration as having more intimate relations with Britain than with any other foreign country. In terms of close and candid consultation ... we have been treated exceptionally – probably uniquely – well.[25]

According to Lord Renwick, who was ambassador to the United States in the 1990s and had visited Washington frequently while Freeman was in post: 'At first, Henry didn't know what to make of this left-wing journalist, who'd previously criticised Nixon, but after only two meetings with John he realised that here is someone on the same intellectual level as himself, and Henry hardly regards anybody else on this planet as his intellectual equal.'[26] Kissinger told Wes Pruden, a journalist then on the *National Observer* who became friends with the Freemans, 'I get along well with John. John doesn't make friends easily and I don't make friends at all, so we get along very well!' He also said of Freeman:

He was one of the most effective ambassadors I ever dealt with. The reason for this was not so simple. His style was unpropitious. Free-man eschewed all flattery; he met socially only those he respected; he made little effort to turn his embassy into a fashionable salon. When he had a message to deliver, he prefaced it with a very formal state-ment that he was speaking under instructions. But he was prepared to go beyond his instructions to express personal views. Since he was a man of superb intelligence and utter integrity, this soon proved invaluable. He had a shrewd geopolitical mind and, as it turned out, rather shared our philosophy of foreign relations.[27]

Whatever John Freeman thought of Henry Kissinger, it did not prevent him making a detached judgement of his work as National Security Advisor, as in this account of a meeting about the Middle East he sent to Sir Denis Greenhill, the head of the diplomatic service, on 5 June 1970. Headed 'Secret, Personal and Guard' Freeman writes: 'I consider some of the views he [Kissinger] expounded, though not completely irrational, both naive and romantic. In fairness to Kissinger I must record my view that he is a man of outstanding intellectual honesty who could be easily influenced by the arguments of others.'

He ended, not for the first time: 'I need hardly point out that the strict protection of Kissinger's confidence concerning a private and obviously indiscreet conversation of this kind is of the paramount importance to our relations with the White House.'[28]

The same day Freeman sent a second letter to Greenhill that reveals the extent of Kissinger's indiscretions and the degree to which he trusted Freeman. It also reveals an odd triangular relationship between the two and President Nixon. It is so extraordinary it deserves to be quoted at length. Freeman begins by recalling a conversation with Kissinger the previous day:

The President, said Kissinger, was not an easy man to read even by those who knew him pretty well. For years he had represented in Kissinger's eyes all that was most objectionable in political life. But working with him had changed his view. Mr Nixon was a 'good' man, generous in his responses and basically warm-hearted.

Kissinger's main criticism of the President was directed against those who surrounded him. He said: 'I have never met such a gang of self-seeking bastards in my life.' When I observed that the same criticism had been levelled at other national leaders and that perhaps this sort of thing was always said, he replied: 'No, I used to find the Kennedy group unattractively narcissistic, but they were idealists. These people are real heels.' I find this convincing testimony.

Finally, I hope you will not misunderstand my motives in reporting, as I think I should, a very bizarre incident that took place later the same evening and is clearly related – though I'm not sure how – to the conversation with Kissinger. At about 11.30 p.m. my telephone rang, and the President was on the line. He said he was relaxing with Kissinger. Kissinger had been telling him that we had had a long and intimate talk earlier in the day. He was glad to hear this and hoped we would do so whenever the opportunity offered. He wanted me to know that Kissinger much valued my friendship and was stimulated by our conversations. After some further amiable remarks, the President rang off.

I am completely unable to interpret this incident.

Freeman added in his handwriting:

I think Mr Nixon spoke seriously and appeared completely rational. Thus, while the telephone call was probably made on impulse, I don't doubt that he was trying to convey *something* he considered of importance.[29]

Freeman hated gossip, but this correspondence was political gilt-edge. It rises up the security hierarchy to SECRET, PERSONAL AND GUARD, ADDRESSEES EYES ONLY. Sir Denis adds in his handwriting to his private secretary 'keep among our private pps'. In 2015 I asked Dr Kissinger if he recalled this incident and, if so, could he tell me what the 'something of importance' was that Freeman referred to? He said it was obvious: 'The President wanted Freeman to know that he knew all about our conversation the previous day.' I asked how he knew; was Dr Kissinger 'bugged'? 'How would I know if I was?' he replied.

In the same conversation, I asked Dr Kissinger what President Nixon had thought of Ambassador Freeman:

> He liked him. He thought he had made an impossible job work because of his intelligence and straightforward manner. He liked his analytical mind. John imposed no strain. He did not flatter the President, he did not want to become close to him. He was reticent; did his business and left.[30]

What did Freeman think of Nixon? He certainly grew to admire him over the first two years of his first administration, before Watergate. At his farewell audience in January 1971 he thought the time had come for him to apologise for his 1962 article. Nixon brushed him aside but he persisted: 'I'm apologising not for my manners but for my judgement. I got you so wrong.'

Nixon replied: 'Ah, I understand. Well, you couldn't have said that before without browning your nose' – the language of 'a ruffian' is probably how Freeman would have described that, as he did the talk of much of Washington society. Wes Pruden remembers him speaking highly of Nixon and Lord Renwick has no doubts that Freeman got Nixon right:

I honestly think before he went to Washington, JF didn't understand how intelligent Nixon was. He found, much to his surprise that before Watergate Nixon actually was a good President. He and Kissinger started winding down the war in Vietnam, preparing for the opening up of China and the détente with Russia. Henry deserves 80 per cent of the credit for this but Nixon instinctively took the right position on these issues; he had a feel for foreign policy. He was quite a brilliant person with a severe character flaw. I know John thought that Watergate was a completely unnecessary tragedy that showed he was right about this flaw [i.e. Nixon's totally self-serving character].[31]

Freeman's admiration for Nixon went further than foreign affairs. He once said that, 'Nixon remains America's greatest undiscovered US President.' This was true in more ways than one, because as the historian Alistair Horne put it:

Nixon wanted to remain undiscovered: he was a paid-up misanthrope [meaning that he disliked the human species and abhorred more contact than necessary]. He shunned Washington society, talked in abstractions about the working class without having any desire to 'press the flesh' in public, and preferred the written memo to any kind of discussion.

Peter Rodman, who was Kissinger's Special Assistant during these years, added, 'Basically Nixon hated people.'[32] Much the same has been said about Freeman; indeed he said it about himself.

Freeman had first-hand experience of how badly Washington society treated the President:

I remember one not uncharacteristic example of this at Mrs Alice Longworth's house one evening. Over drinks before dinner she asked me what I thought of the new President. I gave some sort of respectful reply. Alice then hushed the whole company, saying in her wickedest voice: 'How extraordinary! Listen. The ambassador thinks well of Mr Nixon! Such a common little man!' And her guests all roared with laughter. Nixon was treated abominably by Georgetown society. It was not just a question of political disagreements. Really beastly attitudes were on display towards him, largely to do with class.[33]

The ambassador disliked socialite Washington, too, and was only too happy to creep into the shadows (as Barbara Castle had observed years before) and leave the limelight to Catherine. Her view of Nixon was less than sympathetic:

I sat next to the President at one grand dinner in the White House. I was wearing a Jean Muir evening dress. It was black velvet, with full black organza sleeves. Mr Nixon plucked at one of these sleeves and said, 'All women should wear clothes like this all the time' – a familiarity not really suitable in the circumstances. Then he went on to refer to an aide's wife: 'She's a terrible woman. She refuses to come to Washington to be with him. Women like that should be shot!' So I replied, 'Or drowned at birth, perhaps?' He looked at me and then turned away.[34]

It was his wife's lack of deference to the President of the United States that her husband found hard to cope with. On the other hand, Catherine very much liked Henry Kissinger. He was 'a sophisticated European in America, warm, accessible and amusing'. She saw his insecure side too. In March 1970, they met at a party held by the publisher and hostess Katherine Graham: 'He looked absolutely shaken. He had just come from a confrontation with former academic colleagues about the bombing of Cambodia. He had a vulnerable side, which I found sympathetic.'

If Freeman's success was due to the 'intimate relations', in Nixon's phrase, which he established with the White House, then the success of the ambassador's wife was the atmosphere she created at 3100 Massachusetts Avenue. Washington is a capital of gossip and show and the British embassy was in the spotlight. By all accounts Catherine was a huge success, which reflected well on Freeman whether he liked it or not. As in New Delhi, she entertained with flair. 'The days of the absolutely conventional diplomatic entertaining are over,' she declared to a journalist. One of her Washington friends from this period is a former lawyer, Corinna Metcalf:

> She was the perfect ambassador's wife. She was formal and casual at
> the same time. She knew how to talk to anybody. She knew who to
> sit next to who. She knew about food, about menus, how to treat
> staff. She knew how to give people a good time. Everyone in the dip-
> lomatic corps thought she was the tops.[35]

Another friend, Joanna Rose, who dates her friendship with Catherine from university years at Oxford, met up with her again in New York: 'Catherine was a huge success. She made friends everywhere. You do what you like and she was good at it. John's success in Washington was in large part due to Catherine.'[36]

Freeman hated the 'flummery', as he put it, so that he frequently sloped off early to 'read his telegrams'. Joanna Rose thought he had 'inter-personal problems' ever since she attended the British embassy Christmas party of 1969, an important date in the social calendar, when the ambassador broke with tradition by refusing to play Father Christmas. His own preferred entertainment was watching the Washington

Redskins football team with Wes Pruden, incognito. They 'eschewed', as he may well have said, the Honours Box to sit in the cheap seats and drink Tennent's lager from cans that depicted a 'lager lovely' stripped down to her bikini. Nanny Cynthia Gomes recognised the private side of John Freeman:

> What a good man he was. In Washington in the evenings, whenever he came home I used to hear him coming and he used to come up to the nursery when I'd been making the children's tea and he used to say to me, 'Can I join them for tea?' And I would make them scrambled egg on toast, or Marmite toast or whatever I was doing for the children, and he would sit there eating it with the children.
>
> He was a very simple man actually, Mr Freeman. He didn't like all this posh thing. He liked anything for peace and quiet. He was like that.[37]

The volatile issue during the first year of Freeman's ambassadorship was the Vietnam War. The United States and her Allies wanted to extricate themselves from the war without losing face; the Vietnamese government wanted to extract the most advantageous peace terms possible. Britain was an ally with a small 'a' because although Wilson supported the American intervention, he refused to do so with any military involvement. Freeman's role was to ensure good relations between a President anxious to maintain popular support during his first term in office and a Prime Minister aware of the unpopularity of the war in Britain at a time of an impending general election. It was not easy. He probably found Nixon easier to deal with than Wilson because the former took a global view of foreign affairs while the latter seemed mildly paranoid and parochial. To make matters worse, the American massacre of Vietnamese civilians at My Lai (called Songmy at the time), that came to light in November 1969, and then the bombing of civilians in Cambodia beginning the following April, further inflamed public opinion in both countries and unsettled their governments.

In November 1969, Wilson complained to Freeman that he was not given special treatment by the White House. Exposing his insecurity, he said in a personal letter to his old political friend that despite feeling slighted he had no wish to visit Nixon:

> As John Freeman, rather than HM ambassador, will understand, we are in a pre-election period. There is no mileage whatsoever in a visit to Washington. Any visit would mean a total endorsement of Nixon's Vietnam position and public opinion in this country is, if anything, less in support of Vietnam than public opinion in America.[38]

Freeman replied with a tactful warning: 'There is no effective substitute for personal contacts. If we miss the opportunity to cement personal relationships with the President in his critical first year, they will less easily come by in the future.'[39]

Shortly after came revelations about the 'Massacre at Songmy' the previous March when up to 500 unarmed Vietnamese civilians had been killed in cold blood by American troops. This caused global outrage and Wilson summoned Freeman to London for discussions about the British response. No doubt this was window dressing, but on his return Freeman was given an abject apology from Secretary of State Rogers, which he communicated to London: 'He had no doubt that disgraceful and almost certainly criminal actions had taken place. He was filled with the utmost horror and shame.' Then Rogers added a warning: 'There is no prospect that public opinion will change the President's mind to get out of Vietnam as fast as possible compatible with national honour.'[40] This meant 'not yet'. In a forceful but diplomatic secret and personal memo to Sir Denis Greenhill on 15 December, Freeman warned against any backsliding in American support:

> Special resentment would no doubt be felt against any foreign gov-
> ernment that could be argued to have stabbed the United States in
> the back over Vietnam. This ought to be in the forefront of minis-
> ters' minds considering any change in HMG's policy at this late stage
> in the war from general support to general opposition to American
> war aims in Vietnam.[41]

So Wilson made a speech in the House of Commons backing Nixon's policy and the same day Nixon rang up Freeman and asked him to convey his thanks: 'I wanted him to know I appreciated it.'

At the end of January 1970, Wilson did come to Washington. According to Kissinger, Nixon was not impressed by Wilson's manner:

> He distrusted his views and resented the way he greeted the Presi-
> dent with the avuncular good will of the head of an ancient family
> that has seen better times but is still able to evoke memories of the
> old wisdom, dignity and power that had established the family name
> in the first place.[42]

Apparently Wilson suggested Christian name terms but 'a fishy-eyed stare from Nixon squelched the idea'. Not withstanding this, Wilson was rewarded by Nixon with a rare honour to attend the security council together with his Foreign Secretary and ambassador. This was planned by Kissinger and Freeman.

Three months later the USAF launched Operation Menu, dropping 110,000 tons of bombs on Cambodia followed up by military operations on the ground. Kissinger informed Freeman the day before, in 'sombre mood', and Freeman wasted no time informing the Foreign Office:

> Kissinger invited me this afternoon to see a final draft of the President's speech due to be delivered at 2 a.m. BST tomorrow. He asked me that even more care than usual should be taken to protect his confidence since for the first time he was confiding in me without the President's authority.

Freeman then relayed the news and ended, as always, that he hoped London would support the invasion: 'Our good relations stem largely from the President's appreciation of the understanding he has received from HMG, often in difficult political circumstances.'[43]

The Foreign Secretary, Michael Stewart, did defend the bombing in a speech to Parliament. Perhaps this is why Freeman was able to obtain for him a meeting with the President the following month. This did not go according to plan. At the last minute Stewart told Freeman that he did not expect to be Foreign Secretary after the general election and, therefore, 'as one of his last efforts, he wanted to speak with exceptional candour to the President about his anxieties'. In effect, he wanted to complain about American aggression in Vietnam and Cambodia and he intended to ask the President to withdraw US troops from Vietnam. Freeman and Kissinger sat in on the meeting so that Freeman's complaint to Sir Denis afterwards has the merit of an eyewitness:

> He [the Foreign Secretary] did not speak very diplomatically. He fell into the trap of hammering the President about matters on which he had not been properly briefed and his tone may have been a bit too schoolmasterly for the President. The President's demeanour

throughout was attentive, polite and cheerful. I am not sure this represented his true feelings. Kissinger was much irritated and did not conceal this from me. I can't rid my mind of the thought that we may have used up quite a bit of goodwill to not much purpose and that my welcome at the White House next time may be cooler than usual.[44]

Sir Denis replied:

Addressee's eyes only.

I can see it all only too vividly from your description. I spoke to the Foreign Secretary this morning. He did not feel the President took any umbrage. I can well understand Kissinger's attitude as much as I regret it. It is most extraordinary thing that the last two presidents have attracted to them the same type of European-born guru who is absurdly jealous of other influences on his chief.[45]

On 7 May 1970, Catherine held one of her most glittering social events. The press dubbed it 'Cinderella's Night':

All of a sudden, thousands and thousands of pink and white cherry blossoms floated down into the champagne glasses on the terrace of the British embassy in Washington. The entire 'Salon Operetta' evening, which Ambassador and Mrs John Freeman planned, to benefit the Friends of the American Museum in Bath, was enchanting. The Freemans erected a blue-carpeted stage in the Wedgwood blue and white Great Hall, set up hundreds of gold chairs and presented 'Cendrillon' by Pauline Viardot.

Guests found themselves face to knee with the Freeman's charming sons, Matthew, eight, and Tom, six, dressed in their best blue blazers and white ducks, who were permitted to stay up past their bedtime to greet each celebrated arrival with a very British 'Good evening' and boyish handshake. And since no one likes to miss a British embassy affair, all the Washington *illustrati* were there in full regalia. The gypsy look, chiffon and antique jewels were big.[46]

Only two days later, the atmosphere in Washington changed dramatically. Three days before, the Ohio State Guard had opened fire on a peaceful demonstration against the Vietnam War at Kent University and killed four students. The immediate result was incendiary. Four hundred and fifty universities closed and four million students went on strike. On 9 May, 100,000 people demonstrated in Washington. One of Nixon's speech-writers recalled: 'The city was an armed camp. The mobs were smashing windows, slashing tires, dragging parked cars into intersections, even throwing bedsprings off overpasses into the traffic down below. That's not student protest, that's civil war.'[47] Catherine Freeman remembers leaflets stuffed through the window of the ambassador's Rolls-Royce and rioting in Massachusetts Avenue.

The anti-Vietnam riots were the political sharp end of a new culture sweeping America in the late '60s. Its musical expression was the 'tribal love-rock musical' *Hair*, which opened in Washington in 1969. A product of the hippy counter-culture and sexual revolution of the 1960s, several of its songs became anthems of the anti-Vietnam War peace movement. Catherine Freeman's social secretary, Judith Mitchell, was in her element. She loved *Hair*, went round the residency in bare feet and performed the South African political protest dance *toyi-toyi*, to an appreciative audience. Classical music was not her thing – she told Robert Cassen on an evening out that she had not been to a concert before – but she was in tune with the counter-culture.

This was a difficult time for the Freemans, and it did not get better.

When they holidayed with Joanna and Dan Rose at the exclusive summer colony of the Hamptons, Joanna noticed there was tension in the air. After Wes Pruden had taken Catherine and Corinna Metcalf down to Arkansas to show them his family roots, he tried to describe the trip to John at the next Redskins football game. 'I said "We had a really good trip" and he said "I'm sure you did" and then he started to talk about the tactics of the game we were at. Wasn't interested.' Freeman had become so cold that Catherine was drawn to ask if he was having an affair? 'You have the mind of a housemaid to ask such a question,' he replied. This, of course, was not an answer but it had the desired result of silencing her. That summer he went on his own to a dinner party given by the outspoken socialite Barbara Howar. She raised her voice down the table and asked him, 'What's all this about Edna O'Brien?' Freeman froze her out: 'I've no idea.' He must have realised he was treading on thin ice.

The more Freeman distanced himself from Catherine, the closer Judith moved to her. She became a kind of confidante. She was skilled at hairdressing and would put Catherine's hair up most evenings before parties, and in turn Catherine lent her evening dresses when she needed them. All this irritated the ambassador. Then, completely out of the blue during that summer of 1970, Judith handed in her notice. Catherine was stricken and begged her not to go. Judith seemed equally upset but insisted that family duties in South Africa came first. The '3100 REPORT', edited by Matthew Freeman age nine, noted the departure of Miss Mitchell. 'We had a great party with a cookout and champagne. Lots of people cried. Mum made a good movie so we have something to remind us. Dad added:

Judith Mitchell came alone
And buried herself on the telephone,

Judith Mitchell, lovely girl,
Left the house in a glorious whirl.

The atmosphere in Massachusetts Avenue was now bleak. Freeman seemed hostile and Catherine reacted badly. There were scenes, sometimes witnessed by others. Robert Cassen, now working for the World Bank in Washington, was invited to several embassy dinner parties because, he said, he had the advantage of the single male:

> I always thought John had a shell, a polished, glassy exterior, which covered a dark and mysterious interior. He seemed to have your measure while you did not have his, which was intimidating. He was extremely charming, formidable in a sense that he did what he said he wanted to do and wouldn't bend one inch from that. Quite a cold person.

On one occasion he asked the ambassador for career advice:

> He took me out to lunch and I remember distinctly he said, 'You should change your entire way of life every ten years.' I didn't know then that this was said with huge irony because it wasn't many months after that lunch that he resigned from the embassy and broke up with Catherine.[48]

In 1970 the Freemans had been together for thirteen years.

When the Conservative Party surprisingly won the general election in June 1970, Freeman did not expect he would be retained as United States ambassador. Nor did he want to be. He had already written to Michael Stewart implying that he wanted to leave Washington even if Labour were returned to office. In fact, Edward Heath invited him to stay on but Freeman had made his mind up and, as usual, that was that. He turned down the offer of a peerage, saying to Catherine that 'if it could be proved that an Honour would help me do my job better, then I might consider it. Until then, I don't want one.' Despite his success, it was time to start a new life. About this time he was sounded out to be the next editor of *The Times*, an appointment he said he would have accepted, but it came to nothing. In public he gave his usual reason for leaving as the need to earn good money. In private he said that he was bored. In fact, in 1967 he had given an 'indeterminate promise' to David Frost that he would join London Weekend Television as possible chairman when he left the diplomatic service and since then he had been written in, confidentially, as deputy chairman. Once again, if this career change worked out in practice, he would have been offered a job rather than having sought it.

The following week Freeman called on Prime Minister Edward Heath at 10 Downing Street with a *tour d'horizon* of the American scene. He gave him the President Nixon view that, with the withdrawal of American troops from Cambodia at the end of June, he had 'weathered the worst of domestic reaction'. There would be 'an honourable settlement in due course', probably after peace negotiations in the spring of 1971. The President was now turning his attention to the Middle East.

The Henry Kissinger/John Freeman hot line had one further revelation, this time for the new HMG. In a meeting on 17 July Kissinger told Freeman that there had been two recent occasions when Washington and Hanoi had held highly secret peace talks. They had failed because of deep mistrust on either side. This information was of 'peculiar delicacy' Kissinger told Freeman, because probably even the state department did not know about it, or 'if they did then there was no one there who would understand the significance. The information was known only in the most restricted circles of the White House.'[49]

There can be no stronger evidence of Freeman's success as United States ambassador than this. He was able to pass on to a foreign government such hugely important information pertaining to the end of the Vietnam War that even the US state department possibly did not know about it.

In September 1970 a political crisis blew up that diplomats must dread; it blew in from nowhere and could have spiralled out of control. Freeman was involved not only as go-between but also as advice giver. On 6 September, terrorists of the Popular Front for the Liberation of Palestine (PFLP) hijacked three jetliners shortly after they took off from European airports towards the United States. Hijackers on the El Al. flight from Amsterdam were subdued in mid-air and the plane landed safely in London, so the PFLP retaliated by hijacking a fourth jet, diverting it to Cairo and blowing it up. The remaining two hijacked planes landed on a desert strip in Jordan called Dawson Field, where they were joined by a fourth hijacked plane three days later. Nearly 500 passengers from these TWA, Swissair and BOAC planes were marooned in the desert, now renamed Revolution Field. The aim of the hijackers was to trade these hostages for imprisoned Palestinian terrorists in Israel, Germany and Switzerland, from where these planes had flown, and from Britain too because a PFLP terrorist, Leila Khaled, had tried to hijack the El Al. flight from Amsterdam and was now under guard in London.

Edward Heath's new British government was in a quandary. Sixty-five of the hostages were British. Should it 'give in to fedayeen blackmail and save lives, or take a very stiff stand and run the risk of losing lives?' It's task was made more difficult because it needed to act in unison with the governments of the United States, Germany and Switzerland (the so-called 'Berne Group') and Israel too; and 'any response needed to be concerted in Washington'. That is why

Freeman was heavily involved. In essence, Israel refused to negotiate, the Berne Group was ready to trade hostages in Jordan for terrorists in their countries, organised through the International Committee of the Red Cross (ICRC), but the United States refused to put any pressure on Israel. And Israel's cooperation, obviously, was crucial.

By 11 September, 375 of the passengers had been released and the planes blown up, but fifty-six hostages remained in the desert, Jews and Americans. Now tempers between Washington and London became frayed. Freeman was required, sometimes during the night, to convey messages between a rattled Alec Douglas-Home (British Foreign Secretary) and a nettled William Rogers (American Secretary of State). On 13 September, Prime Minister Heath announced that the British would negotiate come what may, and feelings boiled over in this transatlantic phone call between Joseph Sisco, a top White House aide, and Denis Greenhill:

'I think your government would want to weigh very, very carefully the kind of outcry that would occur in this country against your taking this kind of action.'

Greenhill replied, 'Well, they do, Joe, but there is also an outcry in this country,' expressing concern that 'Israel won't lift a bloody finger and our people get killed. You could imagine how bad that would look, and if it all comes out that we could have got our people out but for the obduracy of you and other people so to speak ... I mean people say, "Why the bloody hell didn't you try?"'[50]

Freeman's attitude, as usual, was to warn against any split with the United States. And with his usual ability for lateral thinking he proposed a way of keeping a united front but still securing the release of the remaining hostages. He suggested to William Rogers that the

Israelis should 'acquiesce through silence' for the ICRC to negotiate with the PFLP, if only to find out exactly what its terms were for the release of fedayeen in Israel. This would, at least, gain time.

And so it happened. Soon the hostage issue was subsumed into a larger crisis. This was the 'Black September' civil war between King Hussein and the Palestine Liberation Organization (PLO) for the control of Jordan, into which Iraq and Syria could easily have been drawn. By the end of September, the Berne Group countries and Israel had all released fedayeen prisoners (including Leila Khaled) and the remaining passenger hostages were released.

Freeman's decision to resign as ambassador was not unexpected but no successor had been approached so there was no hurry for him to leave. Catherine wanted the boys to finish their summer term at Sidwell Friends, a progressive Quaker school in Washington, while she took a temporary job offered her by Ben Bradlee, editor of the *Washington Post*, as TV correspondent. But Freeman was keen to go. On 5 January 1971 he said goodbye to the President and three days later he presented his 'valedictory despatch'. He had three main points to make that most concerned Great Britain:

> Vietnam is now a non-issue. In retrospect, the Cambodian episode appears a justified gamble, which has paid off, though at some cost to the President's position, to national unity and of course to Cambodia.
>
> The President has maintained his usual support for EEC enlargement [i.e. for the UK to join the common market] as a stable bulwark against Soviet pressure, despite opposition from those who fear their commercial interests will be damaged.
>
> When Mr Nixon invited me to say goodbye to him on 5 January he said that he wanted me to be in no doubt that he regarded Britain as his closest and most trusted ally.

His signing-off was formal and courteous, without the tongue-in-cheek eighteenth-century parody he had adopted in New Delhi:

> I now leave the service, of my own choice but with many regrets, after six very full and happy years. You will be losing a cuckoo from the diplomatic nest. But, if I may be permitted to say so (and for what it is worth), I leave as a committed and affectionate supporter of HM Diplomatic Service and of all it stands for, out of the infinitely resourceful and agreeable men and women who compose it.[51]

In *The Washington Embassy: British Ambassadors to the United States 1939 –1977*, John W. Young summed up Freeman's six years as a diplomat:

> He adapted to world diplomacy easily as High Commissioner in India, won the respect of professional diplomats and proved a success in Washington despite the worst possible start to his ambassadorship. He was an astute observer of the Washington scene and realistic about the influence London could wield there. His ambassadorship provides ample evidence of the way in which key individuals could keep the 'special relationship' in a healthy state even when its overall significance was declining.[52]

Lord Renwick is specific:

> Of the ambassadors I served with, the best were Freeman, Christopher Soames [ambassador to France, 1968–72] and Nicholas Henderson [ambassador to West Germany and then France, 1972–79]. One of the three [Henderson] was a career diplomat, the other two weren't. When it comes to political appointees to the Foreign Service, if the person is of sufficient calibre, he is going to do just as well as a career

diplomat, but only if he is of the highest calibre. Freeman was, it is true, rather remote, cold and not naturally gregarious. His temperamental inability was to do the glad-handing, but it's not a serious weakness compared with all his qualities.[53]

As for Dr Kissinger, he wasted no time contacting former Foreign Secretary George Brown to correct the statement in his autobiography *In My Way* that his appointment of Freeman to Washington was 'a mistake':

> I can tell you that just the opposite is true, that indeed you can consider this appointment one of the wisest decisions you ever made. Starting his assignment under somewhat of a cloud, John has moved with great skill and charm to gain the admiration of all of us here. He is not only a highly able and effective representative of your country, he is a man with very fine human qualities. I count him a close friend as well as a respected colleague. (Henry A. Kissinger, The White House, 7 November 1970)

In 2015 I asked Dr Kissinger if he had been surprised and disappointed when Freeman decided to leave Washington – after only twenty months into his years of a successful ambassadorship? His answer was revealing. He said he had always assumed that Freeman left because of the change of government from Wilson to Heath. This shows how little Freeman discussed his life even with those few who considered themselves friends. Nor did Dr Kissinger realise how 'compartmentalised' Freeman's life was, to use his own word. 'I guess I never really knew him. He never talked about himself.'

On their final evening in America, John and Catherine were guests of Dan and Joanna Rose at a smart Manhattan restaurant, La Lutèce.

Henry Kissinger was there, Wes Pruden with Corinna Metcalf, David Frost with the actress Diahann Carroll. There were toasts and speeches. The next day a photographer caught the ambassador crying as he left the residency, a most unusual sight and perhaps a sign of the strain he was under. Catherine had no idea what was about to happen.

The family moved back to London into a small rented house in South Hill Park in Berkshire, which had been found by Lizi. The house was ugly and the atmosphere miserable. After three awkward days of near silence, Catherine could bear it no longer. She asked Freeman what was wrong: 'You're very quiet. Why? You've stopped the job you didn't enjoy and now we are all safely back at home.' Freeman replied that he was unable to stay with her any longer, that he would go mad if he didn't get away. For the second time in their life together she asked if there was somebody else. This time he said, 'It's Jude.' She remembers:

> At first I couldn't think what or who he meant, then it dawned on me that he was talking about Judith and that he had planned all this with her in advance. He had sent her to South Africa while he detached himself from the Foreign Office and his family, and then he would be off to South Africa too. Later on, I realised that he must have started an affair in Washington when they had gone ahead to prepare the residency.[54]

Freeman could not leave straight away because of diplomatic protocols. He needed to attend a farewell dinner at Chequers so he begged Catherine to accompany him 'otherwise it would look odd'. He left for South Africa a few days later. The very next day, bizarrely, Catherine was rushed to the Middlesex Hospital with acute appendicitis, leaving her mother and the ever-loyal Cynthia to look after the children.

Back in the United States their friends were in a state of shock. 'We were all dumbfounded,' said Joanna Rose. 'She deeply, deeply loved him. She did not know about the Edna O'Brien story, she did not know about the affair with Judith; not a clue! Not a clue! It was cruel for Catherine. She was hurt for a very long time. He was the love of her life.'

After the shock came the speculation. The press took the view that the former ambassador had a low boredom threshold and liked to change careers and wives regularly. Every ten years was the figure John Freeman had given to Robert Cassen, probably sounding semi-flippant. Joanna Rose said the view in Washington and New York society was that Catherine was too much for John, too demanding, too extrovert, while John behaved like a Roman, cold and sensual. Corinna Metcalf agreed with both views:

> Catherine asked me once why I thought John left her. I said, 'You are a young man's woman and John is not a young man.' She had a lot of energy. She liked doing things and by the time of the Washington years he was tired. He probably wanted life in a lower key and Judith had none of Catherine's sparkle and brilliance but she was undemanding, very easy, quite different. Also, John never stayed long with any woman during his most virile years. He had several wives and mistresses. That really is the key to John's character. He didn't do anything very long in his life, whether it was marriage or a job. Why he had to close these doors, keep changing everything, including children, I don't know. It's one for a psychiatrist.[55]

Dan Rose's thoughts went in the same direction. 'Professionally he was very impressive, knowledgeable, tough-minded and clear thinking. His interpersonal relationships were odd. Troubled. Abnormal.

I think at the time we felt that. Either he was born that way or he acquired it through childhood experiences. He was a wounded person; no empathy.

Lord Renwick took a professional view: 'I don't think he resigned as ambassador because of the scandal. The Foreign Office by then could take divorce in its stride, why not? The fact is that after Washington there is nowhere else to go. You have occupied the most important foreign post. Where do you go after that?'

It would have been very difficult, however, for Freeman to continue as ambassador for a second term with the former social secretary at the embassy as his official mistress; particularly when his wife had had such a high profile and admired reputation. Freeman must have realised that.

Chapter 11

Media mogul

THE ORIGINS OF John Freeman's seventh career may be traced to a BOAC flight from London to New York on 21 January 1967. The current maker and shaker of British television, David Frost, had an inspired idea. Borrowing a typewriter from another passenger he excitedly tapped out a letter to High Commissioner Freeman who was in New Delhi. He invited him to 'control and direct the whole programme output' of an 'unstoppable *television* [his italics] team' that would take on the 'moguls' of the commercial television industry in a bid to start a new weekend television service in London. This would become London Weekend Television, LWT for short.

Freeman replied that he was interested: 'It would be a wonderful achievement for the practitioners of television to seize part of the franchise from the moguls and I should like to be associated with it. Whether I can is a more difficult question.' On 9 February, David Frost flew to New Delhi and made a secret deal with the High Commissioner. Freeman told Frost that his India posting would probably end in July 1968, after which he would like to become ambassador to either the United States or the Soviet Union: nothing else would do. Nevertheless, he was enthusiastic about heading LWT at some stage. Frost suggested that the solution was to name him, confidentially, as deputy chairman on the bid to win the weekend franchise. 'The date on which he would join us,' wrote Frost, 'would be the conclusion of his service in India, unless he was asked to serve in Washington or Moscow, in which case he would join following his service there.'[1] This deal was to have repercussions throughout the history of LWT.

Why Frost pinned his hopes on a diplomat who might be out of the country for six years and had no experience of the rapidly evolving commercial television industry, although he had been a celebrated performer for the BBC, we do not know. Probably he would have agreed with Lord Renwick that if the newcomer was of sufficient calibre he would cope as well if not better than the professionals, but only if he was of the highest calibre. In fact, when a desperate David Frost did eventually call on Freeman's services in March 1971, poor management at LWT had reduced the station to meltdown. Its very survival was at stake. To appreciate the mess that Freeman had to clear up – he said the offices reminded him of a casualty clearing station after a major battle – we need to go back to 1967.

The 'television team' that set up LWT in the first place, to use Frost's stress on the word 'television', considered themselves the best in the business because they were the elite of BBC TV departmental heads, led by none other than the director-general-in-waiting of the BBC. They had defected as a group to join the opposition, which says much for the insouciance of Frost, the money on offer and the well-known saying 'no one is *entirely* loyal to the BBC'. The reason Frost chose them in opposition to 'the moguls' who he implied ran the rest of commercial television, thus pitting the Greeks against the Philistines, as it were, went back to the Pilkington Report of 1962 on the future of the broadcasting services in the UK.

The high-minded writers of the report had been extremely critical of the contention of the commercial TV 'moguls' that their job was simply to provide programmes the public wanted to watch: 'Those who say they give the public what it wants begin by underestimating public taste, and end by debauching it.' Instead, the Pilkington Committee wrote in a succinct and careful sentence, broadcasting 'should give people the best possible chance of enlarging worthwhile experience'.[2] What better way of doing this, David Frost thought, than by assembling a team of television practitioners from the heads of BBC TV's children's, arts, music and comedy departments and placing them under the controller of the main BBC channel, BBC One, the universally admired Michael Peacock? (see Chapter 5). The new team lost no time announcing that their first principles were to show respect for the creative talents of those who made programmes and for those who watched them, and whose differing interests and tastes aspired to new experiences.

This is what the Independent Television Authority (ITA) wanted to hear. The ITA was, as always, in a difficult position. It was a public authority established by Parliament to maintain the standard of programmes provided by a handful of public limited companies, financed largely by advertising and answerable to shareholders. In practice, this meant that the ITA invited ITV companies from different parts of the UK to submit their programme schedules in order to obtain a licence to broadcast for a limited period. The ITA selected the best on offer in a competitive process and then tried to ensure that the successful companies lived up to their submissions. From time to time, in a head-masterly way, the ITA issued guidance as to what it meant by 'public service broadcasting'. This had to be less stringent, less demanding than the standards expected of the BBC, which, after all, was paid for by a compulsory licence fee. It was a question of where to draw the line. There was bound to be tension between the ITA's regulatory remit and the commercial needs of ITV companies. From the time Freeman arrived at LWT in 1971 to the time he left in 1984 he challenged basic ITA assumptions, from its awarding of contracts to its definition of public service. That, however, was for the future.

In 1967 the ITA was hugely impressed by the manifesto of David Frost's new team. It had complained for some time that the stand-ard of children's, arts, music and comedy programmes on ITV was too low and here were the former heads of those very departments at the BBC promising to lift them. The chairman of the ITA, Lord Hill, wrote: 'It is an understatement to say that the authority liked this application. It was difficult to resist the thought that here was a group who would bring new thinking, fresh ideas and a lively impe-tus to weekend broadcasting. It had to have its chance, whatever the repercussions.'[3]

On 12 June 1967, the ITA took away the franchise for supplying commercial television in the London area at weekends (Friday to Sunday) from Associated Rediffusion and awarded it to what became LWT. 'Bloody hell,' thought Frost, 'we've really got to do it now.' The bid had taken just three months to put together, from start to finish – but that was the easy part.

The new management team gave themselves an effective voice in the running of LWT because they had a substantial equity holding. They saw no reason why, as people who cared about television and made television, this should be otherwise. But they suffered from a handicap familiar later to BBC programme makers who left to set up independent companies in the 1990s, which was that they had no business or legal or personnel background. Neither the chairman, Aidan Crawley, nor Michael Peacock had run a company before. They stuck to the mantra that the quality of the programme was what really mattered, but their weekend schedules in the early days were naive to say the least.

On Saturday evenings, when viewers in the London area wanted to relax, all LWT had to offer was a mixture of 'Brecht, Britten, some uninspired situation comedies and uninteresting variety programmes'.[4] Up against this, a ruthless BBC responded to the challenge by offering its best police series, *Dixon of Dock Green*, *The Val Doonican Show* and *Match of the Day*. Unsurprisingly, audiences in the early months of LWT dropped by 16 per cent from the size of audiences obtained by Associated Rediffusion. This could not be allowed to continue.

The LWT board, composed of business men and investors with non-executive powers, regarded Peacock as impossibly arrogant, spoilt by the BBC and sheltered from economic realities. He resented board members' interference and dismissed them as ignorant about television. The press saw the scenario of Hard-Faced Business up against Creative Talent, and put like that there was no doubt who would win. On Monday 8 September 1969, Michael Peacock returned from holiday, hoping that his new autumn schedules would rescue the channel. Instead, he was summoned to Aidan Crawley's office and invited to resign. The prime movers behind this happened to be friends of John Freeman, the banker Lord Montague and the chairman of the *New Statesman*, Lord Campbell. *The Times*'s verdict: 'For all the splendour of his reputation as a broadcaster, Mr Peacock was in fact running a company that was providing neither the commercial success that had been expected nor the programmes of the quality that had been promised.'[5]

In early October, department heads resigned in protest. They were mostly the former BBC talent, the LWT heads of drama (Humphrey Burton), entertainment (Frank Muir) and children's, religious and adult education (Doreen Stephens). It was the end of a brave experiment.

There were three further reasons why the early LWT failed. The faults were not directly those of management but Freeman had to correct them when he arrived. The other ITV companies resented LWT because of its 'best boy' status with the ITA, and they had considerable power to undermine it. This was because no one company could fill its schedules entirely with its own programmes so the major companies like Granada, Thames, ATV and LWT were obliged by the ITA to produce a range of programmes that they offered to one another in order to form a network schedule – that is a selection of programmes that were shown by every company. Crucially, it was left to individual companies to choose when to schedule these network programmes. Jealous of LWT's reputation and wanting to maximise their own audiences, the other companies were known to schedule LWT programmes at unfavourable times in their own regions. They also offered their own best programmes to Thames TV, the weekday supplier in London, despite pleas from LWT to show them at weekends. Worse than that, some companies like ATV in the midlands scheduled against LWT by placing some of their own poor programmes at the weekend so that the inherited audience for LWT output was minimal.

Then there was the economic climate. Commercial TV might have been in its early days 'a permit to print money', in the words of Lord Thomson who founded Scottish Television in the 1950s, but by 1969 after an economic slump and devaluation the printing presses had certainly stopped. It was hard to make a profit. Advertising revenue was down but the government continued to impose a large tax on it. In 1970, LWT actually made a modest profit, nearly £3 million, but this was reduced to a small loss after payment of a levy larger than the profit itself.

Finally, there were the trade unions, obstructive and expensive. LWT was forced to take over Rediffusion's obsolete studios in Wembley, where the staff, demoralised and suspicious, delayed the start of programme production for two months. Then they pulled the plug on opening night, 2 August 1968, when, ironically, Frank Muir was introducing *We Have Ways of Making You Laugh*. The Association of Cinematographic and Television Technicians (ACCT) members were responsible. They had claimed, and been given, 'a golden handshake' when they left Rediffusion and an enhanced pay packet when they joined LWT the following week. When its members came up against John Freeman a few years later, they would not find the youthful socialist of 1945 who thought trade union power was the gateway to a New Britain; more the *Panorama* interviewer of 1960 who was prepared ruthlessly to expose trade union malpractice.

The one person who might have resolved this was the most important figure in LWT, David Frost himself. He was barred from membership of the board because he was a star performer; *Frost on Friday*, *Frost on Saturday* and *Frost on Sunday* were the staple output of the channel. Yet he had founded LWT, drawn up the franchise bid before Peacock joined, sat in on board meetings and had a seat on the programme committee. He also ran his own talent company, David Paradine Productions, which packaged shows for LWT and had under contract star entertainers like Tommy Cooper, Ronnie Barker and Ronnie Corbett. Peacock, understandably, criticised this as a conflict of interest and resented Frost's salary that was far higher than his own. Then he tried to prevent Frost opening another chat show in the United States, pointing out that this might jeopardise his primary commitment to LWT. He said he had nightmares that Frost might be over the Atlantic when he got his cue to be on air with *Frost on Friday.* There was deep enmity between the two that did diminish over the years.

On 3 October 1969, Frost interviewed Rupert Murdoch on *Frost on Friday.* Looking back at the early history of LWT this seems almost as significant an event as Frost writing to Freeman two years earlier. The Australian press baron had just bought the *News of the World* and this was his introduction to the British public. Taking the *News of the World* as his evidence, Frost invited the audience to question Murdoch's values and morality. The Australian press tycoon was not a confident TV performer and he hated the 'trial by television'. Frost thought it made good viewing and he invited Murdoch for a drink afterwards. Murdoch stormed out, pausing as he left the studios to vow revenge, as legend has it: 'I'm going to buy this place,' he declared.[6]

Gradually, he bought up shares in LWT, encouraged by Peacock's successor as managing director, Dr Tom Margerison, who saw him as an ally and admired his media savvy. Murdoch's motives were not just revenge and certainly not philanthropy. He intended to turn the company round and, by July 1970, as he owned or had been offered over a third of the non-voting shares, he had the power to do so. He injected £500,000 of his own money for a seat on the board. He and his team toured the studios, 'like the Mafia' said one LWT old hand, demanded changes and installed their own man, Bert Hardy, as director of sales.

It soon became clear that although Murdoch was a non-executive director he was behaving, de facto, as if he was running the company.

When Tom Margerison pointed out to him that he had no right to appear at programme meetings, he stopped attending them but invited the programme bosses round to his house at weekends instead. This was too much for the managing director; he had wanted Murdoch's support but not his takeover. He complained to chairman Crawley, but the board had lost confidence in Margerison by now so Crawley used this row with Murdoch as an excuse to demand his resignation. A new executive committee was set up to run LWT under Murdoch. This was in February 1971. A few days later, Murdoch announced that LWT could no longer afford Frost's salary. He must either accept less money or take his talent elsewhere. In under eighteen months, Murdoch's revenge seemed complete.

By now LWT had become a subject of mockery and vilification in the press. The other ITV companies were circling like sharks waiting for a kill. All sorts of rumours and suggestions reached the ITA. Thames wanted to take over LWT: the other major companies wanted to take over LWT jointly and run it like Independent Television News (ITN): the ITA should take over LWT and control it directly. LWT was obviously in melt down.

The ITA had to act decisively and it did. On 25 February, the new director-general of the ITA, Sir Brian Young, invoked the Television Act. This stated that the authority could intervene if a newspaper proprietor was taking an executive role in a commercial TV company that is 'leading to results contrary to the public interest'. Further, it disqualified individuals who were 'not ordinarily resident in the United Kingdom' from being programme contractors. That put an end to Murdoch's ambitions. The ITA gave LWT just six weeks to get its house in order. In effect, it demanded that LWT must appoint a new managing director and re-apply for its licence. Murdoch went off to Australia in a sulk.[7]

The deadline pumped Frost's adrenaline. Acting with his customary self-assurance he devised a rescue plan. This centred on John Freeman, his original choice as chairman, but before he approached him he had to gather support. First, he contacted the ITA and secured the assurance of Sir Brian Young that he really did want LWT to survive. Then he contacted the three men on the LWT board whose backing was essential if he were to invite Freeman to become the new managing director. Lord Montague was sceptical. Lord Campbell was positive: 'I thought that John Freeman had the same qualities as Murdoch – he wanted to do what he did as well as it could be done, which is what we needed.'[8] That left Murdoch. His consent was conditional on what proved to be the final casualty on the LWT battlefield: Aidan Crawley had to go.

Frost approached Freeman. They had kept in touch since 1967, mostly through Catherine. Indeed, Frost had attended their final farewell party in New York back in January. By early March, John was in South Africa with Judith Mitchell but when Frost spoke on the phone with Catherine, who was still in hospital recovering from appendicitis, she suggested that John might be open for the LWT job. The timing could not have been better.

Freeman was out of work and knew he 'had to go out and earn a living. It was quite fun being an ambassador but you don't get rich on it'. He was fifty-six and as he had never bothered to include wealth management among his many skills, he had few savings. If he remained in the diplomatic service until he was sixty he would have to retire, with less chance then of landing a well-paid job. As it was, LWT was offering a reasonable salary plus a large block of shares. Then of course, the offer fitted his philosophy – a radical challenge in a new job every decade. What the 'deputy chairman of LWT' would have done if the company had been riding high in 1971 is speculation. Having already succeeded in politics, journalism and broadcasting there was not much left. As it was, there was an interesting offer on the table.

First, he imposed his own terms. He wanted absolute authority so he insisted on being both managing director and chairman. Crawley disappeared upstairs to become president, in name only. 'This is a blow we must bear with equanimity,' Freeman said drily to Frost.[9] Then he needed the assurance from Murdoch that he would be given a free hand to sort out LWT. Murdoch gave it in a phone call from Australia, but Freeman pressed the point: 'You do realise that a free hand applies to you as well as to everybody else – I really do want a free hand.' Murdoch assented. The stage was set for Freeman to enter, *deus ex machina*.

All of this begs the question, why did Freeman think he could succeed where the best of the BBC had spectacularly failed? The answer is that basically he did not care whether he succeeded or not provided he did his best. Many adopt a similar rationale but then their feelings get the better of them and they find they do care about failure, to the extent of shying away from the challenge in the first place. This certainly was not Freeman. The essence of his leadership was that he had confidence in his own superb judgement and underneath this lay a cold temperament so that any emotion he may have felt was suppressed. As he put it, he 'didn't give a bugger':

> I had very strong views about how the company should be run, but frankly I didn't give a bugger whether I stayed or not – I merely had to do the best I could. I intended to run the company my way and to hell with anyone who wanted it done differently. I always treated Murdoch with the respect he commands personally, because he is a very formidable and able man, but I simply did not concede that he had any right to interfere in the day-to-day running of the company.[10]

Polite, quietly arrogant, ruthless; that was John Freeman.

Back in South Hill Park, he had left behind a scene of desolation. Cynthia Gomes was at the centre of it:

> When Mrs Freeman told me that Mr Freeman had left, we both wept. I stayed with her because the children needed me and Catherine needed me very badly. It was a very difficult time. It was very hard for Matthew; he had to be put on a special medication. It was difficult for Tom; Tom's world came to an end because his dad had gone. And Lucy – it was so hard for her – why had her daddy gone? Had she been naughty or something? And for me, I had been with Lucy from a baby, one day old I handled her. Matthew then was ten years old. So you can imagine how I felt. They were like my own children. I felt a lot for Catherine and like I say my loyalty is to both of them, you know.
>
> Mr Freeman came to the house and he used to come a lot. I used to take the children to visit him [Freeman had rented a flat in Prince Albert Road near Regent's Park] and that was the time too when he was attending to my visa and passport and he got everything done for me and he brought me the paperwork.
>
> I was in-between in this situation. I know personally because I lived with them that to me they were a very happy family and then when this happened it broke. My world had come to an end. The children, the children!

I asked Cynthia if she knew why the marriage had broken up? By this time in our conversation, over forty years after the events in question, she was virtually in tears:

> I don't know. I don't know. All I can say is that I was so close to Mr and Mrs Freeman and I kept my place as a governess and respected

the family. But when you take somebody as your friend and confide in that friend, and that friend is the one who is taking something away from you, where do you go? Where do you turn? What do you say to yourself? How shocked you are when that happens! All I can say is when Mrs Freeman told me that, she and I were crying together … that's all that I can tell you. When I look at her even now, I feel for her. She's never forgotten Mr Freeman. Never. Never! It's still there. It's still there.[11]

On 9 March 1971 the appointment of John Freeman as chairman and chief executive of London Weekend Television was announced. His very first job was to move the executive suite of LWT from Old Burlington Street, Mayfair, into the main production offices at Station House, a grim twenty-storey office block in Wembley that overlooked a railway goods yard. No respecter of social status, this probably made no difference to him but it had a morale booster effect on the staff. When the former HM ambassador was seen queuing up in the canteen and saying simply, 'This is where the work is done', he was greeted with acclaim. Staff asked about his programme tastes? He was tactful but admitted he was no fan of high camp: 'The one show I can't stand is *Come Dancing*.'[12] Within a few weeks he would be presenting LWT's case to the ITA, on which his staff's jobs depended.

Freeman's appointment was seen as a major coup for LWT as well as further proof of Frost's powers of persuasion. Freeman was already hugely respected in television. He was charismatic, dignified and polite, qualities that in LWT had not been much in evidence. He was the sort of leader who inspires confidence. David Docherty, whose book *Running the Show; 21 Years of London Weekend Television* I gratefully acknowledge, said that Freeman behaved in his thirteen years at LWT like a hero played by James Stewart or Gary Cooper in Frank Capra's

1930s films like *Mr Smith Goes to Washington,* crossed with Lewis Elliot, the central figure in C. P. Snow's *Strangers and Brothers.* What he meant was that Freeman seemed a 'profoundly humane character' (Frank Capra) and a leader who 'revelled in command, loved the arts of management, had the strength of will to carry through his ideas but also possessed a stubborn disregard for alternative views' (C. P. Snow). James Stewart and Gary Cooper, of course, always got their girl, which in Freeman's case needs to be in the plural.

Journalists were keen to meet 'the formidable Mr Freeman', as Ivan Rowan called him in the *Sunday Telegraph* of 14 March 1971. His attempt to discover 'who he really is' was as unsuccessful as if the meeting had never taken place:

> It was like arriving at a house for a long deferred appointment, and being greeted by a tall, sandy-haired man with flat blue eyes and a voice as delicate and precise as a vicar's. 'I am afraid the *real* Mr Free-man was called away five minutes ago. I know he would have been delighted to see you. Is there any message?'

Derrik Mercer of the *Sunday Times* got a bit closer, sitting opposite the new chief executive in his office: 'Ruddy, freckled face, blond hair brushed to an immaculate smoothness, graceful hands that he is obviously very proud of, eyes watchful behind heavy rimmed glasses, he looks impressive enough. But what are his qualifications to revive a shaky television company?'[13] He did not get an answer, any more than other journalists. 'That's a fair, even interesting question,' responded Freeman unhelpfully. Former Prime Minister Harold Wilson fared no better. He came round to LWT for a television interview and hoped to catch up with his old colleague's news over lunch. He was told: 'Mr Free-man sends his apologies but he has gone out for a lunch appointment.'

In early March, the ITA had handed LWT a searching question-naire. It wanted written answers 'covering all aspects of the company's structure and operations: financial, managerial, creative and techni-cal'. In effect this required a re-application for the franchise. It asked the company's senior executives and board members to assemble at the ITA offices at eleven o'clock on 22 April for a grilling. It was the day of decision. Frost had been assured by Sir Brian Young that the ITA wanted LWT to survive, for the obvious reason that to fail was too terrible to contemplate for ITV; it would have necessitated major re-organisation. Further, the appointment of John Freeman gave the ITA a way out. But the result was not a foregone conclusion.

LWT fielded a team of ten, headed by Freeman and including Mur-doch, Lord Campbell and Lord Montague. According to Sir Brian Young, who was sitting across the table from LWT, Freeman was clearly in charge of his board. He answered most of the questions himself; he knew his facts, was clear about the direction in which he wanted to take the company, was committed to public service broadcasting and 'filled the authority with confidence that their problem child was about to grow up'.

Freeman's opening statement was an assertion of ideals: 'LWT still believes in the ideals it presented to the authority in its original appli-cation. Indeed we can claim to have fulfilled many and most of the intentions set out.' It was also an admission of serious failings: 'Our setbacks have derived from administrative, executive and commercial shortcomings, for which both board and management must accept a due share of responsibility.'[14] The ITA was satisfied. It renewed the contract and expressed pleasure that uncertainty about the future of LWT had been removed. LWT would now enjoy the same security as the other ITV companies throughout the remaining contract period.

It must have been a masterful performance by a man who six weeks before knew nothing about the television industry or running a company. Further, he had been out of the country for the previous six years and was in the midst of an awful marriage break-up. 'He was,' said the *Daily Telegraph,* 'one of those rare men of parts who seem to be able to do anything better than anybody else.' No wonder he became bored quickly; even the most demanding job was just too easy.

Freeman was at his best leading a team to present evidence before a committee. His army chief-of-staff training came to the fore. For a start, he was a great believer in preparation or, as the army puts it, 'prior preparation prevents piss-poor performance'. At LWT he would make a practice of assembling the executive directors in his office for a thorough dress rehearsal before facing the LWT board or the IBA. Then he would field all the questions himself before handing over to, say, the director of entertainment, in order to give him precious seconds to prepare his answer: prosaic but effective. Then, of course, his manner was anything but prosaic – a charismatic presence and a voice that was always polite but demanded to be heard.

As often happens when a new manager takes over a team, a period of good fortune followed. LWT sold the hugely successful comedy series *Doctor in the House* and *Doctor at Sea* to the USA. The government halved the levy on advertising and thus restored confidence in the industry. By the end of the year, ITV's overall revenue had reached its highest annual increase since 1964. This left Freeman to see off one predator threatening the company from the outside, Thames Television, and one challenger to his authority from the inside, Rupert Murdoch.

Thames TV had wasted no time suggesting to Aidan Crawley that a merger of sorts should take place between the five-day-a-week TV supplier in the London area and the weekend supplier. Crawley was interested but Freeman saw this as the thin end of the wedge. At a working dinner at Crawley's house, Freeman and his new programme controller Cyril Bennett went head to head with the Thames chairman Lord Shawcross (an old colleague of Freeman's from the Attlee government); his managing director, Howard Thomas; and his director of programmes, Brian Tesler. Freeman did not mince his words. He complained that Thames had been traducing LWT and then, as a diplomatic gesture, offered a few crumbs of cooperation like sharing Outside Broadcast units. Shortly afterwards he persuaded the ITA to ask Thames to beef up its current affairs output, thus taking the burden off LWT, and show fewer high-rating US programmes, thus allowing LWT to replace them with its own buy-ins without overstepping the quota. After this decisive intervention, relations between LWT and the whole of ITV improved.

Freeman said:

> It was my job to hold Murdoch in check, because to have allowed him to continue interfering in the company would have spelt simple and rapid disaster. We had a rather odd relationship over quite a long period and became, I hope, friends. I certainly became, and remain, fond of him, and I think he is a decent and much abused man. However, our relationship was based on the fact that I had to prevent him doing what he wanted to do until eventually, and quite inevitably, he decided to focus his energies elsewhere.[15]

On another occasion, he said of Murdoch: 'I trust Rupert. I don't trust him to be nice, you know, but I trust he will do what he says he's going to do.'[16] Soon, Murdoch quit the board because he got involved in United States ventures and nominated Bert Hardy, the director of sales, to replace him. In 1979 he sold nearly all his shares in LWT at a profit. He always acknowledged that 'undoubtedly, John Freeman saved the company'. David Frost switched allegiances too. He signed a contract with the BBC and sold his LWT shares in 1976.

Freeman's impact was making itself felt. At the regular IBA Policy Committee Meetings (in 1972 the Independent Television Authority became the Independent Broadcasting Authority when radio was added) the chairmen of all fifteen companies would sit round a table with the IBA top brass and, in the case of the main ITV companies, their directors of programmes too. This is where Brian Tesler got to know John Freeman:

> For four years at least, John and I sat next to each other, joining in the discussions of programme policy, strategy, and so on. [Tesler was then director of programmes for Thames TV.] Naturally, we got to know each other rather well. He had an agile and very clear brain and a magnificent way of expressing himself. I mean when John Freeman spoke, you listened. It sounded good, even if it possibly wasn't right, it was convincing. And there was magnetism about the man that he never lost. And he looked so good! This tall, straight, very handsome man, with quiet confidence. You knew he was a man of great power and strength but I never saw him lose his temper, nor vilify anyone. With this agile brain, with a marvellous use of language … how could he not succeed?[17]

One of Murdoch's recruits to LWT had been an East End boy, Ron Miller, who became head of sales working under Bert Hardy. He and Freeman joined the company roughly at the same time and became good friends:

> I first met John a few days after he joined the company in an office in Old Burlington Street. There was a complete suite of offices empty

as Rupert Murdoch had fired most of the executives. He was sat behind a desk and he rose as I walked in. The first thing that struck me was his physical presence. He was tall, very upright and he had a magnificent head of hair. And then, of course, there was the voice. I remember him from his *Face to Face* days. Before I did my National Service I simply made a date to watch every one of these shows. I was already in awe of him.[18]

Not long afterwards, Freeman asked Miller to organise a drinks party in Old Burlington Street (where the sales team had remained in the heart of the advertising district) so he could meet them all. What happened became an instant LWT legend:

Halfway through, Elizabeth Wagg, John's secretary, came in. She said to him, 'President Nixon is on the line.' John turned to me and said, 'Ron, would you mind if I take this call?' I just laughed. When he had put the phone down he turned to the room and said, 'It's a pity there are no advertisers here.'

Very soon Freeman announced how he intended to resolve the contradiction between the public service duty demanded by the ITA and the commercial *raison d'être* of ITV. He told advertisers in November 1972:

The significant duty that LWT has to learn the hard way is that at weekends, against the relentless build-up of entertainment programming of BBC One, minority programmes at peak-time lose not only their own time period but the entire evening's viewing. Our specialist programmes must be strategically placed with very great care. We will make these programmes because they are essential for our prestige and because they are important in their own right; however, we will quarantine them and ensure that high ratings programmes are not infected.[19]

From then on, with the few exceptions such as *Aquarius* and later *Weekend World*, money was put into programmes that would earn high audiences and therefore could charge high advertising rates. Under the director of programmes, Cyril Bennett, whom Freeman described as 'a sort of genius', such home-grown programmes as *Upstairs, Downstairs*, *Budgie*, *Please Sir!* and *On the Buses* soon began to dent the BBC's weekend ratings, and were networked. *The World of Sport* rivalled *Match of the Day* while the arts programme *Aquarius* was loved by the arts reviewers and *Weekend World* became a benchmark in analytical current affairs programming. For a while the ITA was satisfied. Other companies followed LWT's definition of public service broadcasting the ITV way and soon John Freeman with Denis Foreman, the chairman of Granada, became the leading spokesmen for the companies on the IBA Policy Committee.

The chief executive was no Grace Wyndham Goldie. He rarely aired his own views about LWT output and stuck to a management overview. For him a programme was a product that needed the right audience appeal and the right placing in order to attract the right revenue. He did occasionally express an opinion, such as a long and esoteric exchange of notes with the producer of *Upstairs, Downstairs* about whether or not butlers in Edwardian England wore moustaches.

In June 1972, LWT moved from Wembley to a new building that became as celebrated as its chief executive. Kent House, as it is still known, occupies a site by the South Bank Centre on the Thames, the hub of the British media arts world. The facilities were state of the art; it was glossy and glamorous. Some called it Camelot. Keen to project this image, Freeman suggested that the new weekly arts programme presented by Melvyn Bragg should be called *The South Bank Show*.

Freeman became worried about Cyril Bennett's workload – 'You may be interested that neither the Prime Minister nor the President of the United States carry your load of day-to-day detail' – and urged him to delegate by appointing a head of light entertainment. Bennett had his eye on young Michael Grade, then running his father's talent agency because Leslie Grade was convalescing in France after serious medical treatment. This required tact, not least because the three Grade brothers, Lew, Leslie and Bernard, were forces to be reckoned with throughout the British film and TV world. Freeman offered to visit him in France and 'ask for his son's hand in marriage'. This he did, to the surprise and pleasure of Leslie, who told his son he had respected Freeman for years. 'Doesn't that show the sheer class of the man!' Ron Miller exclaimed to me. Michael Grade's admiration for Freeman thereafter knew no bounds:

> Inspirational! He just had to turn up! It was enough to know he was in the building to feel safe. You felt his presence even when he wasn't in the room. He had absolutely no enemies in the company. He had time for everybody, without being patronising.
>
> We all saw him as a quintessential English gentleman of his generation. He had immaculate manners and never displayed emotion: reserved and private, yes, but I don't accept this 'enigma' description of John. His defining feature was a lack of ego. He had no need to impress anyone, and there was no point in flattering him. He was just John.
>
> He was of course very formidable. He was definitely not a man you would tell lies to.[20]

Cyril Bennett's next big appointment was the producer of *The Frost Programme*, John Birt, who came from Granada Television to beef up the current affairs output. Freeman said, 'I became very high on him – he was extremely good news.'[21] Birt was attracted to LWT because while it was now stable, indeed 'on the up', the exodus of talented programme makers in 1969 meant 'it was still something of a green-field site; in terms of current affairs the cupboard was bare'. Granada, on the other hand, 'was stuffed with talent'. Birt started the mould-breaking *Weekend World* in 1972 and that was followed by *The London Programme*, both highly regarded by the serious-minded Brian Young, now director-general of the IBA.

Freeman's next task, in order reduce Cyril Bennett's workload and to plan for his own succession, was to appoint a deputy. Although Brian Tesler was expecting to succeed Howard Thomas as managing director of Thames Television, there happened to be a break in his contract. Having ascertained that he could approach Tesler without impropriety, Freeman invited him over to his house in Kew. They walked round the garden, discovered they had a common birthday, a shared like of American crime fiction, and a dislike of Oxbridge intel-lectual snobbery; soon the deal was done. In May 1974, Tesler joined LWT as deputy chief executive on the understanding that he would succeed Freeman in two years if his probation worked out.

Freeman sprang a probationary test soon after Tesler's arrival. Despite Michael Grade's initiatives, comedy programmes were disap-pointing. At one of the occasional staff meetings held in a large studio someone wanted to know why. Instead of asking Bennett or Grade for their views, Freeman turned to Tesler, catching him unawares:

> The only thing I could think of saying was, 'It reminds me of my
> uncle who invented a drink called *One Up*, and it didn't work. The
> following year he invented another drink and he called it *Two Up*,
> and that didn't sell. And in successive years, *Three Up*, *Four Up* and

Five Up didn't sell either so he threw in the towel. The following year someone invented *Seven Up* and made a fortune.' The implication was that we will carry on trying and get there in the end. There was a big laugh. On the way out, John said – and here's the Jewishness of LWT coming out – 'Congratulations, that was your Bar Mitzvah.'[22]

The chief executive belonged to the school of management that believes a light hand on the tiller when the company is doing well is the best way to attract new talent. It is the hiring and firing that is important. In three years LWT had recruited three of the outstanding leaders of the British TV industry of the future. Lord Grade became chief executive of Channel 4, chairman of the BBC and then executive chairman of ITV; Lord Birt became director-general of the BBC; and Brian Tesler CBE became managing director and chairman of LWT, as well as governor of the British Film Institute, vice-president of the Royal Television Society and similar honours. There was one other key appointment to come. John Birt said Freeman reminded him of football manager Sir Alex Ferguson; he was an astute talent scout and he planned ahead. No one called him a 'people person', in the sense that he rarely gossiped, but the consensus at LWT was that he was a shrewd judge of people. As Robert Cassen had discovered in Washington: 'John seemed to have your measure but you never seemed to have his.'

Despite the glamorous South Bank image, the new studios and the display cabinets of awards in the foyer, LWT was no longer 'best boy' with the IBA. In its review of 1974, the IBA criticised the lack of resources and time given to programmes about religion, on adult education and for children. Freeman objected to its headmasterly tone and demanded clarification. When it came, Freeman was irritated further. The IBA now extended its criticism to drama: 'Can there be some causal relationship between the uneven achievement of LWT drama and the proportion of freelance staff in the drama department? Do you have anything that can be described as a drama department at all?' Freeman wrote a draft reply: 'The blunt answer to the first question is "No" and to the second "Yes".'[23]

The IBA did not back down and when it renewed the LWT franchise in 1975 it pointedly repeated its criticisms, as well as noting LWT's many achievements. This criticism went back to the basic belief of Sir Brian Young that 'the answer to the old question whether ITV should reflect or lead the interests and tastes of the public must be that it should do both. The balance it strikes between the two will always be more ambitious than is to be found in a solely commercial service.'[24] Freeman did not object to that in principle but he became increasingly opposed to the IBA practice of awarding franchises to competing companies in the first place. The truth was that he was no friend of the IBA (he had turned down the offer to be considered for the post of director-general as long ago as 1970) and this would become the main issue of his chairmanship of LWT in the years ahead.

In May 1976, Brian Tesler became managing director of LWT and John Freeman moved to the little office next door as chairman. Later that year, Tesler summoned all the senior staff to a three-day brainstorming conference at the Selsdon Park Hotel in Croydon. The aim was to review programming in the light of the IBA criticisms and to inspire some corporate bonding. Tesler had been aware for some time that the management structure at LWT was virtually non-existent. The creative staff worked directly to Cyril Bennett in one-to-one meetings so that they hardly knew what each other was doing. John Birt recalled, 'There was no sense of community or fraternity of programme-makers: there was no forum in which we discussed things in general.' Freeman's style of delegation and laissez-faire was all very well but this was surely a shortcoming. For a former chief of staff who admired army hierarchy and ran the *New Statesman* 'like a quartermaster-general' it seems out of character. According to Tesler, 'John never said to Cyril "something's not right. Where's the organisation? Shouldn't it be like this?" Surprising because John was an organisational man.'[25]

The conference opened with a hard-hitting critique by John Birt – 'when I arrived at LWT it clearly had a flavour of the moment about it; but ideas become sterile, individuals become jaded and programmes become predictable'[26] – and ended in the bar with excited talk and no doubt the telling of in-house jokes. Later that night Cyril Bennett's body was found beneath the open window of his sixth floor flat in Westminster. There was soul-searching at LWT whether the robust self-examination at Selsdon could have been to blame. The funeral was awful, with Birt weeping on Freeman's shoulder. It was left to Tesler to restore morale in the months ahead and to implement a management structure in which each department had a controller who regularly reported to the director of programmes. He in turn held regular meetings with all the controllers to review existing programmes and consider new ones. In February 1977, Grade became the new director of programmes and, when he left LWT in 1981 to work in the States, he was succeeded by John Birt.

In 1976 Judith Mitchell became John Freeman's fourth wife. The gap of five years between his leaving his first family and his remarriage was because Catherine was not prepared to give him a divorce. Initially she could not believe that her husband's liaison would last ('What happens when Judith plays jazz at midnight, Dad?' asked Matthew, aged nine). Nor did she want the children to think she had agreed too easily to the separation that had hurt them so much. And finally, as she now admits, she was prepared to be bloody-minded and make

Freeman wait for the five years that the law at that time required; his betrayal had been too much to accept gracefully. It wasn't so much the divorce itself, or the secrets and lies that led to it, she said, but 'his refusal to engage, to say what the problems were, his blanking out of any discussion. This is what did the damage.'

Freeman was very angry. No longer was he aloof and beyond personal confrontation ('I strove with none for none was worth my strife'). He wrote to Catherine: 'I very seldom choose to fight, but when I do I always win.' Robert Cassen could not believe that John was capable of treating her so badly: 'He behaved in a very chilling way, so chilling that I found it hard to believe. To persuade me she was not exaggerating Catherine showed me some of his letters. They were cold, very cold indeed.'

Were you surprised by this? 'No. I knew that's how he was, though never to me. Catherine was so hurt, so aggrieved, that it was impossible for me to see John again.'[27]

The marriage came to an unseemly end in the Family Court of Registrar Elizabeth Butler-Sloss: John erect and composed, Catherine in tears. He agreed to give her the house in Perceval Avenue, Belsize Park, to which she and the children had moved after South Hill Park, and the sum of £5 a year. That was that.

Slowly, Catherine's life began to improve. In 1976, she was invited by Thames TV to become editor of their daytime programmes, and so began a fruitful period that lasted for twenty-five years. She became controller of documentaries, features and religious programmes at Thames and then an independent producer-director with her own company, Dove Productions. This led to a partial reconciliation with her former husband. She was able to support herself financially and he also appreciated her success. They met for lunch and discussed the children 'without ever disagreeing'. When Matthew became an

adult he took great pride in their achievements. Matt became a leading geneticist and one of the youngest members of the Royal Society.
Tom joined the Merchant Ivory film company as an editor and later
worked for Pixar in America. Lucy read Classics at Oxford, became a
barrister and later a book editor. Freeman was an amiable, if remote,
father and grandfather to Lily, James and Conor. At LWT, the chairman's lifestyle was 'spartan', according to Brian Tesler. He lunched on
his own off a sandwich in his small office. His favourite way of com-
municating was by a handwritten note, and if there was not enough
room on the page he would continue writing round the side. Ron
Miller told me that John Freeman was 'very un-commercial as far as
his own salary was concerned. After he left he told me what his savings amounted to and they were ridiculously small for a man of his
achievement.' In fact, he could have made a lot of money because
LWT became a public company in 1977 and the shares went up far
higher than expected. LWT had a Rolls-Royce and Miller tracked
down the registration plate LWT 1. He offered the car to Freeman
who said, 'I wouldn't be seen dead in it.' According to Michael Grade,
every month the LWT directors would exchange a file of their own
correspondence so others could see what had been going on:

> John had to go to New York for a meeting of UP/ITN that he was
> chairing [see later] and there was a note in the file to the chief account-
> ant at ITN asking for an advance of $100 in cash. Then there was
> another note from John 'I am returning $98 and 50 cents, plus a sub-
> way ticket'! That was John![28]

Freeman was not interested in the trappings of power but he also said at
this time that he did not like power itself: 'Power is a disagreeable element in life. I tend to think those who like it have disagreeable elements

in their personality and I include myself in that.'[29] I read this to John Birt. His reply was unexpected but I think it is absolutely right:

> He certainly did not like power for power's sake, but he was not a proselytiser either. He did not want to impose himself on the world, and that was the theme of his career. He did not want to stand on a platform and parade his views or ask to be loved. He was not self-regarding and he was without ambition.[30]

Was it that Freeman wished to protect himself from self-exposure or simply did not wish to impose himself or his views on others? Probably it was both, but in either case clearly he had not been cut out for political life.

Although Freeman did not enjoy social small talk, when the occasion demanded the LWT chairman was extraordinarily capable of handling it. Michael Grade remembers arriving early at a party for advertisers and Freeman telling him that he did not expect to know any of the sixty or so guests who were coming. Yet when they arrived he handled the introductions impeccably; he knew names, companies and connections. Typically, he had prepared for the event and memorised the guest list. Chan Canasta would have been proud.

A meeting more to his liking was the confrontation with Gavin Waddell, LWT shop steward of the ACTT, over the Bullock Report of 1977 on industrial democracy. Although its radical recommendations for trade union representatives on the board, with shared responsibility for hiring senior staff and disposition of resources, did not strictly apply to LWT because the company had fewer than 2,000 employees, nevertheless the ACTT saw this as an opportunity to increase its power within LWT. 'We will have to meet Gavin,' Freeman told the directors, 'but don't worry, I'll deal with him.' As usual, he had done his homework and thought through the implications for a small company. It seemed Waddell had not. The outcome was similar to the famous Frank Foulkes grilling on *Panorama*. 'Waddell was completely humiliated,' remembers Michael Grade, 'filleted like a kipper! John was coldly polite but knew every trick in the book. He would have made a gobsmacking QC.'

The 1970s was arguably the worst decade in post-war Britain with rampant inflation, a three-day week, widespread industrial strikes, even a sense that the country was ungovernable. Freeman had moved a long way politically from his socialist ideals to a centre-right position. He was a 'dry', as opposed to a 'wet', in the labelling of the times. He believed that his chairman's priority was that LWT should fulfil its contract and if that meant taking on the unions he was ready for it. According to John Birt, he had prepared a management and non-union labour task force that would keep LWT on the air should there be a strike: 'He was unshakable in his resolve.'

The chairman was not always the imperturbable governor of all he surveyed. In November 1978 Michael Grade concluded a secret deal with the Football League whereby ITV won a three-year exclusive contract to televise League football in return for a load of money (£5 million). *Match of the Day* had become 'snatch of the day'. The BBC was livid and threatened court action. Freeman was summoned on his own to the IBA. Somewhat shaken and fearing the worst, Freeman told Tesler that if necessary he would resign to save Tesler and Grade, because they were 'the future of LWT'. To Freeman, loyalty to his team went as far as professional self-sacrifice. In the event, a new deal was struck that allowed both ITV and BBC to show League football – at a much higher price. Grade found out about Freeman's resolve only afterwards.

In the summer of 1980, Freeman led an LWT delegation to the IBA. It was franchise time again, this time a formal presentation and critique before Lady Plowden. According to Ron Miller, 'John was at his brilliant best. After fifteen minutes it looked as if he was interviewing the IBA.' At the end of December, Freeman and Tesler arrived back to be given a sealed envelope. They opened it and read that the LWT contract had been extended for another eight years. The IBA noted its 'diverse good qualities over recent years'. As usual, flattery got nowhere with Freeman. He was not the only ITV leader to criticise the whole franchise-awarding process, but his memo to senior staff at LWT written in August 1981, showed how determined he was to change public opinion: in effect to persuade politicians that the system should be abolished and the IBA cut down to size.

Basically, he thought that the system of fixed-term contracts, which required ITV companies to re-apply for their licences, was a huge waste of time and money. Further, the 'amateurish and unrealistic attitudes of the IBA, many of whose members had little qualification beyond assiduous reading of *The Guardian* and *The Observer*, led it to demand changes that were plain wrong.' He gave the example of Southern TV that had lost its licence not because it had made bad programmes but because the IBA considered another company might make better. 'This sort of haphazard selection is a luxury broadcasting can no longer afford.' What would happen to the BBC, he asked rhetorically, if after 'a lean period, the board of governors and top management would be collectively dismissed in the hope that someone else might do better?' He concluded:

> We must challenge the central doctrine of fixed-term contracts followed by open public tender. The public interest and the quality of broadcasting would best be served by a system under which all contracts were either indefinite or rolling; all were subject to constant review; all subject to summary termination if, after due warning,

satisfactory performance was not achieved. The corollary in logic is that the IBA's massive apparatus of control should be substantially dismantled.[31]

'At the end of his time at LWT John found the IBA very irritating and he had not much time for Lady Plowden,'[32] said Sir Christopher Bland, who had been deputy chairman of the IBA in the 1970s and was soon to join LWT. In 1990 the Broadcasting Act changed the award of franchises to an auction process, incorporating safeguards for quality. After the next round in 1991 Lord Thomson, who had been chairman of the IBA between 1981–88, admitted that this was wrong too. The best way, he said, was a system of rolling contracts. This is what Freeman had proposed; but it was wisdom after the event.

By now Freeman was becoming a media mogul himself. Additional top jobs in the media were his without asking – chairman of ITN (1976–81), chairman of Hutchinson (1978–82), governor of the British Film Institute, vice-president of the Royal Television Society. Hutchinson, the publishers, had been bought by LWT in 1977 when, as Freeman said, 'We were flushed with cash.' It seemed a good investment at the time with a mixture of educational books and popular authors such as Frederick Forsyth. However, from 1980 it began to lose money so LWT determined to make many staff redundant. The lot fell to Freeman as chairman, which perhaps accounts for this view taken of him by Terence Blacker, then an editor at Hutchinson:

> I encountered him now and then, usually viewed from a distance at the head of a long boardroom table. He was sleek and weirdly charmless, so glacial and emotionally absent that one felt that, if someone had died in front of him or taken off their clothes, there would have been no flicker of reaction.[33]

Freeman was certainly cold in a crisis and that had been his reputation for years. However, the former senior staff at LWT deny that
this was his nature. 'Perhaps he mellowed,' Brian Tesler remarked.
'I had heard he was a very cold man but all I can say is that none of
us found him like that.' Ron Miller remembers a convivial drinking session with Freeman in Frankfurt when they went to inspect
an outlying financial office. Michael Grade recalls how Freeman put
his head round the door after Grade's marital problems had become
the stuff of Nigel Dempster's gossip column in the *Daily Express* and
said, 'Don't worry, we've all been "Dempstered"!' John Birt enjoyed
lively conversations with Freeman – 'he was incapable of speaking
an ugly sentence'. Aloof, private, not given to talking about himself
and not a 'joiner', but not cold nor humourless either: that was the
consensus at LWT.

Independent Television News (ITN) supplied news to the ITV
companies in return for a budget and the fixed allocation of airtime.
Freeman was chairman in the 1970s, a time of industrial unrest and
staff dissatisfaction at ITN similar to that at LWT but on a much
more disruptive scale. Coincidentally, at exactly the same time as the
Selsdon Park conference at LWT discussed lack of communication
at management level (1976) so at ITN the editor Nigel Ryan com-
missioned the Pearson Inquiry into the same thing. It reported that
'24 per cent of comments and criticisms were the absence of any form
of constructive communications'. Hitherto, when the political editor
Julian Havilland had complained about this to the chairman, Freeman had given him 'a dusty answer' (a favourite Freeman phrase) but
now a management structure was set up not very dissimilar to that
by Brian Tesler at LWT. Soon after Nigel Ryan left, not because of
this but because the board had turned down his proposal to expand
news into current affairs with more programming. Here Freeman was

adamant: 'I held the view that the only way ITN could survive was if it remained a nuts and bolts operation without fancy points.' The ITV companies did not want poachers on their land.[34]

Freeman was also chairman of United Press International Television News (UPITN). This was a partnership between the American television news agency United Press International and ITN, which provided much of the footage and coverage in the United States. UPI was always short of money because it was not directly connected with any of the big American TV broadcast companies. In 1979 it was rumoured that the government of South Africa was indirectly bankrolling it, just when it was supplying an interview with the pro-apartheid Prime Minister John Vorster. This was too much for ITN. Freeman wrote more than a 'dusty' ultimatum: 'My board do not find it acceptable to be associated in any way with a company that is not in a position immediately and unanswerably to refute the allegation that it may have been covertly penetrated by foreign government funds.'[35]

The rumour proved to be true and much to the embarrassment of ITN it had to buy out the South African shares in UPI. Not long afterwards, UPI went bankrupt and in 1985 UPITN became World Television News (WTN), owned by ITN and the American Broadcasting Company (ABC). Apparently, at one stage in the negotiations with ABC in New York, Freeman turned to Elmer Lower, the president of ABC News and said, in exasperation: 'Elmer, it's time to crap or get off the pot.' This revelation comes from Dan Moloney of ITN, who was there. He adds that 'John spoke in his mellifluous voice, likened by one reviewer to a vicar's.'

By 1984 Freeman had enough. He wrote to me in 2004: 'I served a very long sentence in public life of one kind or another, and I believe I have paid my dues in full.' There speaks a man who must have wanted a rest. Now that Tesler, Birt and Miller were 'operating on all legs' as he put it, and the franchise bid had been successful, he thought the sooner he got out the better. Typically, he had ensured his successor was in place. 'I decided what LWT needed was a businessman to look after the affairs of the company. Christopher Bland was young, go-getting and exactly the right sort of person.' He became chairman of the main board of LWT (Holdings) to universal approval on 1 Janu-ary: 'a stellar talent, a toughie' is John Birt's assessment. Brian Tesler became chairman of the TV company, a dual chairmanship that found less than universal approval at first.

One of Bland's first decisions was to abandon the Freeman practice of holding a pre-board meeting in his office with the executive direc-tors to work out their approach to the board meeting itself. 'Whatever happened at the board meeting was choreographed in advance, which made the meetings rather dull,' Sir Christopher Bland told me. 'John didn't like surprises or confrontation.'

Freeman had stayed longer at LWT than in any of his other careers and enjoyed it the most. He told an interviewer:

> My temperament is such that I like to immerse myself in something and then, when I feel I've had all the experience from it I'm likely to get, say yes to something else. LWT was really the first time I hadn't done that. I enjoyed it more than any other job partly because of the company and partly because the problems have been quite dif-ficult ones.[36]

At Freeman's farewell dinner, Ron Miller gave the speech. He con-cluded with a quote from the American political commentator Walter Lippmann: 'The genius of a good leader is to leave behind him a situ-ation that common sense, without the grace of genius, can deal with successfully.' Once again there was the sound of a closing door. Sir

Christopher Bland told me: 'He disappeared: went out of the room and shut the door, absolutely. He didn't shut it on me personally but he didn't ring up and say, "Why have you done that?" None of that. He didn't look back.'

The assumption was that Freeman would now retire. He said so himself, more or less: 'I want to just drop out and spend time with my wife and daughter [Victoria was born in 1978]. I may do some voluntary work. But if anybody wants me to do something, they will have to arouse my interest.' In fact, he had taken up bowls and a few months later he was signed up by Granada TV to commentate on the six-day Superbowl tournament in Manchester. One activity Freeman resolutely turned his back on was writing his autobiography:

> No, no memoirs. I don't think I have anything to say that would be of real interest or edification. And there's nothing I despise more than the sort of people who construct memoirs out of the gossip they have picked up on the basis of other people's secrets. I've never kept a diary, not a single paper. I don't think it's a good way of carrying on.[37]

As ever, he was true to his word.

Chapter 12

University professor

I N THE LATE 1950s John Freeman was travelling by train to
Monte Carlo when he met a young American painter called Dan
Snyder. They shared a bottle of wine and started a friendship.
Dan was also a stage designer who worked for ITV in London on
the glamorous cabaret show *Chelsea at Nine*. Perhaps this appealed
to Freeman. In any event, the friendship lasted over the years. Dan
married Jean, an Anglo-Brazilian ballet dancer, and John and Catherine became godparents to their son. Much later the Snyders moved
to the University of California campus at Davis, near Sacramento,
where he taught in the dramatic arts department. In 1984 the Freemans, John and Judith, were in California so they called in to see
them. They went for a walk together by the lawns, streams and trees
on the rural, car-free, campus.

'This looks a good place to retire to,' said John.

'So why don't you come and teach here?' replied Dan, who was always on the lookout to attract international figures to what was then, in university terms, something of a backwater.[1]

Randy Siverson was then chair of the political science department:

> I got a phone call from the vice-chancellor for academic affairs telling me there was an unusual opportunity to be pursued and he wanted me to come over and have a talk about it. So I went and he said there was a man in the art department by the name of Dan Snyder who had a very good friend by the name of John Freeman. And Freeman had been in the past a British High Commissioner to India, and then ambassador to the US, and he wanted to come to Davis and I think he said to retire.[2]

Larry Wade was on the committee that reviewed academic appointments: 'The feeling was that he had had a remarkable career in public life that would be of interest to our students.' What persuaded Siverson was that Freeman's 'reasonable salary' would come out of the vice-chancellor's fund and not from his department's allocation. What caused him concern was that Freeman had no training as a political scientist and the bureaucracy forbade the creation of new courses. So a schedule for his teaching was drawn up with the history department and together they put him down for 'Political Elites', 'End of Empire', 'British Foreign Policy since 1920' and 'Diplomacy in the Twentieth Century'.

His students were undergraduates, mostly between nineteen and twenty-one, and he was described on the official course lists as visiting lecturer or visiting professor. Larry Wade says his appointment was as distinguished lecturer. The point is that he was fully integrated into the international relations section of the political science faculty;

he taught a regular syllabus three or four times a week for ten week terms, marked essays and set exams. He was not a VIP who gave prestigious guest lectures to an invited audience, nor did he want to be. 'Please do not call me Mr Ambassador, or Professor Freeman, I am just John,' he said.

Professor Larry Berman, now Dean of the Honors College at Georgia State University, remembers:

> Initially, we thought this was a VIP deal, and that would have been great because Berkeley and UCLA got people of his stature so that John was certainly the most distinguished foreign visitor we ever had. What was even better was that he was part of the faculty; he was engaged; he went to meetings. Some people described him as aloof, standoffish. This is NOT the John Freeman I knew at Davis at all.[3]

The appointing staff did not seem concerned that Freeman had no experience as a teacher; that probably did not concern him either. He had already mastered seven very different careers, in advertising, the army, government, television interviewing, editing a political magazine, diplomacy and the TV industry. Why should the eighth create difficulty? In fact Jean Snyder remembers him coming over especially to give a trial lecture, on the stage of the dramatic arts department: 'The powers that be all thought it was wonderful.' So Freeman, Judith and their daughter Victoria moved to rented accommodation just off the campus for the academic year of 1985. He told Randy he was surprised not to find any shelves to put books on. Soon after their second daughter, Jessica, was born.

The following summer the British journalist Hunter Davis arrived to write about this small-town university that had started as an agricultural college, in 1909, and was making a name for itself as among the greenest and most environmentally friendly campus anywhere. Much to his surprise he came across the Rt Hon. John Freeman PC riding around on a bicycle. What was he doing at Davis?

> I must admit that when I told people in London I was coming out here, the only person who had heard of Davis was my wine merchant. He said it was world famous for its oenology department. Hmm. I'd better get a dictionary. I'm not sure how you spell that either.

In his study he gave Hunter Davis a more reflective answer:

> I have got a small number of years left to do something. I thought perhaps it would be rewarding to put back some of what I have taken out. I have had above-average wide experience in my career. I wanted to use it somehow. Some friends in California knew of my feelings, and I was offered this position. So I took it. I've given up all my British jobs, except one, trustee of Reuters.

Today, UC Davis has a high reputation. It is classed as a 'public ivy', that is a publicly funded university to rival in its league the privately funded Ivy League universities like Harvard, Yale and so on. Using the American predilection for rankings, it is the ninth best publicly funded university in the States and the thirty-eighth best overall. Its research departments in Agricultural Science and Veterinary Medicine are among the best in the world and it has first ranking as 'Coolest Campus' for its devotion to environmental sustainability and climate change.

In Freeman's day it was getting there. Although Davis had become a general university in the 1950s, it still carried the legacy of its foundation, which was the farm for the University of California and then an agricultural college. The 'Aggies', embracing vegetarians,

conservationists and ecologists as well as those studying green subjects, were more prevalent than the 'Jocks' (sports hearties) or 'Greeks'
(members of fraternities). The student restaurant, the Blue Mango,
was, in Freeman's day, a workers' cooperative that was vegetarian and
teetotal. 'We at the Mango', proclaimed the menu, 'have defined our
purpose as promoting nourishment, consciousness and creativity.'
According to Hunter Davis, there were more bicycles in the town
per head, 30,000 in all, than in any other American city. He found
it bemusing. At the Blue Mango a student ordered what sounded to
him like a 'Doubledee Caf Cap Togo'. It turned out to be a large, de-
caffeinated cappuccino to take away. Freeman liked it all:

> Yes, their obsession with ecology. It is rather sweet. Their refusal to
> eat salt can be amusing. There must be students who sniff drugs, but
> I've not seen one yet. They're relaxed and friendly. They'll just drop in
> to pass the time of day with the professors. At the same time, I find
> them frightfully intelligent. They work like stink.[4]

Whereas today 40 per cent of the 30,000 students are Asian-American
(and only 3 per cent Afro-American), in Freeman's time the majority of the 19,000 students were from white, middle-class, three-car
families. The small number of foreign students, 1,000, were based at
International House. Here they were looked after by a Scotswoman,
Julia Blair, who told Hunter Davis: 'I have to admit there are a great
many more pro-Reaganites, blond, blue-eyed, south California types,
than you might expect.' A behavioural scientist on the campus had
just carried out a survey of 15,000 Davis graduates from the mid-'60s
to mid-'80s. She concluded that the '80s generation was more serious,
more trusting, more religious and more accepting of authority than
those twenty years before. 'A new kind of student has emerged,' she

concluded. 'They are not like the "me" generation. They seem warm and caring and concerned about other people.' Freeman could not make it out:

> My colleagues told me I would find Davis very laid back, rather Ivy
> League and conservative, which I suppose is true, but they are also
> liberal with a small l. They're rational, quiet and gentle. I've kept
> wondering why this should be so. It is remarkable. I can only think
> a process of self-selection is at work.
>
> I don't feel any dullness here. I don't think the students do either. If
> they did they would do something about it. I've totally fallen in love
> with Davis. It's a new experience for me and it's very stimulating.[5]

Julia Blair put the peacefulness down to Davis being 'a *spiritually* small campus. There aren't wide gaps. The students are all on good terms with the professors. People in Davis are extraordinarily gentle. It's a very safe place.'

The director of International House in 2015 is Elizabeth Sherwin. In the 1980s she was a journalist on a local paper, the *Davis Enterprise*. She obtained Freeman's permission to 'audit' one of his classes because, much as he sought privacy, he had quickly become a local celebrity: 'the English ambassador'. Afterwards she gave 'The Sherwin Notes' to the Weber Museum at Davis. The class she chose, History 155a 'The End of Empire', held in the fall term of 1987, gave Freeman the chance of adding his personal recollections to what the set books had to say. And who can blame him? For once he could use the past in the service of the present.

Regrettably, perhaps, the unique opportunity of being lectured to in rural California by an eyewitness, indeed a maker of modern history, was somewhat lost on his audience. According to Elizabeth Sherwin, few of the class were curious or confident enough to ask questions or respond in any way. Although he was talking about the end of the Raj there were no Indians present (today many of the students at Davis are of Indian descent): 'Professor Freeman lectured and we listened.'

To set the scene: Freeman stood at a classroom podium, lecturing from notes for up to an hour to thirty or forty undergraduates, average age twenty. He was tall and imposing and dressed quite formally with a tweed jacket and tie. He was self-deprecating but not self-effacing. He was a most fluent, relaxed lecturer, who tried to engage with the audience. He did not 'bore on' and he was not 'stagey', Elizabeth Sherwin told me. These are verbatim extracts from her notes.

On David Lloyd George:

> I remember him as a very compelling public figure. He was Welsh, abundantly endowed with gifts as an orator, had a passion for causes, a horror of war, and was prejudiced against the Church, landlords and capitalism. He was one of the most brilliant political figures I ever met but he had a biting tongue and a sense of humour not easily forgiven by those victimised by it. He was involved in scandals you've seen nothing like in this country. He sold peerages. He caused a scandal at the Versailles Peace Conference when he left to play golf. He lived with his secretary. He was a larger than life man but his reputation is now in the trough in the cycle of history.

On the Privy Council:

> It nominates the new monarch, although what would happen if it nominated anyone other than the heir apparent is not known. I certainly remember being appointed to it. I went to the Throne Room, met the

Queen, knelt in front of her and swore an oath of fidelity, to advise truthfully, keep secrets, defend her with my life. I'm glad it hasn't arisen. She
held her hand languidly to be kissed. I did. Then we got up and had a
cup of tea together. I don't know if I would drop my classes if I were to
be called back to England for a meeting of the Privy Council. I might.

On meeting Mahatma Gandhi – a very different account from the
one he gave when he was High Commissioner to India!

I'll tell you the circumstances and show you what a shallow, frivolous,
idiotic person I was. He was an extremely thin gentleman dressed in a
white garment, and a surprising sight. He took a seminar in my high
school when I was eighteen. He spent the evening with us. I had the
privilege of attending but I made nothing of it. It appeared to me at
the time that he was a stupid old man. It would be nice to tell you
I sat at the old gentleman's feet and was a better person thereafter.
But this is a story of juvenile idiocy that I hope won't be completely
strange to all of you.

On Lord Mountbatten:

Mountbatten was a member of the royal family, a good naval officer,
brilliant, impatient, fallible and arrogant. I knew him well. He was
rather like General MacArthur in his forties: susceptible to flattery.
Some of you think I know everyone. Kenneth Galbraith really does
know everyone [the famous economist, diplomat and advisor to
President Kennedy: co-incidentally, his very first job was as assistant
professor of agricultural economics at Davis]. He wrote that Mountbatten was frequently turned to when people wanted more action,
less thought, both of which he provided in full measure.[6]

Freeman did have one fan in this class. She was Cynthia Basinger, a mature student: 'I hung on his every word. "This guy is amazing," I thought. After he told us about the Privy Council I called him "Mr Right and Honourable", though not to his face.' Professor Freeman had marked her essay B+ so she used this as an excuse to visit him in his office:

> The walls were lined with juvenile pictures [no doubt by Victoria who was a budding artist], none of VIPs. He was very approachable and easy to converse with. He smoked a pipe. He told me not to be discouraged by a B+. I ended up baby-sitting for him. 'That will be wonderful,' he said.[7]

According to another colleague at Davis, Geoffrey Wandesforde-Smith, Freeman was one of the few teachers who seemed to like setting and marking exams. These were written at the end of a ten-week course in the Blue Book, an eighteen-page, lined exercise book; three questions had to be answered over two hours. 'It is fair to say John was under-whelmed by the results. He found the students hard-working but not challenging.' He did not attend official staff meetings because he was not a member of the academic senate, but he was punctilious at coming to birthday or leaving parties held for the administrative staff at coffee time; sometimes he was the only teacher there. Perhaps this was Freeman's army background again. He took his duty to 'other ranks' seriously. For instance, back in London he had not only attended the wedding of Cynthia Gomes, but he would also attend the wedding of her son many years later. John Freeman was admired and liked by all his professional colleagues; probably most of his students were impressed that he was on campus but took him for granted, like students everywhere.

That summer of 1987, when Matthew Freeman was studying nearby on the University of California campus at Berkeley, he visited his father at Davis. In order to watch him in an academic setting he attended a political science seminar at which his father was questioned about his political career. Afterwards he wrote to his mother: 'Dad's style was slick, witty, with some sharp observations, but not terribly thoughtful or academic. He acknowledges this as his way and I can see how he flourishes. He acts as a foil to some of the high-minded, intellectual, but perhaps rather dull, professors.'

He included some of his father's one-liners on prime ministers he had known. On Attlee: 'He was saved from anonymity and perhaps even ignominy by his blinkered view.' On Wilson: 'A quick thinker able to turn any situation to his advantage but with no political vision.' On Thatcher: 'I dislike her but would certainly have voted for her.' This last statement obviously provoked the audience because he was then asked about his own change of political allegiance, from hard left to hard right. Matt noted his answer with care:

> I would bore you almost as much as myself if I talked about that at length, but it suddenly struck me, and it now seems self-evident, that if you pursue policies of economic collectivism and dirigiste policies [state directed] – which is what is implied by the left wing in Europe – then you necessarily end up with a dirigiste government. I realised that was something that I did not want, but not until I had already done considerable harm by supporting such ideas.[8]

This reminds me of an interview Freeman had given in his *Face to Face* years. 'The one thing I really care about is dissent,' he told the interviewer. 'All establishments ought to be kicked against, struggled against, teased, prodded and made human. Emblazoned in letters of fire in every classroom should be the words, "Remember, the teacher may be wrong".'[9] For 'teacher' read 'state' and there you have Freeman's dislike of the dirigiste government. That, at heart, was his political philosophy.

For Matt the experience of watching his father required to talk about himself was an eye-opener. 'I learned a lot more about his politics than I've ever managed to get out of him myself.' His father was in the hot seat and the experienced eye could tell that he loathed it: 'You know how reluctant he is normally to discuss his past life,' Matt reminded Catherine, 'well, he was unable to avoid it this time!'[10]

Soon after he arrived, Freeman handed in a proposal 'for an inter-departmental scrutiny of a subject of major international or domestic importance to senior professors in business administration, economics, governmental affairs, history and political science. This recommended an invitation to a statesman of the calibre of Dr Henry Kissinger to give a keynote speech to invited members of the public and students from the different disciplines. It would be called the President's Lecture. It would be followed by a week of scrutiny in group work, which would close with a seminar under the chairmanship of the departmental head most concerned in order to draw conclusions. There would be a rapporteur and video-taping.[11]

The concept does not seem to have been followed up but the proposal did result in the visit of Henry Kissinger in October 1987. As the set piece of a three-day visit organised jointly by Gary Walton, Dean of the Graduate School of Management, and John Freeman, Kissinger spoke to an audience of several thousand, the largest ever gathered at Davis for this kind of lecture. When Cynthia Basinger saw Professor Freeman introduce the former Secretary of State she was amazed, for he had told none of his students about his friendship. Dr Kissinger remembers his visit without the rosy glow of Freeman's 'Indian summer': 'John was in his declining years and working below his capabilities; but he carried out his work without complaint and with aplomb.'[12] Freeman was also responsible for the invitation as Visiting Professor of his old *New Statesman* colleague Paul Johnson, now an historian and author of *Modern Times: A History of the World from the 1920s to the 1980s* (1984). He reported on his visit in *The Spectator* that Freeman was 'universally revered, by staff and students alike, as a fount of wisdom, a mould of everything an English gentleman and scholar should be'.[13]

Freeman developed a particular friendship with Larry Berman, who succeeded Siverson as chair of the political science department. His expertise covered the Nixon years about which he took a critical view. The author of *Nixon, Kissinger and Betrayal in Vietnam*, he held a course called 'Watergate' that was the most popular in the department, attracting up to 300 students. Berman remembers that Freeman took a particular interest:

> John was one of those people who like all Nixon defenders say, 'If not for Watergate…' John greatly admired his foreign policy, his worldview, his détente, opening with China, all of these things. Of course, now we know that Nixon was wire-tapping and tracking Kissinger around wherever he was going, never mind the break in and all those criminal activities. I recall discussing all this with John. As our relationship developed we were having banterings all the time on this. He ended by thinking, yes, he was quite critical of Nixon for his breaking of the law. But he was still a strong defender of his foreign policy.[14]

As early as 1986, Freeman wrote to his old friend Woodrow Wyatt that he 'wished to stay in California'. He added that he had asked Tony Howard 'to get references that would make sure the authorities would allow me to stay'. 'Odd,' adds Wyatt in his diary, 'considering he had been ambassador in America.'[15] It soon became clear to their friends at Davis that the Freemans were not just passing through. They seemed relaxed and happy, although John was showing early signs of prostate cancer, which he never spoke about. The life was ideal for small children; the weather balmy, the avenues free of traffic except bicycles, the play facilities excellent. Victoria went to the local school in north Davis. John cycled around smoking a pipe and wearing blue jeans, a sign for students that he was accessible. He joined a local bowls club, went for long walks, and together with his old friend Dan made a habit of bartering at garage sales (the equivalent of car boot sales). He was particularly fond of the twice weekly farmers' market, where local farmers sold organic produce direct to the public: 'the bounty of California, with berries, figs, olive oil, chestnuts, asparagus and dozens of other offerings,' boasted the local *YOLO County* magazine, acronym for 'You Only Live Once'. Although Davis was a small-town university with a combined population of only 50,000, the social life around campus was cosmopolitan and the Freemans enjoyed the parties.

Geoffey Wandesforde-Smith joked that John was turning into 'Mr Chips', as in the British film of 1939 *Goodbye Mr Chips*, meaning that he was like the rigidly orthodox schoolmaster who married a young wife, moved with the times and ended up as a beloved and inspiring figure round the school. I doubt if Freeman liked that comparison. It looked as if, Wandesforde-Smith continued, he was putting down roots as part of the community, wanting to lead as ordinary a life as possible, the sort of life denied to him before. When Elizabeth Sherwin asked him if she could write a profile for a San Francisco paper, she was given one of his dusty answers: 'No.' As ever he guarded his privacy.

The Freemans bought a typical 1960s ranch-style bungalow, timber-framed, with the kitchen and master bedroom at the front and a 'grand room' (combined dining/sitting room) at the back, facing a patio with a play area. He put in for, and was given, a pay rise. The political science faculty planned for him to continue beyond the age of seventy-five. In 1988, he and Judith left for a long vacation in South Africa, leaving Cynthia Basinger with her two young children to look after the house. On the way they stopped over in London and found themselves in Woodrow Wyatt's *Journal*. He is writing up a dinner party held by Lord Montagu:

> John has removed himself from life like an Indian *sanyasi*. He is teaching at a university in California. He says that he and his plain but nice wife Judith, his fourth, live in a little cottage about a mile off the campus. He is very happy though the poor chap has cancer.
>
> I am very fond of him. He is a strange, interesting man with one of the highest talents I have ever known and a disinclination to use them, not because of laziness but because he is utterly unworldly. He is seventy-four.
>
> He was quite startled when I said of my first wife [Sue Cox, then Wyatt, then Hicklin] that he was the first person with whom she had an affair. I said, 'But this is all over fifty years ago.'[16]

Freeman liked the United States. It appealed to his egalitarian instincts. He wanted to be what Americans call 'a regular kind of guy', though how far he succeeded is debatable. Politically he was increasingly drawn to the free market economy and the libertarian values that are exhibited to the full in California. In fact he intended to end his days as an American citizen, which, for someone who always travelled light and believed life should be a sequence of change, had its own logic. He asked Henry Kissinger and Wes Pruden to act as referees and Pruden is certain that this request was not for an extension of his Green Card, which would expire after five years, in 1990, but to begin the process of citizenship. It was not to be.

Judith probably liked the California life less than he did and she was sure the girls would get a better education in England. John confided to Larry Berman that this time he was going to put his family first, but it was a hard decision. She returned to London with the girls several weeks before John. He remained to finish the term and attend hospital appointments for his prostate cancer. Larry Berman acted as his chauffeur and remembers that when Freeman left him at the airport he was almost too weak to lift his bags unaided. 'We'll stay in touch,' they promised each other, but Berman never heard from him again. Freeman asked Cynthia Basinger to sell his Dodge minivan and when she transferred the money to London he wired back a commission. 'I didn't expect this; he was so gracious, that's the word I always use about him.'

A few months later, Freeman returned to sell the house in Oak Road. The California idyll was over. 'I really enjoyed teaching. I wish I had tried it before,' was his verdict on the Davis experience.

Chapter 13

'The ordinary man'

I N 1990, JOHN Freeman and his third family moved to a 1930s semi-detached house with bay windows looking onto Suffolk Road near the Thames in Barnes, south-west London. He was now looking old, wasted by cancer, though in recovery. So began the ninth of his lives, the two decades of 'the ordinary man'. He had tried to be ordinary at Davis, but he could not avoid standing out as a celebrity, 'the English gentleman and scholar'. In any event, the role he had given himself was university professor and that was now behind him: another closed door. A profile of Freeman written in the 1960s said, 'This is a man who lives in the present; he is rarely an ex or future anything' – and this was as true in the 1990s as it had been then.[1] He was always self-aware and self-controlled, and the part to which he applied himself now, with his usual concentration, was as 'an ordinary bloke', a phrase that kept coming up when I spoke to former friends of his from the Barnes Lonsdale Bowling Club. Forty years before Freeman had written a tribute in the *New Statesman* to the socialist and educationalist R. H. Tawney: 'Man cannot be whole or dignified until he lives in a community where his private motives lead him to seek the public good.'[2] Much as he closed his mind to the past, I wonder if this truth resonated with him in old age?

His girlfriend from university days sixty years before, Susan Hicklin, was clear that the famous Freeman concentration was now being applied to joining a community. When she went to stay with the Freemans for the weekend, John took her shopping at Sainsbury's:

> He inspected every potato thoroughly – he was exact, perfectionist, thorough – he was trying to be appropriate, to fit into a real community, in which he was living for the first time in his life. It was the same thing with his bowls. He wanted to be accepted not as an ex-ambassador or what have you, but as an old man with a place in the local community. After the weekend I sent him a poem by Wendy Cope. I told him, 'This epitomises your attitude.' He liked that![3]

> Being Boring
> *'May you live in interesting times'– Chinese curse.*
> *If you ask me 'What's new?' I have nothing to say*
> *Except that the garden is growing.*
> *I had a slight cold but it's better today,*
> *I'm content with the way things are going.*
> *There was drama enough in my turbulent past:*
> *Tears and passion – I've used up a tankful.*
> *No news is good news and long may it last.*
> *If nothing much happens, I'm thankful.*

I don't go to parties. Well, what are they for,
If you don't want to find a new lover?
You drink and you listen and drink a bit more
And you take the next day to recover.
Someone to stay home with was all my desire
And, now that I've found a safe mooring,
I've just one ambition in life; I aspire
To go on and on being boring.

Freeman and Judith had joined Barnes Lonsdale Lawn Bowling Club before they went to Davis. When they returned the club had closed down and its members had moved to Priory Park in Kew. He had stopped playing serious bowls by then but he would often go along to Sheen Common for a 'roller', that is a casual game to include all-comers. He also played at Richmond Indoors because the playing surface is more of a smooth carpet and, unlike grass, does not require much effort to propel the bowl onwards. He still smoked a pipe and carried it in a holster when he was playing. At Richmond the games were in the morning and John is remembered among the elderly bowls fraternity for frequently arriving late. 'It's not my fault,' he would say, 'I've been taking my little daughter to school.' That was Jessica.

The Freemans were keen club members. They used to watch the club championships on a Saturday; they attended the annual din-ner and were always gregarious. 'They fitted in,' club member Percy Kimber told me. 'They were both really nice people. He always spoke to everyone the same. He was a man who would extend the hand of friendship and he didn't want to say, "I am the big me." He wanted to be an ordinary man. An ordinary man.' His wife Isobel Kimber remembered how John would greet her across the street or in the super-market. 'He would come and give me a big hug,' she said. This would

surprise most of those who knew him from the old days, including his
son Matthew, who described his father's manner as 'distantly polite,
with the carapace of an Edwardian gentleman'.

When the Kimbers visited California on holiday, Freeman collected them from Sacramento airport and took them back to Davis
for the day; the first stop was his bowls club. 'He was a lovely man,'
added Percy, 'and the thing I think about him, he always wanted to
be ordinary. I spoke to Judith at John's funeral and she said, "Yes,
that was him."'[4]

In Freeman's playing days at Barnes Lonsdale Bowls Club he always
'led', meaning that he 'set up the head' or gave a good lead for others to
follow. This requires a steady nerve. You need a cool temperament, the
Kimbers told me, and a killer instinct, I would add, for there is surely
a sadistic pleasure in sending down a fast bowl to knock either the jack
or your opponent's bowls out of play. This is called a 'drive'. The game
played to Freeman's strengths. Percy recalled the first time they played
together in a club pairs competition:

> I really didn't know who he was except his name was John Freeman.
> Things began to get tight. Their skip rolled a bowl out and it got right
> to the head and I said, joking, 'what do you want to go and do that
> for? It's right in my bleeding way.' Suddenly, a voice very quietly in
> my ear says, 'Concentrate, Kimber, concentrate!' And I looked at John
> and he was looking down the green and his face was stony. Stony it
> was – it couldn't have been him that spoke! I always remember him
> doing that. That was him![5]

It is tempting to imagine what Freeman saw as he stared down the green:
the German tanks at El Alamein? Winston Churchill on the opposition
front bench? Tony Hancock sweating with nerves on *Face to Face*? But

then, was it not Chan Canasta who always said, 'Concentrate, concentrate'? Freeman probably just wanted to win a game of bowls.

John's particular friend at Barnes was John Triggs, known by all as 'Triggsy'. The two together, said the Kimbers, were like chalk and cheese, for John was 'the English gent' and Triggsy was all 'gor blimey'. The two started learning bowls together at Barnes Lonsdale in the mid-1970s. Apparently Triggsy was very competitive, whereas John, although competent, preferred the more relaxed club games. Triggsy was a Brentford boy, an ex-boxer who had fought for money in Scottish boxing booths, and was a Barnes building contractor. 'Whereas John would sit quietly in the club house, you always knew when Triggsy was around,' said the Kimbers. He was loud, brash, a 'rough diamond' and no respecter of persons, and John was very fond of him.

Triggsy's widow Janet, his third wife, told me that when the Freemans' daughter Jessica was born in California, the first person Freeman rang, only ten minutes after the birth, was Triggsy. When they first met in the mid-1970s Triggsy had been in the midst of an acrimonious divorce from his second wife that left him with custody of his six-year-old son. He would bring young Jonathan along to Barnes Lonsdale where the two met the Freemans. John was full of admiration for the way Triggsy was bringing up his son on his own and frequently invited them for Sunday lunch in the Freeman household. They were popular with Victoria and Jessica too. In 1984 the Triggs, father and son, were on holiday in Swanage when Freeman arrived with a Harrod's hamper and took them to lunch at Corfe Castle. An evening of very special importance for Triggsy was the black-tie boxing event organised by Ron Miller. He sat at the top table next to the former world heavyweight boxing champion Floyd Patterson, who had come because Freeman had interviewed him for *Face to Face* many years ago, the two sitting in a boxing ring.

When Triggsy introduced Janet, Freeman said, 'I'm delighted to meet you' and gave her a kiss. John was devastated by Triggsy's unexpected death in 2007. Janet recalled: 'There were about 150 people at his funeral and the cortege diverted past his local pub where all his drinking buddies and staff were standing outside.' After Triggsy's death, Freeman and Janet stayed in touch. 'He always gave me a big hug when we met,' she told me:

> Many people couldn't understand why he formed a lasting friendship with this man John Triggs. It was probably because Triggsy treated him like an ordinary bloke. As for John Freeman, he could hold a conversation with anybody, regardless of who they were or where they came from, without pomposity. He treated everyone as equal.[6]

The Freemans last entry in Woodrow Wyatt's Journal was on 7 April 1992:

> Dinner with David Montagu [Lord Swaythling], John Freeman was there with his wife, Judy. John is looking emaciated. He is taller and thinner than I am. He is seventy-eight. He did have some form of cancer but that has now gone out of his system. He now lives in complete retirement in Barnes. I said, 'What do you do all day?' He replied that he looked after the children, such as they were. He has got children by almost every marriage and he has been married four times. He does the household chores and washes up and a lot of the cooking instead of his wife. He said, 'I send her out to work to earn some money.'[7]

Judith taught in a private junior school in the 2000s, where Victoria joined her to teach art. 'Mother and daughter working in the same school – unusual I should think,' wrote John proudly to Geoffrey

Wandesforde-Smith.[8] In 1995 he celebrated his eightieth birthday with a small party. One of the guests was Paul Johnson, who afterwards wrote an effusive encomium for *The Spectator* entitled 'A man of many epiphanies to remind us what England was once about'. Apparently the man concerned sent him a dusty response. His privacy had been invaded.

At this time John Freeman met Nigel Lawson (the Rt Hon. Lord Lawson of Braby PC) at a weekend house party in Northamptonshire. They had much in common. Both had been at Westminster School, both had been editors of political magazines (Lawson was editor of *The Spectator*, 1966–70), both had been in government (Lawson was Chancellor of the Exchequer in the 1980s serving under Margaret Thatcher) and both had moved subsequently into different areas of life (Lawson, for instance, wrote *The Nigel Lawson Diet Book*, became a campaigning critic of climate change and an opponent of the European Union under current conditions). More important, Lord Lawson told me that he shared with Freeman a determination to live in the present and not in the past. He did not keep up with political colleagues, he did not like to reminisce and he moved from one interest to another. He said this 'did not require any explanation'; it was self-evidently the right way to lead your life. He had no intention of writing an autobiography and, moreover, he guarded his privacy. Both had given the broadcasting psychiatrist Anthony Clare a hard time. Despite warning the producer that he was not prepared to be introspective, Lawson had sat *In the Psychiatrist's Chair*. The result had been 'extremely boring for all concerned'.

Lord Lawson said he recognised John Freeman at that first meeting as 'a man of great stature' whom he would like to know better. Subsequently, he realised like everyone else that Freeman was not only fascinating but hard to know. The two went off to Lawson's house in

Gascony where they played *pétanque*, a French form of bowls. More important, Lord Lawson and Sir Christopher Bland nominated Freeman for the Beefsteak Club, an elite dining club in Irving Street, London, for men of the arts, letters and politics, where members sit round one long table and, apparently, call all the waiters 'Charles'. For a radical, anti-establishment man like Freeman this was a gesture towards becoming a 'joiner'. In fact, he thoroughly enjoyed the club and only stopped going when his frail legs could not negotiate the stairs. He told Lord Lawson that one of his few regrets was declining a peerage, because sitting in the House of Lords seemed a congenial way for retired people to spend the afternoon.

When I failed to obtain John Freeman's permission to write his biography in 2004, I asked Lord Lawson to intercede on my behalf. He had tried but replied, 'You will not be surprised to know that I have been unsuccessful.' In 2014 we discussed the subject again:

> I would just say two things. John is a very cold fish, but I think there's something else that explains his reticence. He said to me that he would not write about his life or talk to anybody who might because he was extremely critical of pretty well everybody. Tony Blair, for instance, he finds 'ineffably insufferable'. At the same time he deeply dislikes unpleasantness and therefore he keeps his views largely to himself.[9]

The enigma of John Freeman is that just when you think you understand the man you have spent years thinking about, you discover a contradiction. For instance, those close to him over much of his life would agree that he was, in effect, 'a cold fish', but his colleagues at LWT, the teachers at Davis and the bowlers of Barnes would not agree. His own contradictory opinions of people, however, were clear, as was his tendency to slide away from confrontation behind a smokescreen of politeness. Time and again Freeman was complimentary to colleagues in print or in person but rude about them behind their backs: Harold Wilson is a good example. Whether or not this stems from the deeper psychological trait of disliking others because he disliked himself, as he told Catherine, is getting into Anthony Clare territory. I suggested to Lord Lawson that Freeman's dislike of people might have been affected by his dislike of several of the professions he had spent time in, politics for example? 'Everything he did, he wanted to do really well, because he would have been unhappy if he thought he was doing badly, but that didn't mean he had respect for the people with whom he was working. That was quite different.'

Approaching ninety, life began to close in. The girls left home so the Freemans moved into a small house nearby in Charles Street. John crashed the car into a tree and decided to give up driving. He began losing his balance and found walking difficult, although he kept going for a while on public transport. They wintered in South Africa frequently, where Judith had a small house on the Eastern Cape, but stopped that in 2008 after John had a bad fall. At home he watched television a lot, particularly American football when he could find it. His reading was middle-brow and slightly old-fashioned; authors like Dorothy Sayers and Evelyn Waugh – the latter had been one of his more difficult guests on *Face to Face*. In 2007, he told Geoffrey Wandesforde-Smith that he had set himself the task of re-reading books that had made an impression on him when he was young and comparing his judgements now with then – 'a rewarding and occasionally humbling experience'.

The Freemans sent a letter to friends every year with family news, often with a photograph. Coincidence or not, it normally showed John with his back to the camera. Norman MacKenzie, an expert on Charles Dickens, said they reminded him of the letters that Scrooge

– 'not exactly but something of that sort' – might have written after his change of heart. He meant that for years Freeman had presented a private front to the world – 'John has the capacity to put up the shutters that is excelled by nobody except a shopkeeper during a time of riots' is how he put it once – and now he was sending out a newsletter! It was at this time too that Freeman wrote to me, 'I wish everybody would forget I was alive.' The point is that 'everybody' referred to the public life he had left behind and the 'change of heart' to the 'ordinary' life of family and friends that he was now living. The letters were kind, warm, and upbeat: 'In most respects my health is good and my mind is still active and alert. I am cared for with total selflessness by my beloved Jude and our two daughters who between them make me feel both wanted and part of their exciting and busy lives.'[10]

They entertained old friends from the LWT days, like the Teslers and Blands, and new friends like the Triggses, but reminders of a public life were less welcome. The Kissingers always tried to make contact when they were in London but found Freeman 'inaccessible'. In 2011 Nigel Lawson's son, Dominic, visited Freeman to find out more about his time at Westminster School:

> I arrived at his modest terrace house in Barnes and was shown to his study. Even though he found it difficult to stand, he was still an imposing presence. And his memories were expressed with unfailing precision, in the clear tone of a great broadcaster.
>
> What I found more striking was the nature of his study. A computer, very much in active use (we exchanged a number of emails), some full bookshelves; yet not a single photograph of the owner with famous people, as one normally finds in the homes of a retired politician or diplomat.
>
> Like his character, this was a study in self-effacement.[11]

Freeman told MacKenzie at their last meeting in 2010: 'I don't remember the past because I've always put it behind me. Not just now, I've always been like that. I like to think about the present and even the future but my past is a closed book, even to me.'

In 2012, Freeman's health declined to the extent that he thought he was becoming a burden to his family. He decided he would call on his military service from the Second World War and move into the Star and Garter Home in Richmond for disabled ex-service men and women. So, at the age of ninety-seven, he said goodbye to his friends and closed another door.

'An actress I used to know in New York called Bette Davis said "old age is not for wimps",' Freeman told the family. He described in a last email to Norman MacKenzie in October 2012 what these twilight months were like:

> I've reached the age when life consists of little more than waiting to die without the comfort of knowing when that will be. I find, curiously, that I have a deeply irrational, but I suppose instinctive, compulsion not to do anything at all to end it accidentally. So I sit or lie here twenty-four hours a day trying to make sure I don't have an accident. I don't want visitors. I believe I do not yet suffer from dementia, though others must obviously judge that. I can always understand what people are saying providing I can hear them, but I am now very deaf. And that's about that.

Behind a door with the rather forbidding nameplate 'Major John Freeman: The Rifle Brigade', he lived a solitary life except for family who paid brief visits on a rota. Occasionally he would go out in a wheelchair with Judith. The Star and Garter in Richmond, he said, was by no means 'a grand officers' club: 'It's a tumbledown, ludicrously

335

inconvenient old barn with nowadays only about forty or fifty residents, mostly what we used to call "other ranks". The care, however, is simply first-class, particularly the food.'

Before long he was moved to a new, purpose-built Star and Garter home in Surbiton. But this was one community he did not want to join. When his second son Tom visited from California, where he now lives, to say goodbye, he heard the sounds of 'If you're happy and you know it, clap your hands' drifting from the residents' lounge. Freeman called it 'the last bastion of Pooterism', Charles Pooter being the fictional character in *Diary of a Nobody* who was full of self-importance.

In his last year Freeman was hard of hearing, short of sight and unsteady, but he could use email and he would sit in a chair for a few hours a day. Brian Tesler thought that he had such control over his life that he would celebrate his century in February 2015 and then close the final door. Probably this anniversary meant nothing to him. In December 2014 he carefully arranged for book tokens to be sent to his grandchildren and then, on the morning of Saturday 20 December, he died.

The funeral service was held in the local parish church of St Michael and All Angels in Barnes on 12 January 2015. As the congregation assembled, Matthew escorted Catherine up the isle to the second row of pews. A small, grey-haired woman turned round and said, smiling, 'I'm so glad you came.'

Catherine was puzzled and said, 'I'm sorry, but I don't think we've met.'

The woman replied, 'I'm Judith.' It was an absurd moment and they both laughed, for they had not seen each other for forty years, and so a potentially awkward moment was defused. The families were all there, apart from Tom who was in America and one of Matthew's children, Lily, who was in India. Judith sat with her daughters Tors and Jess in the front pew. Catherine sat behind with her daughter-in-law, Rose, and Cynthia and Javid Akhtar. Lizi was there with her family and Lucy brought her son Conor. The two sat with Matthew and his son James, who were pall bearers. The congregation was predominantly local, many including the Kimbers and Janet Triggs from the bowling fraternity. A few friends from the past paid their last respects – Paul Johnson from *New Statesman* days, Sir Christopher Bland and Brian Tesler from the LWT era, and Lord Lawson. Matthew read Psalm 43 which ends: 'Why, my soul, are you downcast? / Why so disturbed within me? / Put your hope in God / For I will yet praise him / My Saviour and my God'. Victoria read a P. G. Wodehouse short story. At John Freeman's request there was no eulogy. It was, said Catherine, a plain, peaceful occasion. Matthew and Lucy accompanied the coffin to the crematorium and then joined their mother.

Freeman had told Tom Driberg sixty years before that although he lacked the 'the gift of faith', he 'had no difficulty in doing anything officially expected in this field'. Presumably he would have approved of his own funeral. Such an outstanding contributor to British life over the second half of the twentieth century deserved a memorial service, but the very suggestion would probably have received a dusty reply. Catherine's epitaph comes to mind: 'John was a well-known man but he was a man who was hard to know well. And that's just how he liked it.'

> There is a tailpiece. A few days after the funeral, Judith rang Matthew. She confirmed that John had destroyed his papers but a small file remained, which she would send on. It contained the transcript of an interview that Freeman had given in 1989 to John Boe of the San Francisco Jung Institute Library Journal. His last answer explains why this one file was not destroyed: I went to his [Jung's] funeral and

it wasn't very big. I've forgotten how many people were there, but it wasn't a great occasion at all. I remember thinking that I wouldn't mind this for my own funeral because, on the whole, 'the great and the good' weren't there. I expect there were one or two distinguished celebrities there I've forgotten. It was his family, his lovers, and his close associates, and so on. It was wholly people who cared about him. I remember thinking at the time, 'Well, it's a good way to send the old boy off.' Because he really was a very personal man indeed, who had close and intimate relations with these people. And here they were, all gathered to say goodbye to him. And there wasn't a general, or a prime minister, or a pope in sight.

The obituary writers gave the impression that they were surprised Freeman had only just died. Indeed, Norman MacKenzie in *The Times* and Anthony Howard in *The Guardian* had pre-deceased their subject. He was squeezed off the *Today* programme on Radio 4 because of the death later in the weekend of the actress Billie Whitelaw, which would probably have afforded him pleasure had he been able to foresee it. Two of the obituaries took opposing views. Dominic Lawson saw Freeman as a model of achievement and public service who shunned celebrity status; a survivor from a better age:

> On the streets of our cities, people now brandish 'selfie-sticks', camera-phones with extensions, designed so they can photograph themselves with even greater attention to detail and broadcast their poses to anyone who might be interested (or even those who aren't).
>
> What the long and astonishing life of John Freeman reminds us is that it is not who we are, but what we do – and what we do for others – that matters.[12]

Terence Blacker, writing in *The Independent*, shared the general admiration for Freeman but not for the archetype:

> For all the energy and achievement of clever Englishmen of that generation, there is something sad about their disconnectedness, the lack of pleasure in their own or other achievements, the modesty that could be construed as a kind of arrogance, the general sense of an unhappy and lonely upper-class child's progress through adult life.
>
> They have helped shape the world in which we now find ourselves, but the astonishing, melancholy lives of men of achievement such as John Freeman make one feel startlingly grateful for today's messier, more human leaders.[13]

Let those who knew Freeman personally react as they will. I do see him as an extreme example of his age with all the stiff upper lip and the repression that implies. But the fact is that he lived well beyond his age, and those who saw him cycling through Davis or playing bowls in Barnes in the last decades of his life must have recognised a mellow old man trying his best to fit in with the community around him. Whatever his faults, in the words of Thomas Carlyle, 'The history of the world is but the history of great men' – and John Freeman deserves his place in the British history of his time, even though he did not want it.

Acknowledgements

I N A BIOGRAPHY like this that ranges over very different areas of twentieth-century life, I have necessarily relied on several authors whose books have quoted the source material. I am particularly grateful, therefore, to: Francis Wheen, author of *Tom Driberg: His Life and Indiscretions*; Richard Lindley, author of *'Panorama: Fifty Years of Pride and Paranoia*; Paul McGarr, author of *The Cold War in South Asia, Britain, the United States and the Indian Subcontinent 1945–1965*; John W. Young, author of *The Washington Embassy: British Ambassadors to the United States 1939–1977*; and David Docherty, author of *Running the Show: 21 Years of London Weekend Television*.

For interviews, I am particularly grateful to my friend, the late Professor Norman MacKenzie; also to the late Susan Hicklin, the late Anthony Howard, the late Rt Hon. Michael Foot PC and the late Anthony Clare, all of whom I interviewed between 2004 and 2012.

My thanks to those I interviewed in 2013–15. In the United States I spoke to: Dr Henry Kissinger; Joanna Rose; Corinna Metcalf; Wes Pruden; and Professors Larry Berman, Randy Siverson, Larry Wade and Geoffrey Wandesforde-Smith at UC Davis. Also in the US were Jean Snyder, Cynthia Basinger and Elizabeth Sherwin. In the UK I interviewed, in order of chapters: Lizi Freeman; Michael Peacock; Peregrine Worsthorne; Paul Johnson; Margaret Vallance; Lord Renwick; Professor Robert Cassen; Cynthia Akhtar; Sir Christopher Bland; Lord Lawson; Brian Tesler CBE; Ron Miller; Lord Grade; Lord Birt; Matthew Freeman; Isobel and Percy Kimber; and Janet Triggs.

For permission to use archive material, I thank: Elizabeth Wells of the Westminster School archives; K. Petvin-Scudamore of www.findasoldier.co.uk for Freeman's army service record; Jeff Walden of the BBC Written Archives Centre at Caversham; Jason Crawley of the *New Statesman*; and, again, Professor Geoffrey Wandesforde-Smith and Elizabeth Sherwin of the University of California at Davis. I made use of: the British Library; the National Archives at Kew; the Bodleian Library in Oxford for *Cherwell* magazine; Christ Church, Oxford, for Tom Driberg's papers; and the British Diplomatic Oral History Programme at Churchill College, Cambridge.

For permission to quote written extracts I am grateful to: the family of Lord Birkett; Sharon Rubin at Peters Fraser & Dunlop for Edith Sitwell; the Bertrand Russell Peace Foundation; Emma Cheshire at Faber & Faber for Wendy Cope's poem 'Being Boring'; the permissions departments of Arrow Books for *Open Secret* by Stella Rimington, Carlton Books for *Sisyphus and Reilly* by Peter Luke, Random House and Jonathan Cape for Dalton's *The Political Diary of Hugh Dalton* and HarperCollins for Woodrow Wyatt's *Confessions of an Optimist*.

For photographs I thank the Westminster School archives, the Imperial War Museum, the A&I photo library at the BBC archives, and Gigi and Harry Benson. For maps I am grateful to Barry Lowen-hoff and to Frances Walker for helping with copyright clearances. I gladly acknowledge Prakash Dehta, who suggested I write this biography over ten years ago when we met in India. My agent, James Wills of Watson Little, arranged for this book to be published by the Robson Press, where Jeremy Robson and my editor Melissa Bond have always been very helpful – my thanks to them.

Above all, I want to thank Catherine Freeman, without whose constant encouragement this biography would not have been written; also, my wife Margaret Percy, whose research and technical assistance were invaluable.

Notes

Chapter 1

1   See article by Belinda Board and Katarina Fritzon in *Psychology, Crime and Law*, vol. 11, issue 1, 2005, pp. 17–32

2   See files in Westminster School library for Political and Literary Society, Debating Society and UFPF (known as 'ufpuff')

3   *New Statesman*, 5 April and 31 May 1963

4   *The Journals of Woodrow Wyatt, vol. 1*, Pan Books, 1999, p. 255

5   *Confessions of an Optimist* by Woodrow Wyatt, Collins, 1985, p. 58 onwards

6   'Two Faces of Eve' by Susan Hicklin, *Oxford Magazine*, 15 October 1964

7   'The Diplomatic Family Freeman' by Tom Driberg, *Vogue*, November 1968

8   'Misunderstood', *New Statesman*, 21 June 1952

Chapter 2

1   Driberg, 1968, op. cit.

2   *Sisyphus and Reilly by* Peter Luke, Andre Deutsch, London, 1972, p. 58

3   In possession of the author

4   Luke, op. cit., p. 59

5   *The Rifle Brigade 1939–1945* by Major R. H. W. S. Hastings, Gale & Polden Ltd., 1950, p. 104

6   *Hellfire Tonight* by Albert Martin, Book Guild, Lewes, 1996, pp. 142–2

7   *The Poor Bloody Infantry* by Charles Whiting, Stanley Paul, London, 1987, p. 126

8   Luke, op. cit., p. 59

9   Ibid., pp. 83–4

10   Whiting, op. cit., p. 126

11   Luke, op. cit., p. 83–4

12   Letter from the Luke family in possession of the author

13   Luke, op. cit., p. 63

14   Ibid.

15   *History of the Second World War* by B. H. Liddell Hart, Pan Books, London, 1970, p. 306

16   *African Trilogy*, Alan Moorehead, Weidenfeld & Nicolson, new edition 2000, p. 525

17   WO 373/77/374

18   Hastings, op. cit., p. 233

19   WO 169/4251

20   *Macmillan* by Alistair Horne, Macmillan, London, 1988, p. 183

21   Hastings, op. cit., p. 233

22   'The Rommel Papers' by John Freeman, *New Statesman*, 1953
West Herts Post, 19 April 1945

23   Luke, op. cit., p. 87

24   Ibid., p. 88

25   John Freeman interview with William Hardcastle, transcribed in *The Listener*, 12 December 1968

26   *I Am An Alcoholic* by Raymond Blackburn, Allan Wingate, London, 1959, p. 51

27   WO 171/662

28   WO 373/186/1115

29   Fussell quote in Whiting, op. cit., p. 194

30   *West Herts Post*, 19 April 1945

31   WO 171/4393

32   *London Evening News*, 7 May 1945

33   WO 171/4394

34   *London Evening News*, 17 May 1945

35   WO 171/4393

Chapter 3

1   *West Herts & Watford Observer*, 8 June 1945

2   'Night Thoughts of an MP' by John Freeman, *New Statesman*, 7 May 1955

3   Driberg, 1968, op. cit.

4   Hansard, 2 September 1945

5   *Fighting All The Way* by Barbara Castle, Macmillan, London, 1993, p. 191

6   *High Tide and After: Memoirs 1945–1960* by Hugh Dalton, Muller, 1962

7   *Tom Driberg, His Life and Indiscretions* by Francis Wheen, Chatto & Windus, London, 1990, p. 242

8   'Hugh Dalton' by John Freeman, *New Statesman*, 9 February 1962

9   'The Windsor Lad' by John Freeman, *New Statesman*, 9 May 1953

10   Quoted in Wheen, op. cit., p. 210

11   Ibid., p. 226

12   *The Lamberts: George, Constant and Kit* by Andrew Motion, Hogarth Press, 1987, p. 245

13   *Ruling Passions* by Tom Driberg, Stein & Day, New York, 1978, p. 144

14   Wheen. op. cit., p. 192

15   *Wyatt*, op. cit., 1999, p. 255

16   Wheen, op. cit., p. 350

17   Ibid., p. 272

18   Wyatt, op. cit., 1985, pp. 103–4

19   Freeman to Driberg, December 1946 (Driberg papers, Christ Church, Oxford University)

20   'A Bit of a Month in Rangoon' by John Freeman, *New Statesman*, 23 January 1954

21   'London Diary' by Flavus, *New Statesman*, 8 June 1962

22   *Family Inheritance: A Life of Eva Hubback* by Diana Hopkinson, Staples Press, 1954, pp. 184–5

23   Lizi Freeman interview with the author 2014

24   Ibid.

25   *The Political Diary of Hugh Dalton* edited by Ben Pimlott, Jonathan Cape, London, 1986, entry dated 28 January 1951 (all other Dalton diary quotes from this edition)

26   *Daily Mirror*, 8 February 1951

Chapter 4

1   *Never Again, Britain 1945–1951* by Peter Hennessy, Vintage Books, London, 1993, p. 389

2   Pimlott (ed.), op. cit., entry dated 20 February 1951, p. 506

3   *Aneurin Bevan: A Biography, vol. 2, 1945–1960* by Michael Foot, Athaneum, London, 1963, p. 327n

4   Pimlott (ed.), op. cit., entry dated 22 April 1951, p. 536

5   *Nye Bevan: A Biography* by John Campbell, Hodder & Stoughton, London, 1994, p. 226

6   Hennessy, op. cit., p. 417

7   Ibid.

8   Quoted in *Hugh Gaitskell* by Philip Williams, Jonathan Cape, London, 1979, p. 249, n. 80

9   Foot, op. cit., pp. 326–7

10   Williams, op. cit., p. 260

11   Dalton, op. cit., pp. 368–9

12   *Crisis in Britain 1951* by Joan Mitchell, Secker & Warburg, London, 1963, pp. 186–7

13   Pimlott (ed.), op. cit., p. 537

14   Wyatt, op. cit., 1985, p. 213

15   Castle, op. cit., p. 191

16   *The Scotsman*, June 1961

17   *Year of Hope. Diaries, Letters and Papers 1940–1962* edited by Ruth Williams, Hutchinson, London, 1994, p. 165

18   Quoted in Wheen, op. cit., p. 246

19   Ibid., pp. 250–51 (see also: *The Best of Both Worlds* by Tom Driberg, Phoenix House, London, 1953, pp. 52–7)

20 *Back-bencher* by Ian Mikardo, Weidenfeld & Nicolson, London, 1988, p. 120

21 'Scots Welcome The Queen' (12 July) and 'An American Paints the Queen' (13 December) by Mima Kerr, *Picture Post*, 1952

22 Campbell, op. cit., p. 276

23 Foot, op. cit., p. 434

24 *Wilson: The Authorised Life of Lord Wilson of Rievaulx* by Philip Zeigler, Weidenfeld & Nicolson, London, 1993, p. 96

25 *A Life at the Centre* by Roy Jenkins, PaperMac, London, 1991, p. 90

26 'The New Puritanism' by John Freeman, *Queen*, 1963

27 'London Diary' by Flavus, *New Statesman*, 26 February 1955

28 See Wheen, op. cit., pp. 260–64 for Tom and Ena Driberg and failure of their marriage

29 'Wines of Bordeaux' by John Freeman, *New Statesman*, 27 September 1952

30 'Some Thoughts on Scarborough' by John Freeman, *New Statesman*, 25 August 1954

31 'Night Thoughts of an Ex-MP' by John Freeman, *New Statesman*, 7 May 1955

32 'Stafford' by John Freeman (his obituary for Stafford Cripps), *New Statesman*, 26 April 1952

33 Paul Johnson interview with the author, 2014

Chapter 5

1 *Grace Wyndham Goldie: First Lady of Television* by John Grist, New Generation Publishing, London, 2006, p. 222

2 Quoted in *'Panorama': Fifty Years of Pride and Paranoia* by Richard Lindley, Politico's Publishing, London, 2003, p. 37

3 Ibid., p. 37

4 *Facing the Nation: Television & Politics 1936–76* by Grace Wyndham Goldie, The Bodley Head, London, 1977, p. 90

5 Wyatt, op. cit., 1985, p. 239

6 Wyatt, op. cit., 1985, pp. 255–6

7 WAC *Panorama* file dated 22 February 1960

8 Wyatt, op. cit., 1985, pp. 255–6

9 Michael Peacock interview with the author, 2014

10 *The Guardian*, 23 February 1960

11   Freeman's own summary in an article he wrote in the *New Statesman*, 15 October 1960

12   WAC John Freeman file

13   www.bbc.co.uk/archive/gay_rights/12001.shtml

14   Driberg, op. cit., 1953, pp. 162–5

15   L. Freeman interview with author, 2014

16   WAC John Freeman file

17   Ibid.

18   *De Gaulle* by Aidan Crawley, The Literary Guild, London, 1969, p. 351

19   Catherine Freeman interview with author, 2015

20   Peregrine Worsthorne interview with author, 2014

21   'Constant Loudspeakers' by John Freeman (his review of *The Birth of Broadcasting* by Asa Briggs, OUP, 1961), *New Statesman*, 27 October 1961

Chapter 6

1   Notes by Hugh Burnett with release of BBC DVD set of *Face to Face* in 2009

2   Extracts from interviews with Lord Birkett, Carl Jung, Bertrand Russell and Edith Sitwell all from *Face to Face with John Freeman*, BBC Books, 1989

3   Michael Parkinson written tribute to publisher, 2015

4   *The Guardian*, 6 May 1961

5   *Woman's Day*, 12 August 1961

6   'The Grillers Grilled', *Tatler*, 1961

7   WAC *Face to Face* file

8   Burnett, op. cit.

9   Jung letter, cited in *Wounded Healer of the Soul* by Claire Dung, Continuum, London, 2000, p. 200

10   Letter from Jung in possession of Freeman family

11   WAC *Face to Face* file

12   *Jung: A Biography* by Deirdre Bair, Little, Brown, Boston, 2003, p. 620n

13   This and above references from John Freeman's 'Introduction' to *Man and His Symbols* conceived and edited by Carl G. Jung, Doubleday Books, New York, 1964

14   *Tony Hancock: The Definitive Biography* by John Fisher, HarperCollins, London, 2008, p. 272

15   Anthony Clare's interview with John Freeman at Davis, California, in 1988 (full transcript in *Face to Face with John Freeman*)

16   Fisher, op. cit., pp. 279–80

17   WAC *Face to Face* file

18   *The Guardian*, 19 September 1960

19   WAC *Face to Face* file

20   Ibid.

21   Ibid.

22   Ibid.

Chapter 7

1   John Freeman's 'Introduction' to *The New Statesman, The History of the First Fifty Years 1913–1963* by Edward Hyams, Longmans, London, 1963, p. x

2   Quoted in *The Life, Letters and Diaries of Kingsley Martin* by C. H. Rolph, Victor Gollancz, London, 1973, p. 335

3   Norman MacKenzie interview with author, 2012

4   Freeman in Hyams, op. cit., p. x

5   *New Statesman* (centenary edition), 19 April 2013

6   Rolph, op. cit., p. 316

7   Ibid.

8   *Crossman: The Pursuit of Power* by Anthony Howard, Jonathan Cape, London, 1990, p. 191

9   Ibid., p. 192

10   Ibid., pp. 192–3

11   Rolph, op. cit., p. 328

12   *Enlightening Letters 1946–1960* by Isaiah Berlin, Random House, 2011, pp. 176–7

13   Rolph, op. cit., pp. 334–5

14   'Tell Me Again on Sunday, Agent X' by Anthony Howard, *The Times*, 1996

15   *New Statesman*, 19 October 1962

16   'Spies Like Us' by Hugh Purcell, *New Statesman*, 24 May 2013

17   Ibid.

18   *The Journey Not The Arrival Matters*, Leonard Woolf, Hogarth Press, London, 1969, p. 139

19   Rolph, op. cit., pp. 232–4

20   Margaret Vallance interview with the author, 2014

21   *New Statesman*, 21 August 1956

22   Rolph, op. cit., p. 323 (see also: 'Learning to Love the Bomb' by Hugh Purcell, *New Statesman*, 21 March 2014)

23   Paul Johnson interview with the author, 2014

24   Hyams, op. cit., p. 291

25   Rolph, op. cit., p. 324

26   *The Scotsman*, June 1961

Chapter 8

1   Quoted in Rolph, op. cit., pp. 334–5

2   Hyams, op. cit., p. xi

3   Ibid., p. 303

4   *The Scotsman*, June 1961

5   'Meet the Man from London' by Francis Hope, *New York Times*, January 1969

6   For full account of this episode see Rolph, op. cit., pp. 335–42

7   Norman MacKenzie interview with the author, 2004

8   Ibid.

9   Ibid.

10   Hope, op. cit.

11   MacKenzie interview with the author, 2004

12   John Freeman interview with William Hardcastle, *The Listener*, 12 December 1968

13   'Learning to Love the Bomb' by Hugh Purcell, *New Statesman*, 21 March 2014

14   *New Statesman*, 25 October 1962

15   Norman MacKenzie to Paul Johnson (letter in possession of the author)

16   *The Love Object* by Edna O'Brien, Jonathan Cape, London, 1968, pp. 13–46

17   'Obituary of John Vassall' by David Leitch, *The Independent*, 9 December 1996

18   *News of the World*, 12 May 1963

19   Freeman interview with Hardcastle, 1968

20   *Diary of a Cabinet Minister* by Richard Crossman, Hamish Hamilton, London, 1977, p. 280

21 'New (Acting) Statesman' by Nicholas Tomalin, *Sunday Times*, December 1968

22 *Daily Mail*, 7 January 1965

Chapter 9

1 Hardcastle interview, 1968

2 John Freeman interview with Cyril Aynsley, *Daily Express*, 12 January 1965

3 'Man with passion for truth to represent UK in India', *Sunday Standard*, India, 31 January 1965

4 Freeman interview with Aynsley, 1965

5 John Freeman interview with Erskine Childers, *Ten O'Clock*, BBC Home Service, 11 January 1965

6 'Gandhiji, Symbol of Revolution'; *The Times of India*, 1 February 1965, p. 9

7 *Open Secret: The Autobiography of the Former Director-General of MI5* by Stella Rimington, Arrow Books, London, 2001, p. 54

8 Ibid., p. 58.

9 Ibid., p. 57

10 *Calcutta* by Geoffrey Moorhouse, Penguin Books, London, 1983, p. 252

11 Catherine Freeman interview with the author, 2014

12 John Freeman to Sir John Johnston, 13 April 1966 (PREM 13/967 The National Archives)

13 Ibid.

14 Prem Shankar Jha interview with the author, 2007

15 Kushwant Singh letter to the author, 2007

16 Driberg, 1968, op. cit.

17 Catherine Freeman interview with the author, 2014

18 Ibid.

19 Robin Renwick, Baron Renwick of Clifton, interview with the author, 2014

20 Rimington, op. cit., p. 57.

21 John Freeman to Arthur Bottomley, 'Three Weeks War', 19 October 1965 (DO 196/387 TNA)

22 *The Cold War in South Asia: Britain, the United States and the Indian Subcontinent 1945–1965*, Paul M. McGarr, Cambridge University Press, 2013, p. 301

23 Ibid., p. 310

24 Ibid., p. 311

25   John Freeman record of conversation with General Chaudhuri, 25 August 1965 (as reported to CRO in despatch dated 27 August)

26   McGarr, op. cit., p. 316

27   Ibid., p. 317

28   Ibid., p. 318

29   Ibid., pp. 319–20

30   Ibid., p. 320

31   Ibid., p. 320

32   John Freeman to Arthur Bottomley, 6 September 1965 (DO 133/178 TNA)

33   Freeman to Bottomley, October 1965, op. cit.

34   McGarr, op. cit., p. 339

35   Prime Minister Wilson's reply to F. Noel-Baker in New Delhi telegram, No. 60, 5 January 1966 (PREM B/1051 TNA)

36   McGarr, op. cit., p. 339

37   *The Labour Government 1964–1970: A Personal Record* by Harold Wilson, Weidenfeld & Nicolson, 1971

38   Joe Garner to Harold Wilson, 17 June 1971 (CAB 164/887 TNA)

39   Sir Burke Trend to Joe Garner, 2 July 1971 (CAB 164/887 TNA)

40   McGarr, op. cit., p. 342

41   John Freeman valedictory despatch, 21 June 1968 (PREM 13/2158 TNA)

42   John Freeman despatch to Herbert Bowden, 25 May 1967 (PREM 13/1574 TNA)

43   Freeman to Bottomley, October 1965, op. cit.

44   Sir Peter Hall interview with Jimmy Jamieson for the British Diplomatic Oral History Programme, Churchill College Cambridge, 8 November 2002 (www.chu.cam.ac.uk/media/uploads/files/Hall.pdf)

45   Renwick interview with the author, 2014

46   Akhtar interview with the author, 2014

47   C. Freeman interview with the author, 2014

48   John Freeman to Herbert Bowden on Mrs Gandhi, 25 May 1967 (PREM 13/1574 TNA)

49   C. Freeman interview with the author, 2014

50   Freeman to Bowden, May 1967, op. cit.

51   John Freeman valedictory despatch, op. cit.

52   Hall interview with Jamieson, 2002, op. cit.

53   *Wilson: The Authorised Life* by Philip Ziegler, Weidenfeld & Nicolson, 1993, p. 219

54   Renwick interview with the author, 2014

55   Rimington, op. cit., p. 74

56   John Freeman valedictory despatch, op. cit.

57   Robert Cassen interview with the author, 2014.

58   John Freeman valedictory despatch, op. cit.

59   'Call by Mr Freeman on the Prime Minister on 31 July 1968' briefing paper (PREM 13/2158 TNA)

60   *The Diaries of a Cabinet Minister Vol. III* by Richard Crossman, Jonathan Cape, 1977, p. 166

Chapter 10

1   *The White House Years*, by Henry Kissinger, Weidenfeld & Nicolson, 1979, p. 95

2   *In My Way: The Political Memoirs of Lord George-Brown* by George Brown, Victor Gollancz, 1971, p. 131

3   *Special Relationships: A Foreign Correspondent's Memoirs from Roosevelt to Reagan* by Henry Brandon, Atheneum, 1988, p. 321

4   'Pragmatic New British Envoy to US' by John Freeman (interview with Anthony Lewis), *New York Times*, 5 March 1969

5   Covering note to John Freeman with brief on United States, 26 Jul 1968 (PREM 13/2158 TNA)

6   *Ambassador to Sixties London: The Diaries of David Bruce, 1961–1969* edited by Raj Roy and John W. Young, Republic of Letters Publishing, 2009, entry dated 2 December 1968

7   Brandon, op. cit., p. 321

8   *The Washington Embassy: British Ambassadors to the United States, 1939–77* edited by John W. Young et al., Palgrave Macmillan, 2009, p. 172

9   Brandon, op. cit., p. 321

10   *The Memoirs of Richard Nixon* by Richard Milhous Nixon, Sidgwick & Jackson, 1978, p. 371

11   *Bruce*, op. cit., entry dated 25 February 1969

12   Young et al. (ed.), op. cit., p. 173

13   Ibid., p. 173

14   Hope, op. cit.

15   Ibid.

16   Akhtar interview with the author, 2014

17   C. Freeman interview with Ernestine Carter, *Sunday Times*, January 1969

18   'At the British embassy these days, the entertaining isn't quite as formal' (interview with C. Freeman), *New York Times*, July 1969

19   David (Allan) Burns, CMG, CBE interview with Malcolm McBain for the British Diplomatic Oral History Programme, Churchill College, Cambridge, July 1999 (www.chu.cam.ac.uk/media/uploads/files/Burns.pdf)

20   Sir Andrew Wood GCMG interview with Jimmy Jamieson for the British Diplomatic Oral History Programme, Churchill College, Cambridge, June 2007 (www.chu.cam.ac.uk/media/uploads/files/Wood.pdf)

21   Brandon, op. cit., p. 321

22   PREM13/2158 TNA

23   *Sunday Times*, 15 November 1970

24   *The White House Years* by Henry Kissinger, Simon & Schuster, 2011, pp. 95–6

25   Young et al. (ed.), op. cit., pp. 175–6.

26   Renwick interview with the author, 2014

27   Kissinger, op. cit., pp. 95–6.

28   John Freeman to Sir Denis Greenhill, 5 June 1970 (PREM 13/3081TNA)

29   Ibid.

30   Henry Kissinger interview with the author, 2015

31   Wes Pruden interview with the author, 2014

32   *Kissinger: 1973, The Crucial Year* by Alistair Horne, Simon & Schuster, 2009, p. 24

33   *Nixon: A Life* by Jonathan Aitken, Weidenfeld & Nicolson, London, 1993, p. 371

34   C. Freeman interview with the author, 2014

35   Corinna Metcalf interview with the author, 2014

36   Joanna Rose interview with the author, 2014

37   Akhtar, interview with the author, 2014

38   Harold Wilson 'Secret and Personal' letter to John Freeman, 5 November 1969 (PREM 13/3428 TNA)

39   John Freeman 'Secret and Personal' letter to Harold Wilson, 17 November 1969 (PREM 13/3428 TNA)

40   Freeman to Greenhill, 2 December 1969 (PREM 13/3552 TNA)

41   Freeman to Greenhill, 15 December 1969 (PREM 13/3552 TNA)

42   Zeigler, op. cit., pp. 328–9

43   Telegram No. 1388, Washington to FCO, 30 April 1970 (PREM 13/3081 TNA)

44   Freeman to Greenhill, 15 May 1970 (FCO 73/131 TNA)

45   Greenhill to John Freeman, 19 May 1970 (FCO 73/132 TNA)

46   'Cinderella's Night', *Women's Wear Daily,* 7 May 1970

47   Director Joe Angio, *Nixon: A Presidency Revealed,* History Channel, 15 February 2007

48   Cassen interview with the author, 2004

49   Washington (G. E. Millard) to Greenhill, 20 July 1970 (TNA)

50   Greenhill telephone conversation with Joseph Sisco, 13 September 1970, quoted in *Britain in Global Politics Vol. 2: From Churchill to Blair* by John W. Young et al., Palgrave Macmillan, 2013, pp. 166–7

51   John Freeman valedictory despatch, 8 January 1971 (FCO 82/42 TNA)

52   Young et al. (ed.), op. cit., p. 183

53   Renwick interview with the author, 2014

54   C. Freeman interview with the author, 2014

55   Metcalf interview with the author, 2014

Chapter 11

1   *An Autobiography Part 1: From Congregations to Audiences* by David Frost, HarperCollins, London, 1993, pp. 259–65

2   Cited in *Running the Show: 21 Years of London Television* by David Docherty, Boxtree, London, 1990, p. 7

3   *Independent Television in Britain: Vol. 3 Politics and Control 1968–1980* by Jeremy Potter, Macmillan, London, 1989, p. 34

4   Docherty, op. cit., p. 40

5   Potter, op. cit., p. 42

6   Docherty, op. cit., p. 60

7   Potter, op. cit., p. 49 (see also: Docherty, op. cit., p. 71)

8   Docherty, op. cit., p. 76

9   Sir Christopher Bland interview with the author, 2014

10   Cited in Docherty, op. cit., p. 82

11   Akhtar interview with the author, 2014

12   'Face to Face with the New Boss', *Sunday Times*, 14 March 1971

13   Ibid.

14   Potter, op. cit., p. 55

15   Docherty, op. cit., p. 82

16   Nigel Lawson, Baron Lawson of Braby, interview with the author, 2014

17   Brian Tesler interview with the author, 2014

18   Ron Miller correspondence with the author, 2014

19   Docherty, op. cit., p. 90–91

20   Michael Grade, Baron Grade of Yarmouth, interview with the author, 2014

21   Cited in Docherty, op. cit., p. 99

22   Tesler interview with the author, 2014

23   Docherty, op. cit., p. 96

24   Cited in Potter, op. cit., p. 232

25   Tesler interview with the author, 2014

26   Cited in Docherty, op. cit., p. 116

27   Cassen interview with the author, 2014

28   Michael Grade interview with the author, 2014

29   John Freeman interview with Ivan Rowan, *Sunday Telegraph*, 14 March 1971

30   John Birt interview with the author, 2014

31   John Freeman memorandum to executive directors of LWT, August 1981 (cited in Docherty, op. cit., p. 148)

32   Bland interview with the author, 2014

33   *The Independent*, 22 December 2014

34   *And Finally…?: The History of ITN* by Richard Lindley, Politicos, London, 2005, pp. 174–6

35   Ibid.

36   'Face to Face with John Freeman' by Sue Summers, *Sunday Times*, February 1984

37   Ibid.

Chapter 12

1   Jean Snyder interview with the author, 2014

2   Professor Randy Siverson interview with the author, 2014

3   Professor Larry Berman interview with the author, 2014

4   Ibid.

5   Ibid.

6   Elizabeth Sherwin notes on Freeman's lectures (collated by Professor Geoffrey Wandesforde-Smith, Weber Museum, UC Davis)

7   Cynthia Basinger interview with the author, 2015

8   Letter written by Matthew Freeman to his mother, 21 September 1987 (in possession of C. Freeman)

9   *The Grillers Grilled*, 1961

10   M. Freeman letter to his mother

11   John Freeman proposal, 11 June 1985 (Special Collections Library, UC Davis)

12   Kissinger interview with the author, 2015

13   *The Spectator*, 4 March 1995

14   Berman interview with the author, 2014

15   Wyatt, 1998, op. cit., p. 140

16   Ibid., pp. 595–6

Chapter 13

1   *Daily Mail*, 7 January 1965

2   John Freeman, *New Statesman*, 19 January 1962

3   Susan Hicklin interview with the author, 2004

4   Isobel and Percy Kimber interview with the author, 2015

5   Ibid.

6   Janet Triggs interview with the author, 2015

7   Wyatt, op. cit., 1998, p. 688

8   John Freeman letter to Geoffrey Wandesforde-Smith, 3 July 2007 (given to the author)

9   Lawson interview with the author, 2014

10   John Freeman letter to Norman MacKenzie, 26 June 2008

11   *Daily Mail*, 22 December 2014

12   Ibid.

13   *The Independent*, 22 December 2014

Index